(WOMAN) WRITER

OTHER COLLECTIONS OF ESSAYS
BY JOYCE CAROL OATES

(WOMAN) WRITER

OCCASIONS AND OPPORTUNITIES

A William Abrahams Book

E. P. DUTTON | NEW YORK

Copyright © 1988 by The Ontario Review, Inc.
All rights reserved. Printed in the U.S.A.

Published in the United States by E. P. Dutton,
a division of NAL Penguin Inc.,
2 Park Avenue, New York, N.Y. 10016.

Published simultaneously in Canada
by Fitzhenry and Whiteside, Limited, Toronto.

Library of Congress Cataloging-in-Publication Data
Oates, Joyce Carol, 1938–
(Woman) writer : occasions and opportunities / Joyce Carol Oates. —
1st ed.   p.   cm.
"A William Abrahams book."
ISBN 0-525-24652-5
I. Title.
PS3565.A8W56   1988
814'.54—dc19   87-30672

CIP

Designed by Nancy Etheredge

1 3 5 7 9 10 8 6 4 2

First Edition

Again, to my Princeton colleague
and friend Elaine Showalter,
and my husband, Raymond Smith

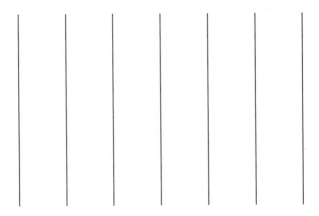

CONTENTS

CONTENTS

CONTENTS

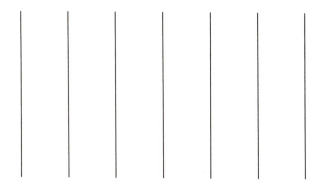

PREFACE:
OCCASIONS AND
OPPORTUNITIES

Of the many forms storytelling can take, surely criticism—literary, cultural, sociological—is the most indirect; one might say the most circuitous and codified. The kind of prose narrative we call discursive, analytical, meditative, non*fictional*—is it perhaps a means of celebrating occasions not, in a sense, our own, but ancillary to our most obvious, most personal concerns? A way of exploring opportunities not otherwise available to us? Essays, articles, memoirs, "appreciations," interviews . . . these forms are wrongly considered unimaginative, or, in any case, considered somehow less significant than the imaginative writer's "real" work. As if one does not speak in a variety of voices, in a variety of modes. The literary critic, like the cultural critic, does after all choose his or her subject even as, to the world, it might appear that his subject—or an editor in search of someone to write of his subject—chooses him. The subject is *out there,* in the world; and not *in here,* in the writer's private world. And surely, at times, that is all to the good?

Writing what is generally called "imaginative" literature is a continuous strain, quite apart from the inevitable strain of using language, choosing the right words to place in the right sequence, because the unconscious, hence unwilled, part of the process makes it erratic and wayward; in a paradoxical sense, impersonal. It is the "white heat" of which Emily Dickinson writes, and the writer's defense against it is *technique:* the dams, dikes, ditches, and conduits that both restrain emotionally charged content and give it formal, and therefore communal, expression.

But there is another kind of writing, another kind of discourse, public, even public-minded: a fully conscious writing in which communication is the primary intention. Not the writer but the subject is *the* subject. And these subjects are freely given, freely chosen; anyone, after all, can write about them, since they are in the public domain. Most of the essays in this volume were written for special occasions and represent, to the author at least, memorial efforts of a kind: unique, unsought, and therefore fortuitous opportunities. Addressing the Thoreau Society in Concord, Massachusetts, from the chastely daunting pulpit of the First Congregational Church . . . giving the keynote address to an audience of Emily Dickinson scholars at the Emily Dickinson conference in May 1986 at the University of North Carolina, Chapel Hill . . . writing prefaces for new editions of *Frankenstein, Moby Dick, Dr. Jekyll and Mr. Hyde,* the short stories of Franz Kafka . . . interviewing, for *Life,* the extraordinary young American boxer Mike Tyson, who was shortly to become the youngest heavyweight titleholder in history. My inchoate thoughts on nature and on the mysterious pleasures and solaces of reading would surely never have crystallized had not Daniel Halpern, editor of the distinguished literary journal *Antaeus,* invited me to contribute to special issues of the journal, nor would I have formalized my uneasy sense of what it means, and does not mean, to be a "woman writer" in our time, had not the organizers of the Twentieth-Century Women Writers' Conference at Hofstra University, in spring 1982, invited me to give the keynote address. My complex and largely unexamined thoughts about Detroit, Michigan, would not have coalesced had not Laurence Goldstein, editor of *Michigan Quarterly Review,* graciously invited me to write a personal piece, a "memory" piece, for a special Detroit issue of that journal, and I would surely—surely!—not have ever driven, let alone "test driven," a Ferrari Testarossa, that sports car sui generis, had not the short-lived glossy *Quality* invited me to do so for their pages. And my essay on "pseudonymous selves," like much of my writing on boxing, though written by invitation, is probably as personal a document, in the interstices of its elaboration of others' obsessions, as anything I have ever written.

Here, then, are a number of memorial efforts of the past several years; oblique, but I hope not circumspect, efforts of storytelling.

1

DOES THE WRITER EXIST?

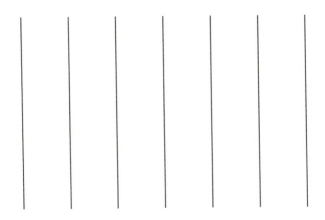

BEGINNINGS

I will maintain that the artist needs only this: a special world of which he alone has the key.

—Gide

I begin with the proposition that the impulse to create, like the impulse to destroy, is utterly mysterious. That it is, in fact, one of the primary mysteries of human existence. We can't hope to explain it but we can't, evidently, resist speculating about it.

Two general theories about the genesis of "art":

- It originates in play: in experiment, improvisation, fantasy; it remains forever, in its deepest impulse,

playful and spontaneous, a celebration of the (child's?) imagination.
• It originates out of the artist's conviction that he or she is born damned; and must struggle through life to achieve redemption. By way of art.

If these theories appear to contradict themselves, to the point, very nearly, of comedy—so, as Walt Whitman would say, they contradict themselves. Sometimes one is self-evidently true; sometimes, the other.

Just as our historical beginnings are utterly mysterious—why are we born? why when and as we are?—so too are the beginnings of works of art and of "artists." Conception (in contrast to the fully public fact of birth) suggests not only the unknowable but the forbidden: our birth dates are matters of public record but our dates of "conception" are permanently shrouded in mystery. Consciousness dominates our thinking about works of art as well as artists, even as we know that the genesis of any creation (in contrast to its execution) must derive from unconscious sources.

Ornamental qualities in prose fiction are invariably the consequence of authorial deliberation and strategy while more powerful qualities—the primitive force fields that generate "theme" (or obsession)—are clearly given. The storyteller experiences the ravishing phenomenon of stories being told through him and by way of him; his single voice generating any number of singular "voices." Is it magic? Is it psychopathology? Is it supremely normal? In Plato's *Ion* Socrates says, "God takes the mind out of the poets, and uses them as his servants, and so also those who chant oracles, and divine seers; because he wishes us to know that not those we hear, who have no mind in them, are those who say such precious things, but God himself is the speaker, and through them he shows his meaning to us. . . . These beautiful poems are not human, not made by man, but divine and made by God; and the poets are nothing but the gods' interpreters, possessed each by whatever god it may be." But this is a logic hostile to the individual; a logic in denial of the wide play of personality that characterizes creative work. For if there is any single quality we associate with art it is the individual, the personal, the unique, the inimitable. One might add: the inevitable. In many writers it comes to seem over a lifetime that a complex and essentially unknowable drama is working itself out by way of the individual; yet, so far as the individual is concerned, each experience is immediate and singular. And the act of writing itself is likely to be felt as purely and radiantly subjective: "the exalted sense of being above time and death which comes from being again in a writing mood" (Virginia Woolf, *Diary*, 8 September 1934).

After the completion of an ambitious project the writer may try to pass judgment on it, "objectively"; he may try to analyze it as a reader; or probe his own motives for writing. "The port from which I set out was, I think, that of *the essential loneliness of my life*—and it seems to be the port also, in sooth to which my course again finally directs itself! This loneliness—what is it still but the deepest thing about one? Deeper, about *me*, at any rate, than anything else; deeper than my 'genius,' deeper than my 'discipline,' deeper than my pride, deeper, above all, than the deep counterminings of art" (Henry James in a letter of 1900). Though such analyses are often astute and startling—recall James Joyce explaining that the labyrinthine *Ulysses* was written "to preserve the speech of my father and his friends"—it surely cannot explain the depth, or the subtlety, or the stark originality, or genius of a work. Virginia Woolf noted that the writing of *To the Lighthouse* seemed to have laid to rest the ghosts of her father and mother, of whom she used to think constantly: "I believe this to be true—that I was obsessed with them both, unhealthily; and writing of them was a necessary act" (*Diary*, 28 November 1928). It remains a surprising (and disturbing) fact to many literary observers that writers should, upon occasion, write so directly from life; that they should "cannibalize" and even "vampirize" their own experiences. But this species of creation is surely inevitable? entirely natural? The artist is driven by passion; and passion most powerfully derives from our own experiences and memories. Writers as diverse as William Butler Yeats, Marcel Proust, August Strindberg, D. H. Lawrence, Ernest Hemingway, even, to a less obsessive degree, Thomas Mann, Willa Cather, Katherine Anne Porter—all were writers of genius whose imaginations were not constrained but positively energized (in Strindberg's case one might say "demonized") by specific events in their lives.

Strindberg, for instance, used not analogous but exact details from his family life, and in particular from his three marriages, for his fiction and plays; his biographer Olof Lagercrantz has noted that he went so far as to create domestic traumas in order to "rectify" his literary material, and, with the passage of time, developed an intuitive symbolist method of creation, in which individuals no longer seemed to exist save as emanations of meaning—*his* meaning. Equally dependent upon his own life—upon what he called "passional" experience—D. H. Lawrence directly fictionalized his own experiences as "son" and as "lover" in virtually all his novels and poetry, from *The White Peacock* to *Lady Chatterley's Lover* and *Pansies*. Thomas Mann was so "excessively precise" in recording his origins and family life in *Buddenbrooks* and *Tonio Kroger* that he directed a French translator to these works of fiction for a biographical portrait. And there falls across much of Albert Camus's work, however obliquely, and allegorically transformed, the presence of the "silent, uncomplaining figure of [my] deaf mother" who instilled in her son fiercely contending emotions of sympathy and helplessness.

Yet how many people, writers or otherwise, have been haunted by families to no productive end! Clearly the powerful unconscious motives for a work of art are but the generating and organizing forces that stimulate consciousness to feats of deliberation, strategy, craft, cunning.

To be *inspired:* we know what it means, even how it sometimes feels, but what is it? Filled suddenly and often helplessly with renewed life and energy, a sense of excitement that can barely be contained; but why some things—a word, a glance, a scene glimpsed from a window, a random memory, a conversational anecdote, the shard of a dream—have the power to stimulate us to intense creativity while others do not we are unable to say. The early Surrealists believed in the empirical world as a "forest of signs"—a rich, largely unexplored region of message forms that lay behind the apparent irrationality of the surface: just as meanings lay behind the apparent irrationality of the dream. Images yield themselves to those who *see*—like Man Ray wandering through Parisian streets with his camera, forcing nothing, anticipating nothing, but leaving himself open to document *disponibilité;* or availability; or chance. Surrealism's most striking images were, at the outset, purely ordinary images, decontextualized and made strange—as Lautréamont said, "Beautiful as the chance encounter of a sewing machine and an umbrella on a dissection table."

No less open to *disponibilité* was Henry James, who listened avidly to dinner table conversation in London social circles—for years the popular novelist dined out as many as two hundred times in a single season. He heard, and overheard, any number of gossipy tales; yet chose to write *The Aspern Papers, The Spoils of Poynton, The Sacred Fount,* "The Turn of the Screw." (Having heard approximately half of the riveting anecdote that would provide the comical plot of *Spoils,* James asked not to be told the rest: he didn't want his imagination contaminated by mere factual truth.) In revisiting Washington Square after years of absence from the United States, James claimed to have "seen" the ghost of his unlived American self—and wrote that remarkable ghost story, "The Jolly Corner," in which the unlived self, the other James, is both realized and exorcized. After the violent Dublin insurrection of Easter 1916, William Butler Yeats was indignant with the Irish rebels for sacrificing their lives, needlessly, he thought; yet for days he was haunted by a single mysterious line of poetry—a line repeating itself again and again—until finally his great poem "Easter 1916" organized itself around that line: "A terrible beauty is born."

> *I write it out in verse—*
> *MacDonagh and MacBride*
> *And Connolly and Pearse*
> *Now and in time to be,*
> *Wherever green is worn,*
> *Are changed, changed utterly:*
> *A terrible beauty is born.*

Karen Blixen, writing under the carefully chosen pseudonym "Isak Dinesen," transmogrified personal experience, a good deal of it bitter, into apparently distant, if not mythical images; yet the biographical element in her work is consistent if one knows how to decipher the clues. For instance, in a late parable, "The Cardinal's Third Tale," of *Last Tales,* a proud virgin contracts syphilis by kissing the foot of Saint Peter's statue in the Vatican after a young Roman worker has kissed it before her—a detail that aroused a good deal of negative criticism for its apparent "frivolity" since, at the time of the book's publication, the secret of Dinesen's own syphilis, also "innocently" contracted, was not generally known. Young Jean-Paul Sartre was so profoundly struck by the hallucinogen-induced vision of a tree's roots that *La Nausée,* his first novel, virtually shaped itself around the hieratic image; an image that has consequently come to represent, however misleadingly, the Existentialist preoccupation with things in their mysterious and usually malevolent *thingness.*

In 1963 the poet Randall Jarrell received a box of letters from his mother, including letters he himself had written at the age of twelve in the 1920s; he immediately embarked upon what was to be his last period of creativity—virtually plucking poems, his wife has said, from the air. The title of the book says it all: *The Lost World.* Before this, Jarrell had been inactive; after this, he sank into depression. He died in 1965. The poet Theodore Weiss, having written a twenty-line poem, was inspired to work on it in subsequent days—and months—and, finally, years: twenty years altogether. Each line of the poem mysteriously "opened out into a scenario," shaping itself finally into Weiss's first book-length poem, *Gunsight.* Eudora Welty was moved to write her early story "Petrified Man" by hearing, week after week, the most amazing things said in her local beauty parlor in Jackson, Mississippi—in this story the writer effaces herself completely and allows the voices to speak. While driving in the Adirondacks, E. L. Doctorow happened to see the sign "Loon Lake"—in which everything he felt about the mountains ("a palpably mysterious wilderness, a place full of dark secrets, history rotting in the forests") came to a point. And there suddenly was the genesis, the organizing force, for his novel *Loon Lake:* "a feeling for a place, an image or two."

For John Updike inspiration arrives, in a sense, as a "packet of material to be delivered." In 1957, revisiting the ruins of the old Shillington, Pennsylvania, poorhouse, a year or two after his grandfather's death, Updike found himself deeply moved by the sight: "Out of the hole where [the poorhouse] had been there came to me the desire to write a futuristic novel"—a highly personal work cast in the form of a parable of the future. So Updike's first novel *The Poorhouse Fair* was conceived, the very antithesis of the typical "autobiographical" first novel. Norman Mailer's first novel, *The Naked and the Dead,* was, by contrast, a wholly deliberate effort, "a sure result of all I had learned up to the age of twenty-five." Mailer's characters were conceived and put in file boxes long before they were ever on the page; he had accumulated hundreds of such cards before he began to write, by which time "the novel itself seemed merely the end of a long active assembly line." But Mailer's second novel, *Barbary Shore,* seemed to come out of nowhere: each morning he would write with no notion of how to continue, where he was going. Where *The Naked and the Dead* had been put together with all the solid agreeable effort of a young carpenter constructing a house, *Barbary Shore* "might as well have been dictated to me by a ghost in the middle of a forest." Similarly, *Why Are We in Vietnam?,* Mailer's *Huck Finn,* was written in a white heat of three ecstatic months, dictated in a sense by the protagonist's voice—"a highly improbable sixteen-year-old genius—I did not even know if he was black or white." Joseph Heller's novels typically begin with a first sentence that comes out of nowhere, independent of theme, setting, character, story. The opening line of *Catch-22*—"It was love at first sight. The first time _____ saw the chaplain he fell madly in love with him"—simply came to Heller for no reason, could not be explained, yet, within an hour and a half, Heller had worked out the novel in his mind: its unique tone, its tricky form, many of the characters. The genesis for *Something Happened* was the inexplicable sentence "In the office in which I work, there are four people of whom I am afraid. Each of these four people is afraid of five people." And though, a minute before, Heller knew nothing of the work that would absorb him for many years, he knew within an hour the beginning, middle, and ending of the work, and its dominant tone of anxiety.

Joan Didion began *Play It as It Lays* with no notion of "character" or "plot" or even "incident." She had only two pictures in her mind: one of empty white space; the other of a minor Hollywood actress being paged in the casino at the Riviera in Las Vegas. The vision of empty space suggested no story, but the vision of the actress did: "A young woman with long hair and a short white halter dress walks through the casino at the Riviera at one in the morning. She crosses the casino alone and picks up a house telephone. I watch her because I have heard her paged, and recognize her name: she is a minor actress I see around Los Angeles but have never met. I know nothing about her. Who is paging her? Why is she here to be paged? How exactly did she come to this? It was precisely this moment in Las Vegas that made *Play It as It Lays* begin to tell itself to me."

In his *Paris Review* interview of 1976, John Cheever speaks of the way totally disparate facts came together for him, unbidden: "It isn't a question of saving up. It's a question of some sort of galvanic energy." The writing itself then becomes the difficult effort to get the "heft" right—getting the words to correspond to the vision. Surely one of the strangest of all literary conceptions is that of John Hawkes's *The Passion Artist.* In a preface to an excerpt from that novel in Hawkes's anthology *Humors of Blood & Skin,* Hawkes relates how, when he and his wife were spending a year in southern France, he found himself inexplicably unable to write, in the midst of a profound and paralyzing depression; "whenever I entered our house I thought I saw my father's coffin. . . . I had this vision even though both my parents were buried in Maine. Each morning I sat benumbed and mindless at a small table. Each morning Sophie left a fresh rose on my table, but even those talismans of love and encouragement did no good. All was hopeless, writing was out of the question." Then came an invitation for lunch. Hawkes was told a lively bit of gossip about a middle-aged man who went one day to pick up his young daughter at a school in Nice, only to discover accidentally from one of the child's classmates that the daughter was an active prostitute, already gone that day from the playground to a sexual assignation. Hawkes listened to the anecdote; saw himself walking toward a lone girl and some empty playground swings. . . . One or two further associations, seemingly disjointed, and he had the plot of what would be *The Passion Artist.* The paralysis had lifted.

The most admirable thing about the fantastic, André Breton said, is that the fantastic does not exist: everything is real.

In *A Portrait of the Artist as a Young Man,* Stephen Dedalus explains the Joycean concept of the "epiphany": "A sudden spiritual manifestation, whether in the vulgarity of speech or of gesture or in a memorable phase of the mind itself. He believed it was for the artist to record these epiphanies with extreme care, seeing that they themselves are the most delicate and evanescent of moments." That Joyce's concept of one of the most potent motives for art has become, by now, a critical commonplace, should not discourage us from examining it. In his own practice the young Joyce, in his late teens and a student at University College, Dublin, began to collect a notebook of "epiphanies" fueled by the ambition not only to write but to write works of genius. He collected approximately seventy epiphanies—sudden and unanticipated moments of "spiritual manifestation"—of which forty survive. Many were to be used with little or no change in *Stephen Hero* (Joyce's early uncompleted novel) and in *Portrait;* the stories of *Dubliners* are organized around such revelations, rather like prose poems fitted to a narrative structure. It might be said that *Ulysses* is a protracted celebration of epiphany fitted to a somewhat overdetermined intellectual (Jesuitical?) grid: a short story tirelessly inflated to encompass the cosmos. (In fact, *Ulysses* had its formal genesis in a story for *Dubliners* titled "Ulysses," or "Mr. Hunter's Day"—a story that, according to Joyce, never got beyond its title.) The epiphany has significance, of course, only in its evocation of an already existing (but undefined) interior state. It would be naïve to imagine that grace really falls upon us from without—one must be in spiritual readiness for any visitation.

Yet is the writer in truth the triumphant possessor of a secret world to which (in Gide's words) he alone has the key?— or is he perhaps possessed by that world? The unique power of the unconscious is that it leads us where it will and not where we might will to go. As dreams cannot be controlled, so the flowering of any work of art cannot be controlled except in its most minute aspects. When one finds the "voice" of a novel, the "voice" becomes hypnotic, ravishing, utterly inexplicable. From where does it come? Where does it go? As in any fairy tale or legend the magic key unlocks a door to a mysterious room—but does one dare enter? Suppose the door swings shut? Suppose one is locked in until the spell has lifted? But if the "spell" is a lifetime? But if the "spell" *is* the life?

So, the familiar notion of a "demonic" art: the reverse in a sense of Plato's claim for its divine origin—yet in another sense identical. Something *not us* inhabits us; something insists upon speaking through us. To be in the grip of a literary obsession is not so very different from being in the grip of any obsession—erotic love, for instance, in its most primary and powerful state. Here the object of emotion is fully human but the emotion has the force of something inhuman: primitive, almost impersonal, at times almost frightening. The very concept of the "brainstorm": a metaphor nearly literal in its suggestion of raging winds, rains, elemental forces. The extravagance of William Blake's visions, for example; the ecstasy of Kafka in writing his early stories—writing all night! tireless! enthralled!—no matter that he is in poor health and physically exhausted. "Odd how the creative power at once brings the whole universe to order," Virginia Woolf observes, 27 July 1934, but she might have gone on to observe that the "universe" is after all one's own very private and unexplored self: "demonic," "divine."

The genesis of Mary Shelley's *Frankenstein* is nearly as primitive as the appeal of that extraordinary work itself: after days of having failed to compose a ghost story (in response to Lord Byron's casual suggestion) Mary Wollstonecraft Godwin Shelley had a hypnagogic fantasy in her bed. "I saw the pale student of unhallowed arts kneeling beside the thing he had put together. I saw the hideous phantasm of a man stretched out, and then, on the working of some powerful engine, show signs of life. . . . His success would terrify the artist; he would rush away [hoping] this thing . . . would subside into dead matter. He sleeps; but he is awakened; he opens his eyes; behold the horrid thing stands at his bedside, opening his curtains." One of the central images of *Frankenstein* is that of a stroke of lightning that seems to issue magically in a dazzling "stream of fire" from a beautiful old oak, blasting it and destroying it: a potent image perhaps for the violence of the incursion from the unconscious that galvanized the author's imagination after a period of strain and frustration. (It cannot have been an accident that *Frankenstein,* telling of a monstrous birth, was written by a very young and yet-unmarried pregnant woman who had had two babies with her lover already, only one of whom had survived.) Following this waking dream of June 1816, Mary Shelley had her subject—spoke in fact of being "possessed" by it. So too the brilliantly realized vision of the monster comes to us with such uncanny force it is difficult to believe that it owes its genesis to so very personal an experience—and did not evolve from a collective myth. *Frankenstein; or, The Modern Prometheus* was published in 1818 to immediate acclaim; yet with the passage of years the novel itself has receded as an artwork while Frankenstein's monster—known simply and inaccurately as Frankenstein—has achieved dominance. The nightmare vision ends as it began, with a curious sort of impersonality.

Why the need, rising in some very nearly to the level of compulsion, to verify experience by way of language?—to scrupulously record and preserve the very passing of Time? "All poetry is positional," Nabokov notes in his autobiography *Speak, Memory;* "to try to express one's position in regard to the universe embraced by consciousness is an immemorial urge. The arms of consciousness reach out and grope, and the longer they are the better. Tentacles, not wings, are Apollo's natural members." For Nabokov as for many writers—one might say Boswell, Proust, Virginia Woolf, Flaubert; surely James Joyce—experience itself is not authentic until it has been transcribed by way of language: the writer puts his imprimatur upon his (historic) self by way of writing. He creates himself, imagines himself, sometimes—recall Walter Whitman changing his name to Walt Whitman, David Henry Thoreau changing his name to Henry David Thoreau—renames himself as one might name a fictitious character in a work of art. And the impulse can rise to the level of a sacred obligation, at least in a young author's ambition: "There is a certain resemblance between the mystery of the Mass," says James Joyce to his brother Stanislaus in a letter, "and what I am trying to do . . . to give people a kind of intellectual or spiritual pleasure by converting the bread of everyday life into something that has a permanent artistic life of its own . . . for their mental, moral, and spiritual uplift." (One is tempted to note here in passing that it was for their "mental, moral, and spiritual" preservation the citizens of Dublin suppressed Joyce's *Dubliners* and in effect drove him into his life's exile in Europe.)

No one has analyzed the complexities of a writer's life so painstakingly as Virginia Woolf in her many volumes of diaries and to a lesser extent in her correspondence. The slow evolution of an idea into consciousness; the difficult transcription of all that is inchoate, riddlesome; the sense of writing as a triumphant act; the necessity of surrendering to the unconscious (the "subconscious" as Woolf calls it, imagining it as "her"); the pleasure in language as sounds, beats, rhythms—Woolf writes so meticulously about these matters because she is trying to understand them. In a letter to Vita Sackville-West of 8 September 1928, she says:

> I believe that the main thing in beginning a novel is to feel, not that you can write it, but that it exists on the far side of a gulf, which words can't cross: that it's to be pulled through only in a breathless anguish. Now when I sit down to write an article, I have a net of words which will come

down on the idea certainly in an hour or so. But a novel . . . to be good should seem, before one writes it, something unwriteable; but only visible; so that for nine months one lives in despair, and only when one has forgotten what one meant, does the book seem tolerable.

And of style:

Style is a very simple matter, it is all rhythm. Once you get that, you can't use the wrong words. . . . This is very profound, what rhythm is, and goes far deeper than words. A sight, an emotion, creates this wave in the mind, long before it makes words to fit it; and in writing . . . one has to recapture this, and set this working (which has nothing apparently to do with words) and then, as it breaks and tumbles in the mind, it makes words to fit in.

One thinks of the young Ernest Hemingway writing each morning in a Parisian café, groping his way into what would be his first book, *In Our Time:* writing at first with extreme slowness and difficulty until he set down his "one true sentence"—usually a brief declarative sentence—and could throw the earlier work away and begin his story. One thinks too of William Faulkner's composition of his greatest novel, *The Sound and the Fury,* which began as a troubling and inexplicable image—the vision of an unknown little girl with muddy underpants climbing a tree outside a window— and slowly expanded into a long story that required another story or section to amplify it, which in turn required another, which in turn required another, until finally Faulkner had four sections of a novel, published in 1929 as *The Sound and the Fury.* It was not until two decades later when Malcolm Cowley edited *The Portable Faulkner* that Faulkner added the Appendix that is now always published as an integral part of the novel.

"I am doing a novel which I have never grasped. . . . There I am at p. 145, and I've no notion what it's about. I hate it. Frieda says it's very good. But it's like a novel in a foreign language I don't know very well—I can only just make out what it is about." So D. H. Lawrence writes in a letter of 1913 in reference to his work-in-progress *The Sisters*. So vague and unformed was the young author's sense of his novel in its early "crude fermenting" he had intended it to be a potboiler of a kind: the novel that would eventually become *Women in Love.* He made several false starts in its composition before realizing that he must give his heroine some background: this background rapidly evolves into the germ of a new, separate novel about three generations of Brangwens—a social history of the English Midlands from before the industrial revolution to approximately 1913. In short, the "background" for the heroine of *The Sisters* became *The Rainbow,* published in 1915. (*Women in Love* was published in 1920: the two novels are radically different in structure, style, narrative voice, tone.)

Is it as a consequence of Lawrence's method of composition, or in defiance of it, that he published within a few years two of the great novels of the twentieth century, *The Rainbow* and *Women in Love?* Lawrence was the most intuitive of writers, yet he was willing to write numerous drafts of a work and even to throw away as many as one thousand pages, as he claims to have done with *The Rainbow.* His deep faith in himself allowed him the energy to experiment in following his voice and his characters where they would lead; temperamentally he was the antithesis of James Joyce, who imposed upon his work a purely intellectual scheme meant to raise it to the level of the symbolic and the archetypal. "Don't look for the development of [my] novel to follow the lines of certain characters," Lawrence says in a letter of 1919; "the characters fall into the form of some other rhythmic form, as when one draws a fiddle-bow across a fine tray delicately sanded, the sand takes lines unknown."

The sand takes lines unknown. What more beautiful and precise image to suggest the very imprecision of the creative enterprise?—the conjunction between inner and outer forces we try in vain to understand and must hope in the end only to embody?

POSTSCRIPT

On the genesis of my novel *Marya: A Life.*

In 1977 I wrote a short story, very short, deliberately spare and uninflected, which I decided to call "November Morning." It was about a boy of eight whose father has been killed, though the boy himself doesn't quite understand what has happened. He is taken to see his father's corpse, in a county morgue; but his father has been so badly beaten or mutilated (it isn't clear which, to the reader) that the boy doesn't seem to recognize him. The story is told not by the child but by way of his limited consciousness and his reluctance to understand what has happened in his family. The setting of the story was rural: naturalistic but dreamlike. The time was several decades ago.

I finished "November Morning" in a few days, and sent it out. Though I went on to other projects I found that I was still thinking about the story, haunted by it, as if I hadn't really finished it. My practice as a writer might be defined as an active pursuit of "hauntedness": I can't write unless I am preoccupied with something, sometimes to the point of distraction or obsession. But rarely am I haunted by a piece of writing, after I have finished it. . . . Though the story was accepted by a magazine, I decided I didn't want it published in that form; but when I tried to withdraw it from publication I learned that I had waited too long. So the story, incomplete, teasingly "wrong," was published.

The test of a work's integrity is its appearance in print: you know then, if you didn't know beforehand, if it is honest or not.

(Cocteau said that writing is a force of memory which is not understood. Certainly there are times when the prospect of writing leaves me virtually faint with longing; a yearning, a desire so palpable it's almost physical, bound up in some complex, undefinable way with memory. This yearning can't be satisfied except by the head-on plunge into work, in which, somehow, God knows how, raw instinct and critical acuity come into some sort of equilibrium. People who don't write might think it is easy. Or, considering me, as a writer labeled "prolific," that it is easy for *me:* but nothing is farther from the truth. Writing is not easy for most writers nor is it easy for me.)

So I rewrote the story another time. At some point it struck me that the protagonist should have been a girl, and not, as I'd thought, a boy. And that would make all the difference.

Except for the bare outline of the plot everything was recast entirely: tone, texture, rhythm, the silences and spaces between words. Immediately I had my "real" character; I knew her thoroughly; Marya, Marya Knauer, eight years old as the story opens but already in my imagination an adult woman—the thirty-six-year-old woman she would be when the novel ends. (I seemed to know too that Marya's story could not be eight pages long but would be novel-length. Many pages, many years, many experiences would be necessary to bring her into focus and to the culminating point of her life.) I had the ending, now; the final image; I had a number of scenes, "dramatic interludes," in the middle; I saw, or seemed to see, the ghostly outlines of characters whom Marya would encounter, who would act upon her in crucial ways, if not radically alter her life. Most of all I "saw" Marya—a girl, and then a woman, with a face not unlike my own yet not my own: kin of some kind, perhaps sisterly, but unknown to me.

It wasn't until I had finished a first draft of the novel that I learned, by chance, that the story I believed I had invented recapitulated an incident in my mother's early life. Not my father, of course, but her father had been murdered; not I, but my mother, had been "given away" after her father's death, to be brought up by relatives. Marya is eight years old at the time of the event that changes her family's life; my mother was an infant of six months. Somehow, without knowing what I did, without knowing, in fact, that I was doing anything extraordinary at all, I had written my mother's story by way of a work of prose fiction I had "invented."

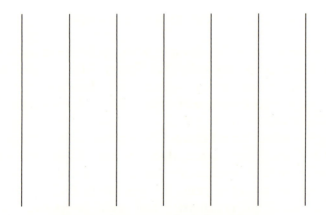

(WOMAN) WRITER: THEORY AND PRACTICE

*To you I am neither man nor woman.
I come before you as an author only. It
is the sole standard by which you have
a right to judge me—the sole ground on
which I accept your judgment.*
    —Charlotte Brontë, to a critic

I.

What is the ontological status of the writer *who is also a woman?*

She is likely to experience herself, from within, as a writer primarily: perhaps even a writer exclusively. She does not inevitably view herself as an object, a category, an essence—in short, as "representative." The individual, to the individual, is never a type. And in the practice of her craft she may well become bodiless and invisible, defined to herself fundamentally as what she thinks, dreams, plots, constructs. To paraphrase Emerson, life consists of what a person is thinking day by day.

It would follow, then, that when the writer is alone with language and with the challenging discipline of creating an art by way of language alone, she is not defined to herself as "she." Does the writer require the specification of gender? Is memory gender-bound? Are impressions filtered through the prism of gender? Is there a distinctly female voice?—or even a conspicuously feminine voice? Or is "gender" in this sense an ontological category imposed upon us from without, for the convenience of others? If so, it is likely to be a category that dissolves the uniquely individual in the abstract. The private drama becomes, in Melville's words, a "hideous, intolerable Allegory."

It has been said by Gide that the artist requires a special, secret world to which he (she?) alone has the key; and it is surely true that an unreasoned faith underlies all motives for sustained creativity. If the ideal reader experiences the classic "enlargement of sympathies" by way of serious fiction, it is to be assumed that the writer, immersed in realizing these sympathies, experiences a similar enlargement of vision: at least so long as she is immersed in her art and not subjected to others' assessments of it, and of her.

In a passage in *Speak, Memory,* his autobiography "revisited," Vladimir Nabokov meditates upon the secret motive for art; or, at any rate, the secret motive for his art:

> Whenever I start thinking of my love for a person, I am in the habit of immediately drawing radii from my love—from my heart, from the tender nucleus of a personal matter—to monstrously remote points of the universe. Something impels me to measure the consciousness of my love against such unimaginable and incalculable things as the behavior

of nebulae (whose very remoteness seems a form of insanity), the dreadful pitfalls of eternity, the unknowledgeable beyond the unknown, the helplessness, the cold, the sickening involutions and interpenetrations of space and time. . . . When that slow-motion silent explosion of love takes place in me, unfolding its melting fringes and overwhelming me with the sense of something much vaster . . . then my mind cannot help but pinch itself to see if it is really awake. I have to make a rapid inventory of the universe just as a man in a dream tries to condone the absurdity of his position by making sure he is dreaming. I have to have all space and all time participate in my emotion, in my mortal love, so that the edge of its mortality is taken off, thus helping me to fight the fact of having developed an infinity of sensation and thought within a finite existence.[1]

Who has spoken more frankly, and more eloquently, of the mysterious motive for metaphor?—of the subterranean connection between private emotion and the impulse for art, the making of something permanent out of love with its "edge of mortality"? Writing out of such motives is a purely human, which is to say genderless, activity. It is always bound up with love, though the specific object of the love is hidden—indeed, subterranean. The composing of fiction is not antithetical to "experience" and certainly not an escape from experience; it *is* experience.

And it is directed, ideally, toward the future. The faith of the present is that the effort of *now* will endure *then*.

So the days pass and I ask myself sometimes whether one is not hypnotized, as a child by a silver globe, by life; and whether this is living. It's very quick, bright, exciting. But

[1] Vladimir Nabokov, *Speak, Memory: An Autobiography Revisited* (New York: Pyramid Books, 1968), p. 219.

superficial perhaps. I should like to take the globe in my hands and feel it quietly, round, smooth, heavy, and so hold it, day after day.

This insatiable desire to write something before I die, this ravaging sense of the shortness and feverishness of life, make me cling, like a man on a rock, to my one anchor.[2]

There are writers, born women, who rarely think of themselves, when they write, as women; there are other writers, similarly born women, who believe their writing to be conditioned at all times by their gender. ("I am never as female as when I write," says Marguerite Duras.) A good deal has been made in recent years by French feminists and their American counterparts (see essays on *L'Écriture féminine* by Hélène Cixous and others) of the phenomenon of the specifically female voice, without regard for the fact that voice can only mean voices, if we are being attentive to subtleties of pitch and nuance. And what of subject matter? Is there a distinctly female subject, in contrast to a distinctly masculine subject? (Childbirth clearly the province of the one, war and "adventure" the province of the other?) But subject matter is clearly culture-determined, not gender-determined. And the imagination, in itself genderless, allows us all things.

Our immediate response to a book, which we might succinctly define as an artful assemblage of words, is a response to language, not to a (hypothesized) person. Where can personal identity, let alone personality, reside, in so neuter a phenomenon as *words?* Yet more crucially, where can gender reside? The reader cannot be predisposed to "like" or "dislike" a work of art because its creator (distant, legendary, perhaps long dead) was identified, during his or her life-

[2] Virginia Woolf, excerpted in *A Writer's Diary*, edited by Leonard Woolf (New York: Harcourt Brace Jovanovich, 1954), p. 135.

time, as *male* or *female*. And what, considering the evidence of moldering bones in remote graves, does *male* or *female* now mean?

Our faith in the craft of writing is that it is a form of sympathy. And, being mimetic, being bodiless, consisting solely of words, it demands no displacement or intrusion in the world; it exults in its own being.

II.

A woman is a Muse or she is nothing.
—Robert Graves

In revenge and in love, woman is more barbaric than man.
—Friedrich Nietzsche

LUXURY OF BEING DESPISED

*The sneering shout in the street, the anatomical female
stretched wide across the billboard: St. Paul's contempt.*

*Montaigne instructs us that poetry belongs to women—
a wanton and subtle art, ornate and verbose,
all pleasure
and all show: like themselves.
And Freud, that women have little sense of justice.
And De Kooning, in these angry swaths of paint:
monster-mother women!*

*The fiery sightless eye which is your own.
The booming breasts, the maniac wink.
All is heat, fecundity, secret seeping blood.
Flesh is here: nor are we out of it.*

*And yet what bliss, to be so despised:
the closed thighs all muscle,
the Church fathers' contempt,*

the Protestant chill, what freedom
in possessing no souls!—
what strange delight.

The angry swaths of flesh which are your own.
The blank stare,
the cartoon heart.
Virginity a mallet.
Mad grin worn like a bonnet.[3]

Though it is true that the writer in his (or her) art is bodiless, and transformed by craft into invisibility, what of the writer, born a woman, in the eyes of others? Does the (woman) writer occupy a significantly different space? What is the objective, as opposed to the subjective, nature of her ontological existence?

A woman who writes is a writer by her own definition; but she is a *woman* writer by others' definitions. (Among these others are, of course, women.) The books she writes are assemblages of words but her sexual identity is not thereby dissolved or transcended, unless she writes under a male pseudonym and keeps her identity secret. Books are neuter objects, *its;* writers are *he* or *she.* "A woman's writing is always feminine; it cannot help being feminine; at its best it is most feminine; the only difficulty lies in defining what we mean by feminine"—as Virginia Woolf has wittily said.

The irony, of course, is that while there are "women writers" there are not, and have never been, "men writers." This is an empty category, a class without specimens; for the noun "writer"—the very verb "writing"—always implies masculinity. (Hence the double-edged praise that befalls the

---

[3] This poem of mine originally appeared in *Bennington Review,* in a slightly different version, and is included in *Luxury of Sin,* a special limited edition published by Lord John Press (Northridge, Calif.: 1984).

woman writer when she is told, by men, that she writes "like a man." Which man? I always ask.)

The woman writer thus finds herself—and the usage is deliberate: she does not will, or wish, or invent herself, but *is found*—in a depersonalized category that is her birthright for life. Women can't write, women can't paint—so Lily Briscoe of Virginia Woolf's *To the Lighthouse* has been hypnotized by male authority, against which she, like Woolf, must struggle. "Language conceals an invisible adversary," says Hélène Cixous, "because it is the language of men and their grammar." Of course not all women are despised by all men, at least not all of the time, but it is a commonplace dilemma that a man's quarrel with the feminine in his own nature will be a quarrel with women: the impulse may be abstract and psychological but its fruition is always concrete. One need not consider the misogyny of the ages— for one thing, it is too familiar, and too depressing—for there are always examples close at hand, in even the most well-intentioned of literary forums. For instance, the *Harvard Guide to Contemporary American Writing*, published in 1979, is divided into chapters with the titles "Intellectual Background," "Literary Criticism," "Experimental Fiction," "Drama," etc., and "Women's Literature"—the last-named a potpourri of virtually anyone who writes and is female, with the inevitable emphasis on those writers who write about "female subjects." Being so ghettoized seems insulting until the (woman) writer stops to realize that a ghetto, after all, is a place in which to live; raze it, and she may find herself homeless altogether.

The old prejudice dies hard, that a woman is a muse or nothing—that is, an inspiration to the (male) artist; never an artist in her own terms. As a young writer Charlotte Brontë was assured by Robert Southey, Poet Laureate of England, that "Literature cannot be the business of a woman's life, and it ought not to be"—a remark that has subsequently become famous, though not as Southey might have anticipated. Even if, like Emily Dickinson, she succeeds in creating a remarkable body of work, she is still vulnerable to dismissal by dint of her gender: R. P. Blackmur spoke condescendingly of Dickinson as a woman poet who seemed to have taken up verse in the way that other women of her time took up needlepoint or quilting; Gerard Manley Hopkins states dogmatically that "the male quality *is* the creative gift." Anthony Burgess once dismissed Jane Austen's writing because it "lacks a strong male thrust," and William Gass once said that literary women "lack that blood congested genital drive which energizes every great style." Is this sexual contempt or sexual anxiety? one wonders. Some years ago Norman Mailer acknowledged that, though there were probably some excellent women writers in America, he would not read their work: *could* not, in fact. Even excellence isn't enough to compensate for being female.

And here is John Berryman in a slapstick Dream Song:

> *Them lady poets must not marry, pal.*
> *Miss Dickinson—fancy in Amherst bedding her.*
> *Fancy a lark with Sappho,*
> *a tumble in the bushes with Miss Moore,*
> *a spoon with Emily, while Charlotte glare.*
> *Miss Bishop's too noble-O.*
>
> *That was the lot. And two of them are here*
> *as yet, and—and: Sylvia Plath is not.*
> *She—she her credentials*
> *has handed in, leaving alone two tots*
> *and widower to what he makes of it—*
> *surviving guy. . . .*[4]

[4] In *The Dream Songs* (New York: Farrar, Straus & Giroux, 1969), p. 206.

| | 29 | |

That was the lot. Centuries of women poets are dismissed in a drunk's baby prattle, and those who are considered worthy of special attention are nonetheless "lady poets" the (male) poet would not want to "bed." (And would the objects of Berryman's boozy sexual interest want to "bed" him? A question the poet seems not to consider.)

The recent publication of the monumental *Norton Anthology of Literature by Women,* edited by Sandra Gilbert and Susan Gubar, had the perhaps unanticipated effect of polarizing women writers into two contending camps: those who denied the claims of gender and those who acknowledged them. The anthology was not seen, in some quarters, as complementing existing anthologies (consisting mainly of work by men) but as challenging them; the revisionist work of feminist scholars and critics was judged threatening, dangerous, and subversive. And some of this reaction has been by women writers whose sense of themselves is "genderless," though their writing has been aimed toward a specifically female audience and their literary reputations nourished, in part, by feminist support.

Yet the (woman) writer who imagines herself assimilated into the mainstream of literature, the literature of men, is surely mistaken, given the evidence of centuries, and the ongoing, by now perplexing, indifference of male critics to female effort. Alfred Kazin's recent *An American Procession: The Major American Writers 1830–1930* contains only one woman writer, Emily Dickinson, whom Kazin could hardly overlook. (Kazin has written elsewhere about Edith Wharton, yet excludes her pointedly from the "procession.") A recent essay by Guy Davenport—"Claiming Kin: Artist, Critic, and Scholar as Family"[5]—contains only fleeting references to

---

[5] In *Shenandoah,* Volume XXXVI, No. 1 (1985–86).

women writers (Gertrude Stein, Eudora Welty, H.D., Margaret Mitchell), though it considers, often in meticulous detail, centuries of literary endeavor, from Homer through Shakespeare to O. Henry and Louis Zukofsky. "The principle [sic] concern binding the scholar, the critic, and the artist is the vital one of continuity," Davenport says, but he means only male scholars, male critics, male artists; his "family" consists, mysteriously, of no women, rather like the Christian Trinity. Similarly, Harold Bloom's romantic theory of the psychodynamics of literary influence concerns itself exclusively with father-poets and their "misreading" sons: since women do not exist in the critic's theoretical equation, their texts must be ignored, as if they do not exist either.

As Virginia Woolf predicted in "Women and Fiction," in 1929, the male reader is disposed to dismiss women's writing as offering "not merely a difference of view, but a view that is weak, trivial, or sentimental, because it differs from his own." But even when the (woman) writer's point of view is indistinguishable from the (man) writer's, and she manages to attain some distinction during her lifetime, it frequently happens that she is likely to be devalued and forgotten following her death. Literary scholarship and history, as practiced by homosocial critics like Kazin, Davenport, Bloom, and numberless others, makes no effort to preserve her. For she does not finally belong to the "family" of Man.

Better to be despised, then, than to be ignored; or damned with condescending praise. There is a luxury after all in being despised if it frees energy away from the self and into the work; away from the distractions of visibility and into the permanence of art.

So the (woman) writer has faith in the high worth of the craft to which she has dedicated herself, but she should not be deceived in gauging her relative position within it. Power does not reside with women—no more in the literary world than in the world of politics and finance—and power is never under the obligation to act justly. A writer may be afflicted by any number of demons, real or imagined, but only the (woman) writer is afflicted by her own essential identity.

How can the paradox be accommodated? one asks, and some answers might be: with resilience, with a sense of humor, with stubbornness, with anger, with hope.

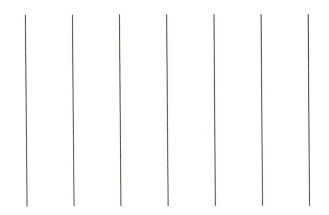

THE ART OF
SELF-CRITICISM

Self-criticism is an art not many are qualified to practice. Despite our best efforts it is problematic that, apart from the most immediate, practical, technical revisions, the writer's effort to detach himself from his work, let alone his oeuvre, is quixotic: knowing too much may be a way of knowing too little; or, conversely, how can we know more about ourselves than we know about anything else? In the human eye no light energy can stimulate the retina at the exit of the optic tract: all human beings carry blind spots with them in their vision. Everywhere we look there are points of invisibility, it might be said; and, since they are invisible, they cannot be seen even as absence. We are all in the position of Lear, who, holding absolute authority over his kingdom, had "but slenderly known himself."

In the long history of literary effort, what eccentric self-critical judgments—amounting, at times, very nearly to self-destruction. The first great poet in the English language, Chaucer, not only came to doubt the worth of his extraordinary work but repudiated it, overcome by Christian repugnance for what he conceived of as the sin of secular creation; Thomas Hardy, author of *Tess of the D'Urbervilles* and *Jude the Obscure*, two of the greatest novels in the language, spoke with dismaying indifference of novel writing as a mere profession, a "temporary" but economically "compulsory" interruption of a poetic career. Franz Kafka's self-criticism, always severe, seems to have developed gradually into a species of self-laceration analogous to the powerful images of his work—masochistic fantasies of punishment, mutilation, and erasure: it is hardly surprising that Kafka asked his friend Max Brod to destroy all his work, including the uncompleted masterpieces *The Trial* and *The Castle*. (Brod naturally refused to do so.)

"Do you know how many years I have to be read?" Chekhov asked his friend Ivan Bunin, at a time when no Russian writer except Tolstoy was so highly praised as he. "Seven years." "Why seven?" asked Bunin. "Well, seven and a half," Chekhov conceded.

Excessive self-consciousness and self-doubt, whether the consequence of ravening egotism or simple humility or, as in the case of Albert Camus at the zenith of his career, a mysterious combination of both, often results in literary paralysis. Jonathan Swift's injunction, *Just get the right syllable in the proper place,* is the perfectionist's nightmare. "I am unlikely to trust a sentence that comes easily," says William Gass. And "I write slowly because I write badly. I have to rewrite everything many, many times just to achieve mediocrity." The psychological phenomenon of paralysis itself, however, can be given an ingenious theoretical twist so that, in contemplating the difficulties of writing one's next book, one is also contemplating the universal human condition; passivity, indecision, and "impotence" in a romantic, post-*Hamlet* vein then become subjects for art, as in Mallarmé, Baudelaire, and others associated with fin de siècle consciousness—that sense that life has played itself out, that language is inadequate to communicate the intransigent facts of the human condition. In our own time it remains a perennial mystery why J. D. Salinger, one of the most praised writers of his generation, stopped publishing in mid-career; and we are all acquainted with writers, once praised as "promising" if not "absolutely brilliant!" who seem to have disappeared from public view, no longer writing or, in any case, no longer daring to publish. Are such writers intimidated by their own highly publicized worth or have they internalized their critics' judgments to the point at which nothing, however good, can appear good enough? I am acquainted with a writer who is in fact one of the finest American writers of his generation, and generally acknowledged as such, but whose self-consciousness in recent years has made it impossible for him to write letters to anyone, even friends—he knows that everything he writes is consigned to posterity (oblivion's other, seemingly more benign, face), so he feels he must compose even casual letters with painstaking exactitude; the effort leaves him exhausted. He makes telephone calls instead.

For some of us, the self's natural doubts are given a mesmerizing amplification by way of critics' negative assessments of our writing. As John Updike has said, you come to feel that the good reviewers are being generous while the others have really found you out. "When reviewers like something of mine," Gore Vidal once said, "I grow suspicious."

More commonly, writers often have virtually no conception of how their work is perceived by others—as if mere intention assured achievement. Herman Melville, the author, as a very young man, of the best-sellers *Typee* and *Omoo,* evidently believed that he had written another best-seller, a bowl of "rural milk" for the ladies, in the savagely opaque *Pierre; or, the Ambiguities* (a novel that comes close to strangling on its own self-loathing and was to prove as dismal an economic failure as *Moby Dick,* the novel that immediately preceded it). Charles Dickens seems to have considered *Great Expectations* a comedy, boasting of the opening section as "exceedingly droll" and "foolish"—material that would strike any reader as clearly tragic, if not horrific. Scott Fitzgerald argued that *Tender Is the Night* was not only a great novel but a far more experimental work of prose fiction than Joyce's *Ulysses;* William Faulkner wanted to believe that *A Fable,* that most strained, willed, wooden, lifeless of novels, set beside which his great works are like precious stones sparkling in a slag heap, was in fact his greatest novel. (Faulkner was also in the habit of speaking of himself as a "failed poet.") James Joyce seems to have been under the impression that, all evidence to the contrary, *Finnegans Wake,* on which he had labored for sixteen years, was in fact a "simple" novel: "If anyone doesn't understand a passage, all he need do is read it aloud." Then again, in a less confident mood, Joyce confessed, "Perhaps it is insanity. One will be able to judge in a century." He seems to have offered no defense to his brother Stanislaus's observation that "{Finnegans Wake} is unspeakably wearisome. . . . The witless wandering of literature before its final extinction. I would not read a paragraph of it if I did not know you."

* * *

No one was more uncertain about her work than Virginia Woolf, perhaps because she thought about it, analyzed it, so obsessively. In November 1936 when she went over the proofs of *The Years,* the novel that had given her the most difficulty of her career, she noted in her journal that she "read to the end of the first section in despair: stony but convinced despair. . . . This is happily so bad that there can be no question about it. I must carry the proofs, like a dead cat, to L., and tell him to burn them unread." But Leonard Woolf said he liked the book; thought it in fact "extraordinarily good." (Leonard is lying, but no matter: Virginia can't know.) She notes in her diary that perhaps she had exaggerated its badness. Then again, a few days later, she notes that it *is* bad. "Never write a long book again." But a few days later: "There is no need whatever in my opinion to be unhappy about *The Years.* It seems to me to come off at the end. Anyhow, to be a taut, real, strenuous book. I just finished it and feel a little exalted." Later, she concedes that it might be a failure after all—but she is finished with it. The first reviews, however, are ecstatic; Woolf is declared a "first-rate novelist" and "great lyrical poet." Almost universally it is said that *The Years* is a "masterpiece." A day or two later Virginia notes:

> How I interest myself! Quite set up and perky today with a mind brimming because I was so damnably depressed and smacked on the cheek by Edwin Muir in the *Listener* and Scott James in *Life and Letters* on Friday. They both gave me a smart snubbing: E.M. says *The Years* is dead and disappointing. So in effect did James. All the lights sank; my reed bent to the ground. Dead and disappointing—so I'm found out and that odious rice pudding of a book is what I thought it—a dank failure. No life in it. . . . Now this pain woke me at 4 A.M. and I suffered acutely. . . . But [then]

it lifted; there was a good review, of 4 lines, in the *Empire Review*. The best of my books: did that help? I don't think very much. But the delight . . . is quite real. One feels braced for some reason; amused; round, combative; more than by praise.

(*The Years,* all improbably, rises to the top of the best-seller list in the United States, where it remains for four months. And we consider it, today, one of Woolf's least successful experiments, curiously dull and soporific—"no life in it"— unlike her genuine masterpieces *To the Lighthouse, Mrs. Dalloway, The Waves,* through which life flows with the quicksilver subtlety of light in a Monet painting.)

Any number of distinguished writers have been drawn into the folly of rewriting and "improving" early work: W. H. Auden, Marianne Moore, John Crowe Ransom immediately come to mind. The energies of youth having passed, the aging and, it sometimes seems, vindictive elder wants to set things right: prune, revise, recast, in line with the doubtful wisdom of experience. His fellow poet George Seferis particularly denounced Auden's tampering with "September 1, 1939" (in which the famous line "We must love one another or die" was altered to "We must love one another and die"— or in another version omitted altogether, along with the stanza that contained it), seeing such revision as "immoral" and "egotistical" since the poem had long passed out of Auden's exclusive possession. W. B. Yeats's lifelong obsession with revising—the "making," as he called it, "of my soul"—was, by contrast, nearly always justified; as was Henry James's, and what we know of Emily Dickinson's. (Dickinson even did numerous drafts of her seemingly tossed-off little letters.) In rewriting early work for his *Collected Poems,* D. H. Lawrence considerably improved it, perhaps because the youthful poems were so bad to begin with. (However, Lawrence was a shrewd enough critic of his own work to understand that "A young man is afraid of his demon and puts his hand over the demon's mouth sometimes and speaks for him. So I have tried to let the demon say his say, and to remove the passages where the young man intruded." Note to *Collected Poems,* 1928.)

Of the innocence of raw egotism there are many, one might say too many, examples: that most macho of celebrated American writers, Ernest Hemingway, boasted of having beaten Turgenev and de Maupassant in fantasized boxing/writing matches, and of having fought two draws with Stendhal—"I think I had an edge in the last one." John O'Hara, the contemporary of such masters of short fiction as Thomas Mann, William Faulkner, Willa Cather, Katherine Anne Porter, Eudora Welty, and Hemingway, frequently boasted that "no one writes short stories better than I do." Robert Frost, even as an elder, much-honored poet, found it difficult to sit in an audience and hear another poet read work, particularly if the work was being well received, and it was wittily said (by John Cheever) that the Russian poet Yevtushenko has an ego capable of "cracking crystal at a distance of twenty feet." Nabokov believed himself superior to, among others, Dostoyevski, Turgenev, Mann, Henry James, and George Orwell.

One is led to conclude that the artist and the self-critic, the "demon" and the "ego," are, with a few felicitous exceptions, forever at odds.

The writer must accept it as a premise of his existence that certain delusions—one of these, in fact, the delusion of "self-knowledge"—are necessary for his career; as necessary as delusions of various sorts are, for all of us, generally. The "life-lie" as Ibsen named it, but Ibsen is being rather cruel: why not erect "life-*ideal*" as a more beneficent term? One can live with ideals but does feel a bit uncomfortable with lies.

This principle, in any case, we must hold if we are to survive as writers, deluded or otherwise: even when all evidence is to the contrary, *we are steadily improving; whatever we are working on at the present time is the best thing we have ever done, and the next book will be even better.* In this sense all writers are quintessentially American—we fear that not to progress is to plunge into the abyss. And we may be right.

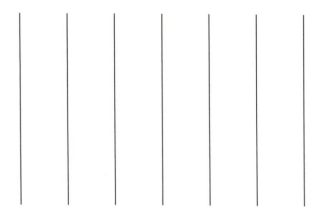

THE DREAM OF THE "SACRED TEXT"

One of the oldest stories we tell ourselves is the dream of the "sacred text."

All writers—all artists?—tell themselves this story, sometimes in yearning, sometimes in despair. Perhaps it is the oldest story: language set down with such talismanic precision, such painstaking ardor, such *will,* it can never be altered; language that constitutes an indissoluble reality of its own—human in origin but more-than-human in essence.

Not *what* is being said, but *how.* For *what* is frequently given to us, *what* is inevitable: it is the *how* that makes, or has the possibility of making, the text sacred.

What is the impulse underlying this old story—dream, delusion, motive-for-metaphor? It might spring from the child's belief in the omnipotence of thought, an early sense that dreams are not (merely) interior but might be shared by others, specifically by adults. One wishes for permanence by way of the medium of language, a command that time stand still. What is curious is that the act of writing often satisfies these extraordinary demands. We immerse ourselves in it so deeply, "writing" in our daydreams, "composing" in our sleep, hypnotizing ourselves with *what* we have been born to tell, that time seems to warp or to fold back upon itself. The writer is always writing, always sounding words, measuring cadences, hearing, feeling, attending to, taking the pulse of . . . secret rhythms. Content yields to, or crystallizes around, form; form is subordinate to "voice." We write by ear, we experiment with "voice" without knowing what it is.

We only know its absence: we hear nothing.

In reading, it seems we search for sacred texts written by others *that we might read them.* The written word leaps to the eye and through the eye to our deepest consciousness: there is nothing quite like it. Reading too is a mysterious process, entirely private, perhaps even secret: a rent in the fabric of time, so to speak, a sudden lifting of the veil that separates one consciousness from another. Sounding the talismanic language of another in our own ears, are we not participating in a reality exterior to our own?—preceding it and fated to outlive it? Unless the exterior "voice" rings false, or there is no "voice" at all.

Henry James in his journal suddenly exclaims, as if

involuntarily, "Sanctities, pieties, treasures, abysses!" And though unprepared for the revelation, one thinks, Yes.

For the writer each work as it is being composed is a part of the sacred text. Often it appears to be *the* text, a powerful summing up of all that has preceded it. For those of us who sometimes write novels—long novels—poetry is the miracle of finitude and exactness: it affords the pleasure of revision, and revision, and yet again revision, in a way that longer forms cannot. We know that to rewrite a page in its entirety is almost inevitably to improve it—what temptation, then, to compose a single text forever! The poem is by definition that which can always be rewritten, unless of course it is a long narrative; it can be sounded yet again in the poet's ear, envisioned yet again in another formal arrangement.

Hence the notorious instinct among writers for rewriting early work in assembling a "collected" volume, an instinct that sometimes leads to folly.

The secret at the heart of all creative activity has something to do with our desire to complete a work, to impose perfection upon it, so that, hammered out of profane materials, it becomes sacred: which is to say, no longer merely personal. Yet the desire brings with it our exclusion from that phase of our lives. To begin a new work invariably involves extraordinary effort but after a while—weeks, months; if one is fortunate, only days—it acquires its own rhythm, its own unmistakable "voice"; it begins, as we so clumsily say, to "write itself." As if any text has ever "written itself" except by way of the effort of the writer . . . drop by drop by precious drop, his or her blood draining into it.

Completing a work of art we're expelled from it. This hurts. This frightens. Sometimes it terrifies—and baffles others. Of course we know that we *should* be eased out, forced to let go; we should not find it surprising that a door closes behind us, and locks. And it really does close; and it really does lock. A book may be many things to many people, but always to the author it is a monument to a certain (past) self, a certain irremediable chunk of time: so many pulse beats, so much effort. Will it never come again? "Never, never, never, never, never"—which is to say, five times never: the cadence of tragedy. For *knowing oneself* after all posits a single self to be known, at a single point in time. And the very rhythms and cadences of language speak to selves—fluidity, movement, ever-unfolding revelations: the search for the elusive "sacred" text.

"The" text.

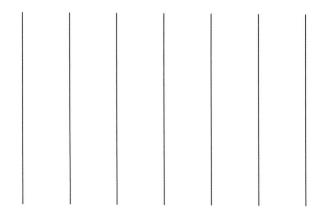

DOES THE
WRITER EXIST?

There are many memorable passages in Virginia Woolf's diaries, but none more poignant than the entry for Sunday, 25 July 1926, which records the visit of the forty-five-year-old Virginia with Thomas Hardy at his home in Dorset. Hardy, seventy-six years old, the greatest novelist of his time, the author of *The Mayor of Casterbridge, Tess of the D'Urbervilles, Jude the Obscure,* now "sets no great stock by literature" but is immensely interested in facts. Whatever one might expect of "Thomas Hardy," it is somehow *not* the "little puffy cheeked cheerful old man, with an atmosphere cheerful & businesslike in addressing us, rather like an old doctor's or solicitor's." Hardy seems to be, at this point in his life, "delivered" of all his work: he is not much interested in his novels, or in anyone's novels; does not in fact read fiction any longer. Much is made of the ease—"I never took long with them"—with which he wrote both novels and poetry. But now it is all very distant, and mildly amusing, the world of literary activity and literary significance:

> The whole thing—literature, novels etc.—all seemed to him an amusement, far away, too, scarcely to be taken seriously. Yet he had sympathy & pity for those still engaged in it. But what his secret interests & activities are—to what occupation he trotted off when we left him—I do not know.[1]

It is not that the elderly gentleman has outlived himself as "Thomas Hardy" so much that the works of "Thomas Hardy" are no longer relevant to Hardy himself. One seeks the author of *Tess* and *Jude* and finds—of course—a stranger.

More amusing, yet scarcely more satisfying, is a quick portrait of George Eliot diffracted through the lens of a (nowforgotten) woman writer named Eliza Lynn Linton, who had in fact enjoyed Eliot's hospitality upon more than one previous occasion.

> Marian Evans ("George Eliot") held her hands and arms kangaroo fashion; was badly dressed; had an unwashed, unbrushed, unkempt look altogether; and . . . assumed a tone of superiority over me which I was not then aware was warranted. . . . She was so consciously "George Eliot"— so interpenetrated head and heel, inside and out, with the

---

[1] *The Diary of Virginia Woolf, Volume 3, 1925–1930*, edited by Anne Oliver Bell and Andrew McNeillie (New York: Harcourt Brace Jovanovich, 1980), pp. 96–101.

sense of her importance as the great novelist and profound thinker of her generation.[2]

(In which case—or so it seems: for can we trust the envious Miss Linton?—"George Eliot" has swallowed up Marian Evans entirely.)

And when writers of equal iconoclastic genius finally meet—James Joyce and Marcel Proust in Paris, May 1921, as reported by observers:

> The two men sat together. Joyce said: "I have headaches every day. My eyes are terrible." Proust replied: "My poor stomach. What am I to do? It's killing me. In fact I must leave at once." "I'm in the same situation," said Joyce. "If I can find someone to take me by the arm." Proust afterward said: "I regret that I don't know Mr. Joyce's work," and Joyce said: "I have never read Mr. Proust."[3]

According to Joyce himself, who seems to have remembered the meeting differently, the two men spoke briefly of truffles: Proust asked him if he liked truffles, and Joyce answered, "Yes, I do." (Joyce had in fact tried to read Proust but found his style "unimpressive"; he envied Proust only his material circumstances—his money and his cork-lined room.)

"That was a profound book. You don't look like you wrote it." So, as reported in a letter to Robert Lowell and Elizabeth Hardwick, in December 1953, spoke a stranger who came up to Flannery O'Connor at a social gathering in Nashville, Tennessee, after the publication of her first novel,

---

[2] From *My Literary Life*, 1889. Quoted in *A Literature of Their Own: British Women Novelists from Brontë to Lessing*, Elaine Showalter (Princeton, N.J.: Princeton University Press, 1977), p. 107.

[3] *James Joyce*, Richard Ellmann (New York: Oxford University Press, 1965), p. 523.

Wise Blood. Flannery O'Connor, whose estimation of herself was generally rather modest, reported that she "mustered up my squintiest expression and snarled, 'Well I did,' but at the same time I had to recognize he was right." She doesn't, she says, look very intelligent. She doesn't look *profound.*[4]

As, indeed, who does?

The examples of course can be multiplied endlessly, the anecdotes cast in darker and more bizarre or more grotesque tones (the last days of Dylan Thomas, Delmore Schwartz, Robert Lowell, for instance; the vision of Edmund Wilson eating spaghetti, so extraordinary a sight, a literary acquaintance reported, it was enough to cause one "to lose faith in the human race"). The contrast between what we *know* of a writer from his or her work—the private self—and what we are forced to *confront* in the irrefutable flesh—the "public" self—is nearly always disorienting. Our conviction is that, as readers, as devoted and sympathetic readers, we can lay claim to the writer as he truly "is"; and it seems to us a violation of nature that the writer in person so rarely "is" the person we anticipate. (For instance, how is it possible to reconcile the poet Robert Frost—author of some of the most extraordinary lyric poems in the English language, in which beauty and wisdom are gracefully combined—with the man who, in August 1938, at the Bread Loaf Writers' Conference in Vermont, was so jealous of his rival Archibald MacLeish that, at MacLeish's public reading, he set a handful of papers on fire, to capture the audience's attention for himself?[5] *It is not possible to reconcile the two!*) Yet more puzzling, perhaps,

---

[4] *The Habit of Being: Letters of Flannery O'Connor,* edited by Sally Fitzgerald (New York: Farrar, Straus & Giroux, 1978), p. 65.

[5] *Robert Frost,* Lawrance Thompson and R. H. Winnick (New York: Henry Holt & Co., 1981), p. 385. (This is the one-volume edition of the biography, edited by E. C. Lathem.)

is Vanity's complete reversal, the split between writer and "person" so great, that, like Charles Dodgson, who irritably returned to senders all correspondence addressed to "Lewis Carroll," there would appear to be active hostility between the two. (It is said that the two sides of Dodgson's face were uneven and did not quite match; but as to which side was "Dodgson" and which "Carroll," we are not informed.)

Jorge Luis Borges has written so powerfully of the split in himself that it is a temptation to quote him in (near) entirety:

> It's to the other man, to Borges, that things happen. I walk along the streets of Buenos Aires, stopping now and then—perhaps out of habit—to look at the arch of an old entranceway or a grillwork gate; of Borges I get news through the mail and glimpse his name among a committee of professors or in a dictionary of biography. I have a taste for hourglasses, maps, eighteenth-century typography, the roots of words, the smell of coffee, and Stevenson's prose; the other man shares these likes, but in a showy way that turns them into stagy mannerisms. It would be an exaggeration to say that we are on bad terms; I live, I let myself live, so that Borges can weave his tales and poems. . . . Little by little, I have been surrendering everything to him, even though I have evidence of his stubborn habit of falsification and exaggerating. . . . Years ago, I tried ridding myself of him and I went from the myths of the outlying slums of the city to games with time and infinity, but those games are now part of Borges and I will have to turn to other things. And so, my life is a running away, and I lose everything and everything is left to oblivion or to the other man. Which of us is writing this page I don't know.
>
> ("Borges and I")

Does the writer exist?

Or, granted his or her (physical, temporal) existence,

does the writer exist in any significant relationship to his or her work? By approaching the person, even by way of correspondence, can one approach the work?—or does the work necessarily retreat, now forever imprinted with the irrevocable face, or voice, or presence, of an actor impostor? "Not by the face shall the man be known, but by the mask," declares a character (himself an impostor) in Isak Dinesen's "The Deluge at Norderney," from *Seven Gothic Tales*. And the living Dinesen deliberately created for herself a kind of death mask by powdering her face dead white, ringing her eyes in black mascara, and swathing her head in turbans; she was the ageless undying sibyl, the storyteller laying claim to being three thousand years old and having dined with Socrates . . . a fictional character more prodigious than any she had created in prose.

For profundity, as Nietzsche has said, loves the mask.

And there is the fear that the work will be betrayed by its author: the one is after all typeface on white (chaste, pristine, innocent) paper; the other is . . . mere flesh. The one may have been revised tirelessly, monomaniacally (in drafts, in galleys, even in page proofs) so that it is as close to perfection as possible; the other has been cast upon the wayward surf of spontaneity, happenstance, the promiscuous energies of Real Life.

The more deliberate the writer is in his art, the more he risks by existing.

Yet, perhaps, the ontological status of "existence" in this case has not been demonstrated: *Does* the writer exist. . . ?

In a surrealist comedy of 1892, "The Private Life," Henry James deals with the problem in his own ingenious manner through the character of a celebrated author named Clare Vawdrey. What are such an author's admirers to make of the fact that, though his novels are extraordinary, his person is so very ordinary? Vawdrey, the most famous English writer of his time, mystifies observers by way of his public self, which is never anything but "totally mediocre . . . loud and liberal and cheerful." His opinions are sound and thoroughly second-rate; he never expresses a paradox or plays with an idea; he has "marched with his even pace and his perfectly good conscience into the flat country of anecdote, where stories are visible from afar like windmills and signposts."

Contrasting sharply with the (Browning-inspired) Vawdrey is that genius of the drawing room, Lord Mellifont. Ah, Mellifont! "The mere sound of his name and air of his person, the general expectation he created, had somehow a pitch . . . romantic and abnormal," says James's narrator. So brilliant, charming, and original is Mellifont, his very legend pales before his reality. He is not merely the perfection of a style, "he *was* a style." When Vawdrey and Mellifont dine together the contrast is embarrassing: Vawdrey's talk suggests the reporter, Mellifont's the bard.

It turns out, however—for this *is* comic surrealism—that Lord Mellifont does not exist at all, apart from society. When there is no one present to observe and admire him, he vanishes "like a candle flame blown out."

Whereas Vawdrey is discovered to be not one but two people: literally two people.

The narrator learns this amazing fact by accident, having left Vawdrey (the public man) in one room, and going to Vawdrey's room to fetch a manuscript, where he happens upon Vawdrey (the private man) sitting in the dark, hunched over a table, *writing.* One man *dines,* the other *writes.* The narrator and his lady confidante breathlessly confer, as narrators and confidantes do so frequently in James's fiction, ferreting out, for our benefit, the knotty truths of a mystification. "It looked infinitely more like him than our friend does himself," the narrator says in deadpan humor. "Do you mean it was somebody he gets to do [his work]?" the lady asks. "Yes, while he dines out and disappoints . . . disappoints every one who looks in him for the genius that created the pages they adore." The genius is forever inaccessible; it is only the "loud and liberal and cheerful" bourgeois whom people know: *he* moves among them as one of them.

James's is a witty parable that illuminates a sober truth: for the novelist Vawdrey (like Browning—or James himself) is not to be encountered, let alone casually befriended, by other people. Genius means inaccessibility, isolation, mystery. That it is a mystery to the writer himself should not be surprising: "You may rely on it you have the best of me in my books, and that I am not worth seeing personally, the stuttering, blundering clod-hopper that I am. Even poetry, you know, is in one sense an infinite brag and exaggeration. Not that I do not stand on all that I have written—but what am *I* to the truth I feebly utter!" (Henry David Thoreau in a letter of 1857, to an admirer named Greene whom, perhaps wisely, he never met.)

It might be argued that most human beings, writers or not, are in disguise as their outward selves; and that their truest and most valuable selves are interior. A way of saying "The kingdom of God is within"—as if we knew, except in metaphor, what the "kingdom" is. And what "God."

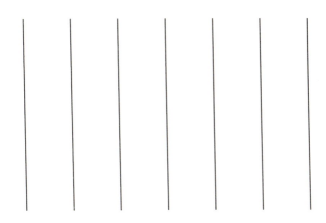

LITERATURE AS PLEASURE, PLEASURE AS LITERATURE

I have always come to life after coming to books.
—Jorge Luis Borges

It might be argued that reading constitutes the keenest, because most secret, sort of pleasure. And that it's a pleasure best savored by night: by way of an ideal insomnia. At such times, lamplight illuminating the page but not much else, the world is writ small, deliciously small, and words, another's voice, come forward. *What I love about wakefulness,* the insomniac says, *is being alone, and reading.*

   Insomnia is a predilection, a skill, a way of being, best cultivated young: in early adolescence if possible. To begin in adulthood would be a pity since, at the very least, so much precious solitude (i.e., occasions for reading) has already been lost.

You know it's poetry, Emily Dickinson says, when it takes the top of your head off. Or when, to use Randall Jarrell's metaphor, you're struck by lightning—as a reader. All great poetry is enhanced by the occasion of its discovery, and by the occasion of its savoring: a poem by night is far more powerful than a poem by day. And there are certain mysterious poems, like this by Walt Whitman—atypical Whitman, it should be noted—that can only be read by night.

A CLEAR MIDNIGHT

This is thy hour O soul,
　　thy free flight into the wordless,
Away from books, away from art,
　　the day erased, the lesson done,
Thee fully forth emerging, silent, gazing,
　　pondering the themes thou lovest best:
Night, sleep, death and the stars.

Love at first sight/hearing: however delusory in human romantic terms, it is nearly always reliable, in fact irresistible, in literary terms. A certitude that darts into the soul by way of the eye provokes an involuntary visceral effect. Not always "pleasant" in the most benign sense of that ambiguous word but always, always exciting.

When you haven't realized you have memorized another's words, poetry or prose, then, as if unbidden, the words assert themselves. Coleridge's "knowledge returning as power." As, one evening in Princeton, a poet friend and I discovered that we could recite in unison an early poem of Yeats's most admirers of Yeats would consider marginal, yet in its angry percussive rhythms, it could have been written by no one else:

TO A FRIEND WHOSE WORK HAS COME TO NOTHING

> *Now all the truth is out,*
> *Be secret and take defeat*
> *From any brazen throat,*
> *For how can you compete,*
> *Being honor bred, with one*
> *Who, were it proved he lies,*
> *Were neither shamed in his own*
> *Nor in his neighbors' eyes?*
> *Bred to a harder thing*
> *Than Triumph, turn away*
> *And like a laughing string*
> *Whereon mad fingers play*
> *Amid a place of stone,*
> *Be secret and exult,*
> *Because of all things known*
> *That is most difficult.*

This too is a poem best savored, perhaps uniquely savored, by night. Like other great poems of Yeats's—"The Magi," "The Circus Animals' Desertion," "The Cold Heaven," "The Wild Swans at Coole," the Crazy Jane poems, to name only a few—which I first discovered in protracted, headachey, but utterly ravishing insomniac spells of reading in my late teens. How hard to maintain the keenest degree of consciousness after having been awake most of the night; how hard, how *willful* the task, to take daylight as seriously as night! Yeats's magisterial imperatives have the authority, shading into contempt, of words engraved in stone: tombstone, maybe. Like those famous lines at the end of "Under Ben Bulben":

JOYCE CAROL OATES

Cast a cold eye
On life, on death.
Horseman, pass by!

"A book is an ax," Franz Kafka once said, "for the frozen sea within." Curious metaphors—particularly the ax. But we know what he means.

There are pleasures in reading so startling, so intense, they shade into pain. The realization that one's life has been irrevocably altered by . . . can it be mere words? Print on a page? The most life-rending discoveries involve what has in fact never been thought, never given form, until another's words embody them. Recall the ingenuous Dorian Gray, of whom it is said he was "seduced by a book." (The book being Huysmans's masterwork of decadence, *À Rebours*.) And have there been innumerable others who were seduced by that book, and Wilde's own masterwork *The Picture of Dorian Gray?* And what, at a morbid extreme, of the young killers Leopold and Loeb, who, having read Nietzsche as undergraduates, decided in the manner of Dostoyevski's Raskolnikov to experiment with taking a human life—having ascended, as they thought, to the level of absolute moral freedom that Nietzsche's Zarathustra preached? Is this pathology, or the greatest possible empathy? The least resistance to the "pleasure" of being overcome by another's voice?

Consider the phenomenon of reading, that most mysterious of acts. It is the sole means by which we slip, involuntarily, often helplessly, into another's skin; another's voice; another's soul. One might argue that serious reading is as sacramental an act as serious writing, and should therefore not be profaned. That, by way of a book, we have the ability to transcend what is immediate, what is merely personal, and to enter a consciousness not known to us, in some cases distinctly alien, *other*. . . . This morning I open a new hardcover book, of moderate size, modestly packaged, not guessing how, within minutes—in fact, within seconds—my heart will be beating more quickly, my senses alert to the point of pain, an excitement coursing through me that makes it virtually impossible to stay seated. The book is *The Collected Poems of William Carlos Williams, Volume I, 1909–1939*, edited by A. Walton Litz and Christopher MacGowen (New York: New Directions, 1986). The poem I begin to read is "Paterson: Episode 17," with its haunting refrain "Beautiful Thing"—first read how many years ago? and reread how many times?—yet still possessed of its uncanny original power. And there are the great "raw" poems we all know and have memorized, "By the road to the contagious hospital," "The pure products of America/ go crazy," "The Widow's Lament at Springtime," and that poem in honor/awe/terror of America—

The crowd at the ball game
is moved uniformly

by a spirit of uselessness
which delights them—

all the exciting detail
of the chase

and the escape, the error
the flash of genius—

all to no end save beauty
the eternal—

So in detail they, the crowd,
are beautiful

for this
to be warned against

saluted and defied—
It is alive, venomous

it smiles grimly
its words cut—

The flashy female with her
mother, gets it—

The Jew gets it straight—it
is deadly, terrifying—

It is the Inquisition, the
Revolution

It is beauty itself
that lives

day by day in them
idly—

This is
the power of their faces

It is summer, it is the solstice
the crowd is

cheering, the crowd is laughing
in detail

permanently, seriously
without thought
    (from *Spring and All*, 1923)

Elsewhere—

What are these elations I have
at my own underwear?

I touch it and it is strange
upon a strange thigh.
    (from *The Descent of Winter*,
                    1928)

And: I enter an empty classroom in the old Hall of Languages Building, Syracuse University, sometime in the fall of 1956, discover a lost or discarded book on ethics, an anthology of sorts, open it at random, and begin reading . . . and reading . . . so that the class that begins in a few minutes, whatever remarks, long forgotten, by whatever professor of philosophy, also, alas, long forgotten, are a distraction and an interruption. How profoundly excited I am by this unknown new voice, this absolutely new and unique and enchanting voice—though I am familiar, I suppose, with some of the writers *he* read, and from whom *he* learned (Shakespeare, Dostoyevski, Emerson), I am not at all familiar with Nietzsche himself—only the name, the word, the sound, mysterious and forbidding. This philosopher who is an anti-philosopher, a poet, a mystic (and anti-mystic); whose genius expresses itself in aphorism and riddle—"philosophy with a hammer." To have read Nietzsche at age eighteen, when one's senses are most keenly and nervously alert, the very envelope of the skin dangerously porous; to have heard, and been struck to the heart, by that astonishing voice— what ecstasy! what visceral unease!—as if the very floor were shifting beneath one's feet. Late adolescence is the time for love, or, rather, for passion—the conviction that *within the next hour* something can happen, will happen, to irrevocably alter one's life. (*"The danger in happiness:* Now everything I touch turns out to be wonderful. Now I love any fate that comes along. Who feels like being my fate?") Whatever books of Nietzsche's I then bought in paperback or took out of the university library—*The Birth of Tragedy, Human, All Too Human, The Gay Science, Thus Spake Zarathustra, Beyond Good and Evil, Twilight of the Idols*—I must have read, or devoured, quickly and carelessly and with no sense of their historical context; under the spell of an enchantment I had every reason to think was unique. And for me Nietzsche *was* unique—one of those voices out of a densely populated world that define themselves so brilliantly, in a way so poignantly, against that world, they become—almost—assimilated into one's very soul.

(Nietzsche died mad. But, mad, lived for a long time—eleven years. In January 1899 on a Turin street he saw a coachman flogging a horse, ran to protect the horse, flung his arms around it, and collapsed; and never recovered. And in his madness, even, what radiance, what bizarre and heart-rending poetry—signing himself "The Crucified" and "Dionysus"—writing letters like this one, to Jacob Burckhardt: "In the end I would much rather be a Basel professor than God; but I have not dared push my private egoism so far as to desist for its sake from the creation of the world. You see, one must make sacrifices however and wherever one lives. . . . What is disagreeable and offends my modesty is that at bottom I am every name in history. With the children I have put into the world too,[1] I consider with some mistrust whether it is not the case that all who come *into* the kingdom of God also come *out* of God. This fall I was blinded as little as possible when I twice witnessed my funeral. . . . We artists are incorrigible." And, in a postscript: "I go everywhere in my student's coat, and here and there slap somebody on the shoulder and say, 'Are we content? I am the god who has made this caricature.' ")

And: I leaf through a bulky anthology of poetry, too many years ago to calibrate though I am probably still in junior high school, and the names are mostly new, mysterious, lacking all associations, therefore talismanic, pure. No mere opinionizing went into the assemblage of this book—

[1] Nietzsche never married, had no child. It is believed his madness was caused by syphilitic infection contracted when he was a student or while nursing wounded soldiers in 1870. (The translation used here is by Walter Kaufmann.)

no literary politics, surely not!—so far as a thirteen-year-old might guess. If I noted the absence of women I have no memory of it and rather doubt that I did, since poetry even more than prose seemed to me then, and seemed to me for many years, a wholly neutral—or do I mean neuter?—genderless activity. (I might have thought—perhaps I still think—*That's the beauty of the enterprise!*) And it would have struck me as rude, vulgar, insipid, trivializing, a profanation of the very page, to read the poetry that excited me most as if it were the product, even, of a human being like myself; as if it were the product of what would one day be called a "female consciousness." For didn't it mean that, being a poet, having been granted the imprimatur of poet, Emily Dickinson had in fact transcended not only the "female" but the "human" as categories?

I don't remember the first Dickinson poems I read; very likely they were the same poems we all read, and re-read, and were puzzled and haunted by, as by a child's riddle of such evident simplicity you feel you must understand it—yet can't, quite. Of the frequently anthologized poems it was the darker and more mysterious ones that struck me as embodying poetry's very essence. The Dickinson who fascinates most is the Dickinson of the great elegaic poems, the poems of "madness," the terse elliptical statement poems that carry with them an air very nearly of belligerence, they are so short, and complete:

> *The competitions of the sky*
> *Corrodeless ply.*[2]

[2] The poems of Emily Dickinson quoted in this essay are from the Thomas H. Johnson edition of *The Complete Poems of Emily Dickinson* (Cambridge: Harvard University Press, 1960).

JOYCE CAROL OATES

And:

> *Fame's Boys and Girls, who never die*
> *And are too seldom born —*

And:

> *We outgrow love, like other things*
> *And put it in the Drawer —*
> *Till it an Antique fashion shows —*
> *Like Costumes Grandsires wore.*

All good poets resist paraphrase; Emily Dickinson frequently resists simple comprehension. And should we "sense" her meaning we are inevitably excluded from her technique, marveling at the rightness of certain images, sounds, strategies of punctuation—the ellipses of a mind accustomed to thinking slantwise—yet unable to grasp the poem's ineluctable essence. (And the identity of the poem's narrative "I," shifting as it does from poem to poem.) When we read Dickinson the nerves tighten in sympathy and wonder. Fragments leap out at us as powerfully as fully realized poems:

> *It is the Past's supreme italic*
> *Makes this Present mean —*
>
> *
>
> *Oh Life, begun in fluent Blood*
> *And consummated dull!*
>
> *
>
> *The Brain, within its Groove*
> *Runs evenly — and true —*
> *But let a Splinter swerve —*
> *'Twere easier for You —*

To put a Current back —
When Floods have slit the Hills —
And scooped a Turnpike for Themselves —
And trodden out the Mills —

Franz Kafka in his stories, parables, fragments, and journal entries rather more than in his incompletely realized novels. . . . Virginia Woolf in her diary and letters, in which her voice sounds forth glimmering and inimitable, rather more than in her frequently stilted, always self-conscious prose fiction. . . . Henry James when he is most Jamesian (as in *The Wings of the Dove*) and then again least Jamesian (as in the unabridged *Notebooks,* in which he addresses himself without artifice, sometimes in melancholy, sometimes in triumph, speaking to his muse whom he calls "mon bon" as if he, or it, were a lover). . . . William James in that great work *The Varieties of Religious Experience,* in which you will find yourself in one or another chapter ("The Religion of Healthy-Mindedness," "The Sick Soul," "The Divided Self, and the Process of Its Integration"). . . . Hardy's great novels, prose poetry as narrative, *Tess of the D'Urbervilles* and *Jude the Obscure* in particular. . . . Robert Frost despite the distracting regularity of certain of his rhymes (which mitigate against, in the ears of many admirers, the deeper music of his art). . . . D. H. Lawrence in his poetry no less than in his prose, and in such "minor" work as *The Lost Girl* as well as in the "major" novels. . . . James Joyce in the very excess of his genius, word-maddened, besotted, not so much crossing the line between sanity and craziness as erasing it—at least in art. And there are the others, the many others, the flood of others, the voices of strangers closer to us than the voices of friends, more intimate, in some instances, than our own. Literature grants us few of the consolations and none of the vatic promises of religion, but *is* our religion nonetheless.

The expression on the young man's face—I am haunted by it, not envious (of it, or of its cause) but wondering, bemused: was it simple surprise, at the masterpiece of short prose fiction we had taken up in our workshop; was it awe?— sheer *interest?* And his eagerness to read more by Hemingway, more of these short tight perfect narratives, written when Hemingway was (as I tell my students gently) not much older than they. The story is "A Very Short Story," one and a half pages of laconic prose, bitten-back rage, "One hot evening in Padua they carried him up onto the roof and he could look over the top of the town"; and it's perfection of a kind, of a kind Hemingway himself only infrequently achieved. It is a young man's record of being wounded, the death of romance, of hope, as powerful in its way as the novel it would later become, and far less sentimental. And the young, very young writers in my workshop to whom "Ernest Hemingway" has always been a name or a reputation are allowed to see that there was a Hemingway who did not know himself Hemingway, could not, so young, have guessed it would turn out as in his most aggressive childlike fantasies he'd dreamt it would: he *was* the real thing, wasn't he? And one of them remains after class wanting to say something further, not wanting the talk of Hemingway to end, or the talk, in any case, of *this* Hemingway to end, this page and a half of perfectly honed and seemingly immortal prose; wanting to ask me something but not knowing what to ask, as at all crucial moments in our lives we want to speak without knowing what to say. What can I tell him of the unfathomable mystery of personality? of personality transcribed and made permanent in art?—in mere finite *words?* Perhaps the young man wants to ask, Can I do it too? Can I try, too? but he would not ask such a thing, would not expose himself so rawly, that isn't Princeton's style. He says, the book still open in his hands, his voice rather vague, searching, "It's so short. It does so much." And I'm thinking, Yes, this is the real thing, this is love, that look on your face, again, always, what pleasure.

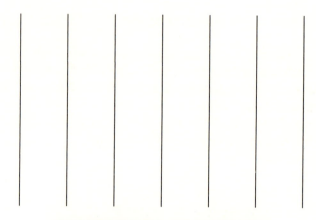

AGAINST NATURE

We soon get through with Nature. She excites an expectation which she cannot satisfy.

—Thoreau, *Journal*, 1854

Sir, if a man has experienced the inexpressible, he is under no obligation to attempt to express it.

—Samuel Johnson

The writer's resistance to Nature.

It has no sense of humor: in its beauty, as in its ugliness, or its neutrality, there is no laughter.

It lacks a moral purpose.

It lacks a satiric dimension, registers no irony.

Its pleasures lack resonance, being accidental; its horrors, even when premeditated, are equally perfunctory, "red in tooth and claw," et cetera.

It lacks a symbolic subtext—excepting that provided by man.

It has no (verbal) language.

It has no interest in ours.

It inspires a painfully limited set of responses in "nature writers"—REVERENCE, AWE, PIETY, MYSTICAL ONENESS.

It eludes us even as it prepares to swallow us up, books and all.

I was lying on my back in the dirt gravel of the towpath beside the Delaware and Raritan Canal, Titusville, New Jersey, staring up at the sky and trying, with no success, to overcome a sudden attack of tachycardia that had come upon me out of nowhere—such attacks are always "out of nowhere," that's their charm—and all around me Nature thrummed with life, the air smelling of moisture and sunlight, the canal reflecting the sky, red-winged blackbirds testing their spring calls: the usual. I'd become the jar in Tennessee, a fictitious center, or parenthesis, aware beyond my erratic heartbeat of the numberless heartbeats of the earth, its pulsing, pumping life, sheer life, incalculable. Struck down in the midst of motion—I'd been jogging a minute before— I was "out of time" like a fallen, stunned boxer, privileged (in an abstract manner of speaking) to be an involuntary witness to the random, wayward, nameless motion on all sides of me.

Paroxysmal tachycardia can be fatal, but rarely; if the heartbeat accelerates to 250–270 beats a minute you're in trouble, but the average attack is about 100–150 beats and mine seemed about average; the trick now was to prevent it from getting worse. Brainy people try brainy strategies, such as thinking calming thoughts, pseudo-mystic thoughts, *If I die now it's a good death,* that sort of thing, *if I die this is a good place and good time;* the idea is to deceive the frenzied heartbeat that, really, you don't care: you hadn't any other plans for the afternoon. The important thing with tachycardia is to prevent panic! you must prevent panic! otherwise you'll have to be taken by ambulance to the closest emergency room, which is not so very nice a way to spend the afternoon, really. So I contemplated the blue sky overhead. The earth beneath my head. Nature surrounding me on all sides; I couldn't quite see it but I could hear it, smell it, sense it, there is something *there,* no mistake about it. Completely oblivious to the predicament of the individual but that's only "natural," after all, one hardly expects otherwise.

When you discover yourself lying on the ground, limp and unresisting, head in the dirt, and, let's face it, helpless, the earth seems to shift forward as a presence; hard, emphatic, not mere surface but a genuine force—there is no other word for it but *presence.* To keep in motion is to keep in time, and to be stopped, stilled, is to be abruptly out of time, in another time dimension perhaps, an alien one, where human language has no resonance. Nothing to be said about it expresses it, nothing touches it, it's an absolute against which nothing human can be measured. . . . Moving through space and time by way of your own volition you inhabit an interior consciousness, a hallucinatory consciousness, it might be said, so long as breath, heartbeat, the body's autonomy hold; when motion is stopped you are jarred out of it. The interior is invaded by the exterior. The outside wants to come in, and only the self's fragile membrane prevents it.

The fly buzzing at Emily's death.

Still, the earth *is* your place. A tidy grave site measured to your size. Or, from another angle of vision, one vast democratic grave.

Let's contemplate the sky. Forget the crazy hammering heartbeat, don't listen to it, don't start counting, remember that there is a clever way of breathing that conserves oxygen as if you're lying below the surface of a body of water breathing through a very thin straw but you *can* breathe through it if you're careful, if you don't panic; one breath and then another and then another, isn't that the story of all lives? careers? Just a matter of breathing. Of course it is. But contemplate the sky, it's there to be contemplated. A mild shock to see it so blank, blue, a thin airy ghostly blue, no clouds to disguise its emptiness. You are beginning to feel not only weightless but near-bodiless, lying on the earth like a scrap of paper about to be blown off. Two dimensions and you'd imagined you were three! And there's the sky rolling away forever, into infinity—if "infinity" can be "rolled into"—and the forlorn truth is, that's where you're going too. And the lovely blue isn't even blue, is it? isn't even there, is it? a mere optical illusion, isn't it? no matter what art has urged you to believe.

Early Nature memories. Which it's best not to suppress.

. . . Wading, as a small child, in Tonawanda Creek near our house, and afterward trying to tear off, in a frenzy of terror and revulsion, the sticky fat black bloodsuckers that had attached themselves to my feet, particularly between my toes.

. . . Coming upon a friend's dog in a drainage ditch, dead for several days, evidently the poor creature had been shot by a hunter and left to die, bleeding to death, and we're stupefied with grief and horror but can't resist sliding down to where he's lying on his belly, and we can't resist squatting over him, turning the body over.

. . . The raccoon, mad with rabies, frothing at the mouth and tearing at his own belly with his teeth, so that his intestines spill out onto the ground . . . a sight I seem to remember though in fact I did not see. I've been told I did not see.

Consequently, my chronic uneasiness with Nature mysticism; Nature adoration; Nature-as-(moral)-instruction-for-mankind. My doubt that one can, with philosophical validity, address "Nature" as a single coherent noun, anything other than a Platonic, hence discredited, is-ness. My resistance to "Nature writing" as a genre, except when it is brilliantly fictionalized in the service of a writer's individual vision—Thoreau's books and *Journal,* of course, but also, less known in this country, the miniaturist prose poems of Colette *(Flowers and Fruit)* and Ponge *(Taking the Side of Things)*—in which case it becomes yet another, and ingenious, form of storytelling. The subject is *there* only by the grace of the author's language.

Nature has no instructions for mankind except that our poor beleaguered humanist-democratic way of life, our fantasies of the individual's high worth, our sense that the weak, no less than the strong, have a right to survive, are absurd. When Edmund of *King Lear* said excitedly, "Nature, be thou my goddess!" he knew whereof he spoke.

In any case, where *is* Nature, one might (skeptically) inquire. Who has looked upon her/its face and survived?

But isn't this all exaggeration, in the spirit of rhetorical contentiousness? Surely Nature is, for you, as for most reasonably intelligent people, a "perennial" source of beauty, comfort, peace, escape from the delirium of civilized life; a respite from the ego's ever-frantic strategies of self-promotion, as a way of ensuring (at least in fantasy) some small measure of immortality? Surely Nature, as it is understood in the usual slapdash way, as human, if not dilettante, *experience* (hiking in a national park, jogging on the beach at dawn, even tending, with the usual comical frustrations, a suburban garden), is wonderfully consoling; a place where, when you go there, it has to take you in?—a palimpsest of sorts you choose to read, layer by layer, always with care, always cautiously, in proportion to your psychological strength?

Nature: as in Thoreau's upbeat Transcendentalist mode ("The indescribable innocence and beneficence of Nature,—such health, such cheer, they afford forever! and such sympathy have they ever with our race, that all Nature would be affected . . . if any man should ever for a just cause grieve"), and not in Thoreau's grim mode ("Nature is hard to be overcome but she must be overcome").

Another way of saying, not *Nature-in-itself* but *Nature-as-experience.*

The former, Nature-in-itself, is, to allude slantwise to Melville, a blankness ten times blank; the latter is what we commonly, or perhaps always, mean, when we speak of Nature as a noun, a single entity—something of *ours.* Most of the time it's just an activity, a sort of hobby, a weekend, a few days, perhaps a few hours, staring out the window at the mind-dazzling autumn foliage of, say, northern Michigan, being rendered speechless—temporarily—at the sight of Mt. Shasta, the Grand Canyon, Ansel Adams's West. Or Nature writ small, contained in the back yard. Nature filtered through our optical nerves, our "senses," our fiercely romantic expectations. Nature that pleases us because it mirrors our souls, or gives the comforting illusion of doing so.

Nature as the self's (flattering) mirror, but not ever, no, never, Nature-in-itself.

Nature is mouths, or maybe a single mouth. Why glamorize it, romanticize it?—well, yes, but we must, we're writers, poets, mystics (of a sort) aren't we, precisely what else are we to do but glamorize and romanticize and generally exaggerate the significance of anything we focus the white heat of our "creativity" upon? And why not Nature, since it's there, common property, mute, can't talk back, allows us the possibility of transcending the human condition for a while, writing prettily of mountain ranges, white-tailed deer, the purple crocuses outside this very window, the thrumming dazzling "life force" we imagine we all support. Why not?

Nature *is* more than a mouth—it's a dazzling variety of mouths. And it pleases the senses, in any case, as the physicists' chill universe of numbers certainly does not.

Oscar Wilde, on our subject:

> Nature is no great mother who has borne us. She is our creation. It is in our brain that she quickens to life. Things are because we see them, and what we see, and how we see it, depends on the Arts that have influenced us. To look at a thing is very different from seeing a thing. . . . At present, people see fogs, not because there are fogs, but because poets and painters have taught them the mysterious loveliness of such effects. There may have been fogs for centuries in London. I dare say there were. But no one saw them. They did not exist until Art had invented them. . . . Yesterday evening Mrs. Arundel insisted on my going to the window and looking at the glorious sky, as she called it. And so I had to look at it. . . . And what was it? It was simply a very second-rate Turner, a Turner of a bad period, with all the painter's worst faults exaggerated and over-emphasized.
>
> ("The Decay of Lying," 1889)

(If we were to put it to Oscar Wilde that he exaggerates, his reply might well be, "Exaggeration? I don't know the meaning of the word.")

Walden, that most artfully composed of prose fictions, concludes, in the rhapsodic chapter "Spring," with Henry David Thoreau's contemplation of death, decay, and regeneration as it is suggested to him, or to his protagonist, by the spectacle of vultures feeding off carrion. There is a dead horse close by his cabin, and the stench of its decomposition, in certain winds, is daunting. Yet "the assurance it gave me of the strong appetite and inviolable health of Nature was my compensation for this. I love to see that Nature is so rife with life that myriads can be afforded to be sacrificed and suffered to prey upon one another; that tender organizations can be so serenely squashed out of existence like pulp,—tadpoles which herons gobble up, and tortoises and toads run over in the road; and that sometimes it has rained flesh and blood! . . . The impression made on a wise man is that of universal innocence."

Come off it, Henry David. You've grieved these many years for your elder brother, John, who died a ghastly death of lockjaw; you've never wholly recovered from the experience of watching him die. And you know, or must know, that you're fated too to die young of consumption. . . . But this doctrinaire Transcendentalist passage ends *Walden* on just the right note. It's as impersonal, as coolly detached, as the Oversoul itself: a "wise man" filters his emotions through his brain.

Or through his prose.

Nietzsche: "We all pretend to ourselves that we are more simple-minded than we are: that is how we get a rest from our fellow men."

Once out of nature I shall never take
My bodily form from any natural thing,
But such a form as Grecian goldsmiths make
Of hammered gold and gold enamelling
To keep a drowsy Emperor awake;
Or set upon a golden bough to sing

> *To lords and ladies of Byzantium*
> *Of what is past, or passing, or to come.*
> —William Butler Yeats, *Sailing to Byzantium*

Yet even the golden bird is a "bodily form [taken from a] natural thing." No, it's impossible to escape!

The writer's resistance to Nature.
    Wallace Stevens: "In the presence of extraordinary actuality, consciousness takes the place of imagination."

Once, years ago, in 1972 to be precise, when I seemed to have been another person, related to the person I am now as one is related, tangentially, sometimes embarrassingly, to cousins not seen for decades—once, when we were living in London, and I was very sick, I had a mystical vision. That is, I "had" a "mystical vision"—the heart sinks: such pretension—or something resembling one. A fever dream, let's call it. It impressed me enormously and impresses me still, though I've long since lost the capacity to see it with my mind's eye, or even, I suppose, to believe in it. There is a statute of limitations on "mystical visions," as on romantic love.
    I was very sick, and I imagined my life as a thread, a thread of breath, or heartbeat, or pulse, or light—yes, it was light, radiant light; I was burning with fever and I ascended to that plane of serenity that might be mistaken for (or *is,* in fact) Nirvana, where I had a waking dream of uncanny lucidity:
    My body is a tall column of light and heat.
    My body is not "I" but "it."
    My body is not one but many.
    My body, which "I" inhabit, is inhabited as well by

other creatures, unknown to me, imperceptible—the small-
est of them mere sparks of light.

My body, which I perceive as substance, is in fact an
organization of infinitely complex, overlapping, imbricated
structures, radiant light their manifestation, the "body" a tall
column of light and blood heat, a temporary agreement
among atoms, like a high-rise building with numberless
rooms, corridors, corners, elevator shafts, windows. . . . In
this fantastical structure the "I" is deluded as to its sover-
eignty, let alone its autonomy in the (outside) world; the
most astonishing secret is that the "I" doesn't exist!—but it
behaves as if it does, as if it were one and not many.

In any case, without the "I" the tall column of light
and heat would die, and the microscopic life particles would
die with it . . . will die with it. The "I," which doesn't exist,
is everything.

But Dr. Johnson is right, the inexpressible need not be expressed.

And what resistance, finally? There is none.

This morning, an invasion of tiny black ants. One by one
they appear, out of nowhere—that's their charm too!—moving single file across the white Parsons table where I am
sitting, trying without much success to write a poem. A poem
of only three or four lines is what I want, something short,
tight, mean; I want it to hurt like a white-hot wire up the
nostrils, small and compact and turned in upon itself with
the density of a hunk of rock from the planet Jupiter. . . .

But here come the black ants: harbingers, you might
say, of spring. One by one by one they appear on the dazzling white table and one by one I kill them with a forefinger, my deft right forefinger, mashing each against the sur-

face of the table and then dropping it into a wastebasket at my side. Idle labor, mesmerizing, effortless, and I'm curious as to how long I can do it—sit here in the brilliant March sunshine killing ants with my right forefinger—how long I, and the ants, can keep it up.

After a while I realize that I can do it a long time. And that I've written my poem.

2

WONDERLANDS

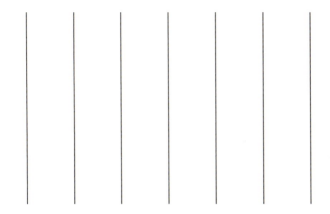

WONDERLANDS

Another world to live in is what we mean by having a religion.
—Santayana

A melancholy conclusion. . . . It turns lying into a universal principle.
—Joseph K. of Kafka's *The Trial*

Humankind has rarely found attractive or convincing the mystic's gnomic pronouncement that the "higher" world is in fact this world, transfigured: *any* world, the unarticulated cry would have it, so long as it is not *this!* How otherwise to account for the proliferation of wonderlands in our culture—anti-worlds, counterworlds, counterfactual dimensions of the spirit: archetypal gardens, celestial cities, landscapes of unspeakable beauty—even, upon occasion, mock Utopias that mirror our own world by way of distortion or nightmare reversal? Here, suddenly, is a mysterious door in a wall, and here is the golden key that will unlock it, one has only to summon forth one's courage and enter. Whatever awaits will not only be strange and unexpected, it will, in a way impossible to explain, *make sense;* and it will be *ours*—as "reality" never is.

How spontaneously our childlike excitement is aroused by the mere notion of a secret world—a secret garden, perhaps, or a world of dazzling radiance; a spectral world that is yet authentic, plausible—contiguous with our own (otherwise how should we enter it?) yet altogether separate and unpredictable. A veritable galaxy of fantasy worlds exists for us to explore, in legend, fairy tale, and imaginative literature; and no less fantastic are the hypostatized worlds of singularities (in physics, "non-places" where all known laws of nature seem to be suspended) and counterfactual conditionals ("possible worlds" accessible only by way of logic). These wonderlands share only their antipathy to the real or historical world; in most respects they never bisect one another, nor do they exhibit common boundaries. Divine legends, Gothic tales, childhood fantasies, moral parables cloaked in the forms of science fiction, the supernatural, the mock-adventure—each makes claim to having penetrated the most secret region of the soul, addressing the soul in its own special language; each vision makes war upon the others. If common images abound—radiance, doorways, gardens—they mean radically different things, like words in foreign languages that merely sound like words we recognize.

Consider the afterworld as an actual place: luminous, yet material; a region of dazzling light; studded with gems, gold, glass; a landscape transfigured by the Divine, filled with what Ezekiel calls stones of fire. Very little is said of the paradisiacal garden of our first parents, in Genesis, but much is said of heaven, in Revelation: that extraordinary region inhabited by God himself, available to the mystic known as St. John the Divine, as a door is opened in heaven and a trumpet sounds, and here is the very throne of God encircled by a rainbow "in sight like unto an emerald." And round about the throne are four and twenty elders clothed in white, with crowns of gold on their heads. And

> out of the throne proceeded lightnings and thunderings and voices: and there were seven lamps of fire burning before the throne, which are the seven Spirits of God. And before the throne there was a sea of glass like unto crystal: and in the midst of the throne, and round about the throne, were four beasts full of eyes before and behind. . . . And when these beasts give glory and honour and thanks to him that sat on the throne, who liveth for ever and ever, the four and twenty elders fall down before him that sat on the throne, and worship him that liveth for ever and ever, and cast their crowns before the throne, saying, Thou art worthy, O Lord, to receive glory and honour, and power: for thou hast created all things, and for thy pleasure they are and were created.

Here follows the apocalyptic vision of the book of the seven seals.

What significance has a deity that cannot be experienced by the senses?—what value has a heaven that cannot be entered by way of a door? Visions must be tangible, tactile; they must not only be seen but entered; the human participant must *feel* the event as material and not merely spiritual. Hence in Roman Catholic tradition the Virgin is *bodily* assumed into heaven; the resurrection of the *body* is promised; in hell—that counter-heaven—sinners suffer excruciating *physical* agony for all eternity (so wretched are the damned, St. Anselm says, they are unable to remove from their eyes the worms that gnaw them).

Though Plato would ban all poets from his perfect state, charging that they have no "mind" but are only "possessed," the very concept of the Republic itself is of course a poetic conceit; and Plato fully exploits the human yearning for fantasy worlds experienced as "real." In Book X of *The Republic,* for instance, in the tale of Er, we learn of a "wonderful region" in which there are two openings in the earth, side by side, and two others in the heaven above, facing them: by one of each pair of openings souls depart, and by the other of each pair souls return, some from earth and some from heaven, some to earth and some to heaven, to serve out the sentences their behavior warrants. The souls arriving from earth have naturally suffered, to a degree; the souls from heaven tell of bliss and of sights "incredibly beautiful." A vision is granted the worthy of the intricate Spindle of Necessity—a cosmic network in which intense light functions as the bond of heaven holding together the universe. According to the tale of Er, men are free to choose their destinies, but, once they have chosen, they are bound to their fates *of necessity:* "The blame is for the chooser; God is blameless." (The destinies are imagined as literal "models of lives" spread out on the ground.)

Though the ostensible theme of *The Republic* is a correct definition of justice, the concept depends upon a precise image of a "wonderful region" and a no less precise image of a counter-heaven—an underground cave where men are chained with their backs to the light, with necks and legs fettered. The famous Parable of the Cave (Book VII) is a labored conceit whose lesson is that men naturally mistake shadows for substance: "Suppose the prisoners were able to talk together, don't you think that when they named the shadows which they saw . . . they would believe they were naming things?" If granted a vision of reality (imagined as brilliant sunshine), men would turn aside dazed and incredulous, preferring the ignorance to which they have become accustomed. The lot of man resembles habitation in prison, and only a very few are capable of perceiving the Idea of the Good ("the cause of all right and beautiful things").

The secret of the divine wonderlands lies in their exclusionary and punitive qualities. Sacred spaces demand profane counterparts: it is pointless to be "saved" unless others are "damned." The radiant afterworld is defined by the lightless region, usually far below, where men (our fallen comrades) suffer the absence of God or the Good. What value has the Divine, if all have access to it?

In Gothic literature, "wonderful regions"—ruined castles, accursed houses, the poisoned garden of a Rappaccini—are dimensions of the psyche given a luridly tangible form, in which unacknowledged (or rigorously suppressed) wishes are granted freedom. Impulse rises at once to the level of action: the unconscious is provoked—the unconscious "awakes"—what has been long buried seizes life and autonomy, as if independent of the mediating self. Frequently in Gothic fiction the innocent are not only victimized but are co-opted by the wicked: the wonderland is a marvelous place where *we* are *they*—our shadow selves given both substance and potency.

The deathly power of the vampire of legend, for instance, is scarcely his or her ability to destroy (for simple destruction is in a sense only Nature—"natural") but to seduce; to transform the "virtuous" victim into the "evil" accomplice. Commingled with loathing is a fairly explicit fascination for what is repulsive and forbidden, even vulgar. Jonathan Harker speaks for many a victim of supernatural forces when he says, in a passionate outburst near the conclusion of Bram Stoker's *Dracula,* "Do you know what the place is? Have you seen that awful den of hellish infamy—

with the very moonlight alive with grisly shapes, and every speck of dust that whirls in the wind a devouring monster in embryo? Have you felt the Vampire's lips upon your throat?" (What Jonathan has actually experienced differs significantly from this account, however. We recall his night at the Castle Dracula many months before when he was approached in his sleep by one of Dracula's sisters. A "fair girl," with "honey-sweet" breath in which there is a faint scent of a "bitter offensiveness, as one smells in blood," she bends over him, gloating, and

> there was a deliberate voluptuousness that was both thrilling and repulsive, and as she arched her neck she actually licked her lips like an animal, till I could see in the moonlight the moisture shining on the scarlet lips and on the red tongue as it lapped the white sharp teeth. Lower and lower went her head as the lips went below the range of my mouth and chin and seemed about to fasten on my throat. Then she paused, and I could hear the churning sound of her tongue as it licked her teeth and lips, and could feel the hot breath on my neck. Then the skin of my throat began to tingle as one's flesh does when the hand that is to tickle it approaches nearer—nearer. I could feel the soft, shivering touch of the lips on the super-sensitive skin of my throat, and the hard dents of two sharp teeth, just touching and pausing there. I closed my eyes in a languorous ecstasy and waited—waited with beating heart.

Jonathan is saved from the extremities of his "languorous ecstasy" by the sudden appearance of his host, Count Dracula.)

Much of the appeal of the Gothic wonderland has to do with the disarming fact that its inhabitants, who resemble civilized and often quite attractive men and women, are in reality creatures of primitive instinct. Gratification is all, and it is usually immediate—to *wish* is to *act*. This counterfactual region functions yet more magically as a reversal of our ethical world, in which, the monstrousness of the vampire given *a priori,* any means are justified in destroying him—or her. Perhaps the most telling episode in *Dracula* occurs midway in the narrative, as reported in Dr. Seward's diary: the painfully graphic scene in which Lucy Westenra's vampire self is killed by men bent upon "saving" her. Here, a communion of blood brotherhood is enacted that parodies the Christian ritual of purification and atonement. The legitimate Lucy, it seems, has died; her sweetness has changed to "adamantine, heartless cruelty"; the blood of a victim trickles over her chin and "stains the purity" of her gown. This is, yet cannot be, the Lucy Westenra they have all loved: she possesses Lucy's beautiful eyes in form and color, but Lucy's eyes "unclean and full of hell-fire, instead of the pure, gentle orbs we knew." Dr. Seward is led to confess that, at that moment, his love for Lucy passed into hate and loathing: had the woman then to be killed, he could have done it with "savage delight." This creature is a "nightmare" of Lucy, with pointed teeth, a bloodstained, voluptuous mouth, the entire "carnal and unspirited appearance" a devilish mockery of Lucy's purity; naturally she must be killed, but only according to ritual.

"Take this stake in your left hand," the righteous Van Helsing instructs, "ready to place the point over the heart, and the hammer in your right. Then when we begin our prayer for the dead . . . strike in God's name, so that all may be well with the dead that we love and that the Un-Dead pass away." With these extraordinary results:

> The Thing in the coffin writhed; and a hideous, blood-curdling screech came from the opened red lips. The body shook and quivered and twisted in wild contortions; the

sharp white teeth champed together till the lips were cut, and the mouth was smeared with a crimson foam. But Arthur never faltered. He looked like a figure of Thor as his untrembling arm rose and fell, driving deeper and deeper the mercy-bearing stake, whilst the blood from the pierced heart welled and spurted up around it. His face was set, and high duty seemed to shine through it; the sight of it gave us courage so that our voices seemed to ring through the little vault.

And then the writhing and quivering of the body became less, and the teeth seemed to champ, and the face to quiver. Finally it lay still. The terrible task was over. . . .

There, in the coffin lay no longer the foul Thing that we had so dreaded and grown to hate that the work of her destruction was yielded as a privilege to the one best entitled to it, but Lucy as we had seen her in her life, with her face of unequalled sweetness and purity.

Where but in a wonderland of "privilege"—a world in which "high duty" mingles with violent sexual sadism—might such an episode take place? The stake pounded into the female vampire's heart is "mercy-bearing"—the entire procedure is performed in the name of God the Father—for by way of the ritual magic of the Gothic wonderland even a violently sadistic fantasy of gang rape is sanctified. (For the sacrifice is after all in the service of the church; one might even argue that it is altruistic.)*

The great appeal of Edgar Allan Poe is surely that, in

---

*In a remarkably similar rite of sadistic purification, young Frankenstein of Mary Shelley's tale butchers the "nearly completed" female creature he has made at the request of his demon, who has begged him for a bride—and for the possibility of living a virtuous life in human terms. Frankenstein's cruelty throughout *Frankenstein* is far more reprehensible than the demon's, which is surely the author's point, but *Frankenstein* is not a Gothic novel so much as a philosophical tract in which ideas are given ponderous but occasionally quite moving dramatic utterance.

his imagination, the very perimeters of the Gothic region—wonders, horrors; how can they be distinguished?—become perverse strengths. Sickness is superior to health; hallucination is superior to mere vision; the dead woman, being dead, exerts an irresistible appeal that is spiritual and not debased by the body. In this overwrought claustral world it is frequently reason itself that is challenged and found inadequate; the supernatural exists as plausibly, perhaps even more convincingly, than the natural. Darkness, Decay, and Death constitute the first principle of existence, yet what *is* Death, when so many of Poe's automatons appear to be dead while alive, and not sufficiently dead when dead?

In that paradigmatic Poe tale "Ligeia," the immediate horror springs from the fact that the Conqueror Worm (its "vermin fangs/ In human gore imbued") has dominion over mortal man and even over the most passionate love. Yet, if one's will is strong enough (to quote Joseph Glanvill, "Man doth not yield him to the angels, nor unto death utterly, save only through the weakness of his feeble will") death can be overcome; one can return to the world of the living if not precisely to "life." (But is "life" ever an issue in Poe's fiction? It might be argued that life—the necessity of *living*—is in fact the primordial terror his personae dare not confront. In the pitiless turbulent daylight of America of the 1830s and 1840s, Poe's hallucinatory fantasies would be destroyed at once, if exposed to "life.") Ligeia returns from the grave in the physical form of the Lady Rowena, as a consequence of her powerful will; but the tale might as readily be interpreted as the narrator's creation of a second wife in terms of the first—*his* potent fantasy projection come to life (again). Poe's women are anima figures exclusively, for in the fiercely claustrophiliac world of his fiction only one personality exists. This is a "wonderful region" of the soul that has no counterworld in historic possibility.

Grotesque as Poe's images famously are, and inter-
larded as his ornate prose is with such key words as "anxiety," "suffocation," "terror," and "dread," it is clear that this
is an icily cerebral vision, an obsessively *willed* art in which
neither human beings nor their emotions legitimately exist.
The tales, even the poems, can be reduced to speculative
propositions; the spectral figures so frequently limned in the
same adjectives, the atmospheres of unrelieved tension, the
near-ubiquitous terror of the putrefaction of the grave—all
suggest an allegorical plane of consciousness in which "this"
world scarcely functions save as a sort of grammar of Gothic
possibility. If anything is finally taboo in Poe's counterworld
it is the commonplace experiences of our own—birth, for
instance, or "normal" love; Poe's chastely narrow imagination disavows such concerns. Birth is mock birth, the return
of a prematurely interred "corpse" from its grave, as in "The
Fall of the House of Usher"; love is a feverish commingling
of souls in which the stronger will possesses the weaker, as
in "Ligeia." In no other Gothic fiction are the terms so exotic, so bizarre, or the mode of discourse more breathless,
yet one reads Poe's fantasies as deftly transposed autobiographical confession; indeed, much of the continuing appeal
of Poe has to do with the fact that he makes shamelessly
manifest the childhood or infantile terrors that maturity ostensibly forbids. The more outsized and lurid and even ri-
diculous Poe's images, the more directly they speak to us,
though we might wish it otherwise.

In "The Imp of the Perverse," for instance, Poe speaks
of matters that strike a startlingly contemporary note, for all
that they are impacted in turgid, editorializing prose. The
parable is witty, cruel, slyly nihilistic—"It would have been
wiser," the narrator argues, "it would have been safer to
classify, (if classify we must,) upon the basis of what man
usually or occasionally did, and was always occasionally doing,

rather than upon the basis of what we took for granted the Deity intended him to do"—making its point that, as a species, we desire not transcendence but annihilation. The horror in horror!—and yet, is there not also delight? "For the very reason that it involves that one most ghastly and loathsome of all the most ghastly and loathsome images of death and suffering which have ever presented themselves to our imagination—for this very cause do we the most vividly desire it," the protagonist declares. And surely he is not speaking for a single aberrant personality.

To be filled with revulsion, to be horrified, to be brought to the very edge of madness and rendered totally impotent as adult human beings—are these finally disagreeable experiences if one considers their alternative? For isn't life the alternative?—the *living* of a life? Literal geographical abysses surely exist, as in, for example, *The Narrative of Arthur Gordon Pym,* but it is the interior abysses that tempt: the suicidal compulsion being so very urgent, so very sweet, even to savor it must be sin. The problematic work that Poe believed to be his crowning achievement, *Eureka,* presents a Gothic cosmology that seems to us, reading it in the late twentieth century (it was written in 1848), as uncomfortably prescient, despite, again, the tortuous quality of its language: for here is a mystic cosmos in which individuals half-consciously long to be assimilated into an original divine power that, many aeons ago, dispersed and diluted itself into its creation. "Each law of Nature depends at all points on all the other laws," Poe states, for his is not a mechanical and spiritless universe from which God has departed, but a living, breathing, *calculating* universe in which individuals, for all their pose of rationality, are but components in a vast ineffable drama. Their terror of dissolution is at once their yearning for assimilation—hence the "naturalness" of what we have come to call the death wish. The Conqueror Worm, the Red Death, the very Imp of the Perverse are agents in mankind's fulfillment of its destiny.

In any case death, being a limit, defines us in a way that life cannot; for life is improvisation, human plenitude, the risk of surrendering childish narcissism to societal obligation. In Poe the sickly paraphernalia of the Gothic wonderland is especially seductive because the images are so striking and the thematic conclusions are known beforehand. "Psyche," Poe has told us repeatedly, is "Holy Land."

In Hawthorne's *American Notebooks* we find the impulse behind the Gothic sensibility, the idea before it is imagined in a coherent and extended work of narrative art. The notebook entries are brief, mere jottings, yet dramatically suggestive: "Our body to be possessed by two different spirits; so that half the visage shall express one mood, and the other half another"; "A man living a wicked life in one place, and simultaneously a virtuous and religious one in another"; "All the dead that had ever been drowned in a certain lake to arise." Most touching is an entry in 1838: "A person to catch fireflies, and try to kindle his household fire with them. It would be symbolical of something." Gothic fiction is very often deductive rather than inductive—by which I mean that the writer knows beforehand the paradoxical proposition he intends to present, and the act of writing itself is an act of explanation. Thus the Gothic imagination is fundamentally didactic and restrictive—its cosmos is already defined.

By contrast, the "wonderful regions" of much of children's literature have the air of spontaneous invention, of artless improvisation; as if by magic—but of course it is magic— they open out from familiar landscapes and are presided over by benevolent (though usually invisible) powers. These are innocent rather than sacred realms of the spirit, protected by love and suffused with a sense of justice and logic.

It is significant that child heroes and heroines are rarely susceptible to the emotions "real" children might feel, except in such nearly naturalistic works as Frances Hodgson Burnett's classic of 1911, *The Secret Garden*. Lewis Carroll's Alice is a model of sanity in a world gone askew; she has been called the "prime heroine of our nation" by the poet Robert Graves—her unfailing judiciousness of behavior being, perhaps, an aspect of her Englishness. Alice's penetration into another realm of being coterminous with our own, yet entertainingly combative with it, allows her an enlargement of personality and perspective that is uniquely satisfying in "children's" literature.

In the opening chapter of *Alice in Wonderland* Alice peers through a small door into "the loveliest garden you ever saw"—her immediate problem being that she is too large to push herself through. Much later, when she does succeed in entering the enchanted garden, it is only to be disappointed: the behavior of the King and Queen turns out to be idiotic, a parody of inexplicable "adult" behavior. Clearly this wonderland is not the expression of the heart's secret desire so much as an oblique comment on presumably civilized behavior aboveground. (In the far more conventional novel by Frances Hodgson Burnett, the "secret garden" is the redemptive factor in the lives of two motherless children, Mary Lennox and her cousin Colin, both of them sickly and ill-natured; the garden becomes an altogether convincing image of their mutual rejuvenation. But of course adults are absent from Burnett's wonderland on the Yorkshire moors.) In *Through the Looking-Glass* Alice willingly plays the role of a pawn whose vision is limited: "It's a great huge game of chess that's being played—all over the world—if this *is* the world," Alice exclaims. The game has innumerable facets; its rules, known to some, are denied to others; underlying the entire adventure is the mystery of who dreams the dream—the Red King (foolishly snoring beneath a tree) or Alice herself (safely returned to childhood again in the book's frame). Much in the *Alice* books has to do with the mind's disintegration in the face of unanswerable questions, but Alice, the "prime" heroine, is strengthened by her experience. Indeed, how comforting and exhilarating the conclusion of *Wonderland,* when the emboldened Alice defies her elders by demanding: "Who cares for you? You're nothing but a pack of cards!" Immediately the dream creatures are routed, the fantasy nightmare ends:

> At this the whole pack rose up into the air, and came flying down upon her; she gave a little scream, half of fright and half of anger, and tried to beat them off, and found herself lying on the bank, with her head in the lap of her sister, who was gently brushing away some dead leaves that had fluttered down from the trees upon her face. . . . "Oh, I've had such a curious dream!" said Alice.

The enduring charm of the story lies precisely in its being contained by a child's deeply moral consciousness.

Underlying Alice's adventures is a strategy of improvisation, an animistic sense of fluidity, flux, constant metamorphosis: amusing at times and at other times highly disturbing. *If* this, *then* this; if *that,* then *that.* If Alice accepts a pair of knitting needles from a grandmotherly sheep, why should they not turn into oars?—why should she not, in an instant, find herself in a little boat, rowing, about to misunderstand the quaint command "Feather"?—if Alice enters a door in a tree, why should she not find herself back at the very start of her adventure? *Drink Me* finds her ten inches high, "shutting up like a telescope"; *Eat Me* finds her enormous, long-necked, suddenly doubtful of who she is ("I'm sure I'm not Ada . . . and I'm sure I can't be Mabel"); merely holding a fan causes her to shrink rapidly, and on the verge of disappearing altogether ("That *was* a narrow escape," Alice says, a good deal frightened at the sudden change). Fantasy improvisation is after all the primary process of the dreaming self; one's identity, in such regions of consciousness, is realized as a verb in the act of expressing itself and not as a passive, stolid, fully defined noun. Is it really the case, as Humpty Dumpty bravely states, that one can be "master" of words—or of anything? Not very likely, as the ground shifts so restlessly, and the very landscape is on the point of dissolving.

Nightmares not specifically identified with childhood are given memorable dramatic shape in both the *Alice* books and in *The Hunting of the Snark: An Agony, in Eight Fits.* The Cheshire Cat's bland assertion that everyone in Wonderland is mad cannot protect Alice (or the reader) from the alarming manifestations of madness she encounters: the croquet game played with living hedgehogs, the furious Queen who wants everyone beheaded, the stasis of the tea party at its perpetual 6 P.M., the frightening idiocy of Tweedledee and Tweedledum. In the King's courtroom rules are invented on the spot; sentences are handed down first, verdicts afterward—a sleight-of-hand assuredly practiced in Charles Dodgson's time, as it is now. If, in Looking-Glass World, time is capable of reversing itself, it is only logical that the White Queen screams before her finger is pricked, to save herself the effort of screaming afterward; and poor Hatta, imprisoned, must wait for the crime he will commit. And it is logical, given the exigencies of time and space, that in order to merely keep one's place (one's existence? one's sanity?) "it takes all the running you can do," as the Red

Queen tells Alice. The good-natured White Knight may very well be senile, for all his sweetness; the amiable White Queen changes into a bleating sheep. "Jam yesterday and jam tomorrow—but never jam today" is a principle for some; for others, like the greedy Walrus and the Carpenter, it is always jam today. (The Walrus and the Carpenter shamelessly devour the young oysters in their charge. "It seems a shame," the Walrus said,/ "To play them such a trick./ After we've brought them out so far,/ And made them trot so quick!"/ The Carpenter said nothing but/ "The butter's spread too thick!") "I can't explain myself," Alice says to the Caterpillar, "because I'm not myself, you see." As the gentlemen who hunt the elusive Snark discover, "soft and sudden vanishings" are the order of the day and not, after all, an awakening from comic nightmare. Time is capable too of coming to an abrupt stop—in mid-sentence.

It is significant, perhaps, that the Alice of fantasy is so much more fully realized than the Alice of the tales' fairly conventional frames. The "real" Alice in the "real" world (presumably of Oxford, England) is after all merely a little girl chattering to herself, and not Lewis Carroll's brilliant distillation of childhood. (At the conclusion of *Through the Looking-Glass* Alice comes rather close to trivializing her own experience, as she speculates about the strange dream she has had and whether "Kitty" participated in it. Who has dreamt whom is a problematic issue in the fantasy, for, after all, if the Red King is indeed dreaming Alice she can go out—"bang!"—like a candle, as Tweedledum says; her very existence is precarious. But the frame makes light of this puzzle as if it is quite inconsequential. And the author's sentimentally elegiac poem "A boat, beneath a sunny sky" makes the point that the tale is a tale, "life" but a "dream," the most banal of observations.) Only in the anarchic counterworld of the imagination could Carroll/Dodgson express himself freely.

Alice's "wonderful regions" are under the protectorate of a benign authorial consciousness; these are, it must be remembered, books for children. Her bravely rationalist position in both Wonderland and Looking-Glass World is one of the sources of our amusement, but she is not seriously, finally, frustrated in her effort to "make sense" of things or to comport herself intelligently and judiciously in the face of outrageous behavior on the part of others. Not a child but a child heroine, a model of sanity and fair-mindedness, a *mature* little girl in the midst of decidedly *immature* adults: it is altogether fitting that the final triumphs are hers. She defeats Wonderland by denouncing its quarreling adults as "nothing but a pack of cards," she defeats the rather more frightening Looking-Glass World by bringing the cannibal banquet to an end and waking up. The author need not take us further, to make the cruel point that his child heroine becomes merely a child by waking up, and that she is saved from harm by returning to the "sane" world that encloses and defines the nightmare. She *does* triumph, she *does* awaken, and the stories end on a note of propriety and tenderness.

Alice in Wonderland (an early title being *Alice's Golden Hours*) belongs to 1865; *Through the Looking-Glass* to 1871. The coldly brilliant comic epic *The Hunting of the Snark: An Agony, in Eight Fits,* published in 1876, was first conceived in the summer of 1874, when Lewis Carroll/Charles Dodgson was forty-two years old. Here, one is struck immediately by a new tone, the absence of a central narrative consciousness, the mockery underlying the droll recitation of events; clearly the haphazard world of *Snark* is not another Wonderland. Standing outside the frame, the nameless narrator tells a nonsense tale that is also a kind of tragedy, or a tragedy that is also a nonsense tale, evincing not the slightest sympathy for his deluded characters. A Bellman, a Boots, a Bonnet-maker, a Barrister, a Broker, a Billiard-maker, a Banker, a Beaver, a Baker, a Butcher: a doomed crew goes to sea with enthusiasm to hunt the deadly Snark.

A triumph of faultlessly measured language, a tour de force of rather black and nihilistic comedy, *Snark* is most striking in the ironic disparity between its jaunty jangling rhymes and the unhappy tale it tells. The Baker says

> *"I engage with the Snark—every night after dark—*
> *In a dreamy delirious fight:*
> *I serve it with greens in those shadowy scenes,*
> *And I use it for striking a light:*
>
> *"But if ever I meet with a Boojum, that day,*
> *In a moment (of this I am sure),*
> *I shall softly and suddenly vanish away—*
> *And the notion I cannot endure!"*

which turns out to be, of course, prophetic. As for the Banker's fate in the seventh fit, when he goes insane, or suffers a stroke:

> *He was black in the face, and they scarcely could trace*
> *The least likeness to what he had been:*
> *While so great was his fright that his waistcoat turned white—*
> *A wonderful thing to be seen!*
>
> *To the horror of all who were present that day,*
> *He uprose in full evening dress,*
> *And with senseless grimaces endeavoured to say*
> *What his tongue could no longer express.*

With equal dispatch the Baker (variously called "Thingumbob," "Fritter my wig," "What-was-his-name") vanishes in the final stanzas:

> *They gazed in delight, while the Butcher exclaimed*
>   *"He was always a desperate wag!"*
> *They beheld him—their Baker—their hero unnamed—*
>   *On top of a neighboring crag,*
>
> *Erect and sublime, for one moment of time.*
>   *In the next, that wild figure they saw*
> *(As if stung by a spasm) plunge into a chasm,*
>   *While they waited and listened in awe.*
>
> *"It's a Snark!" was the sound that first came to their ears,*
>   *And seemed almost too good to be true.*
> *Then followed a torrent of laughter and cheers:*
>   *Then the ominous words "It's a Boo—"*

Then, silence. For the Baker has met his fate, and "not a button, or feather, or mark" remains of him.

> *In the midst of the word he was trying to say,*
>   *In the midst of his laughter and glee,*
> *He had softly and suddenly vanished away—*
>   *For the Snark* was a Boojum, *you see.*

Perhaps it strikes too solemn a note to suggest that the Snark "is" Death, or Fate, or the folly of the Absolute; or that this crew of bumbling fools, led by a madman captain (with a navigational chart showing only ocean) represents our species. No one knows precisely why the men are pursuing the Snark, or, indeed, what a Snark actually is (apart from being a Boojum), but the frenzy of the chase is comically appropriate. "Golden hours" do not pertain here.

Carroll satirizes not only the hoary old archetype of the "heroic" quest but the very principle of adult life itself. Children may be innocently brash, like Alice; but children, safely contained within the wonderlands of childhood fantasy, are after all immortal; they can come to no harm. Adult men, however, are another matter. They act out their wishes under no benign protectorate: if they choose to destroy themselves, why should their folly not be celebrated in nonsense verse? This is the punishment for persisting in childish pursuits—for lingering in Wonderland—when one is no longer a child.

At heart, Lewis Carroll/Charles Dodgson was no more a sentimentalist than the Snark, who cannot be seduced into smiling at a pun.

Images of mystery opening into highly ambiguous "enchantments":

> Two doors down from one corner, on the left hand going east, the line was broken by the entry of a court; and just at that point, a certain sinister block of building thrust forward its gable on the street. It was two storeys high; showed no window, nothing but a door on the lower storey and a blind forehead of discoloured wall on the upper; and bore, in every feature, the marks of prolonged and sordid negligence. The door, which was equipped with neither bell nor knocker, was blistered and distained. . . . "Did you ever remark that door?" [Mr. Enfield] asked. . . . "It is connected in my mind with a very odd story."
> —*The Strange Case of Dr. Jekyll and Mr. Hyde*
> by Robert Louis Stevenson

> He did at the very first sight of that door experience a peculiar emotion, an attraction, a desire to get to the door and open it and walk in. And at the same time he had the

clearest conviction that either it was unwise or it was wrong of him—he could not tell which—to yield to this attraction. He insisted upon it as a curious thing that he knew from the very beginning—unless memory has played him the queerest trick—that the door was unfastened, and that he could go in as he chose.

—"The Door in the Wall" by H. G. Wells

In Stevenson's famous tale of 1886, "the door in the wall" is the door through which Hyde enters, after having brutally trampled a little girl on the sidewalk. (In fact he enters it at four in the morning and returns bearing a check signed by Dr. Henry Jekyll.) The focus of a good deal of speculation, the mysteriously repulsive Hyde appears and disappears by way of Jekyll's rear laboratory door; he is the heir to Jekyll's fortune, though none of Jekyll's friends and associates knows him. What is Hyde's power, that he can provoke, in genteel men, the desire to do violence to *him?* "There is something wrong with his appearance," says Mr. Enfield, "something displeasing, something downright detestable. I never saw a man I so disliked, and yet I scarce know why. He must be deformed somewhere; he gives a strong feeling of deformity, although I couldn't specify the point." His kinsman, the lawyer Utterson, is similarly bewildered by his own response to Hyde:

> [He] was pale and dwarfish, he gave an impression of deformity without any nameable malformation, he had a displeasing smile, he had borne himself to the lawyer with a sort of murderous mixture of timidity and boldness, and he spoke with a husky, whispering, and somewhat broken voice; all these were points against him, but not all of these together could explain the hitherto unknown disgust, loathing, and fear with which Mr. Utterson regarded him. "There must be something else," said the perplexed gentleman.

"There *is* something more, if I could find a name for it. God bless me, the man seems hardly human! Something troglodytic . . . or is it the radiance of a foul soul that thus transpires through, and transfigures, its clay continent?"

Hyde, of course, *is* Jekyll; but he is also an aspect of the men who contemplate him—their morally debased reflection.

It was Henry Jekyll's intention to separate the two distinct natures of man, that the primitive might be divorced from the civilized: "If each, I told myself, could but be housed in separate identities, life would be relieved of all that was unbearable." He has discovered that "man is not truly one, but truly two" and that a pernicious double nature contends for the soul of civilized man; one is thoroughly amoral, the other, presumably, refined and "moral." Jekyll's dangerous experimentation with the nature of man may relate to Victor Frankenstein's similarly doomed undertaking, as it anticipates the cruel science of H. G. Wells's Dr. Moreau, but the crucial difference is that Jekyll experiments with *himself*—a sign of his nobility, but also of his naïveté. His most serious miscalculation is that evil is extraneous to man and not bound up, as he later discovers, "closer than a wife, closer than an eye," to all that is highest in us.

Jekyll takes a drug so powerful it "shakes the very fortress of identity" and causes him to experience "a grinding in the bones, deadly nausea, and a horror of the spirit" suggestive of birth and of death.

Unlike Wilde's handsome Dorian Gray, who exploits others "simply as a method of procuring extraordinary sensations," Stevenson's Edward Hyde is a mere brute, given to coarse (and but vaguely defined) appetites. With the passage of time he begins to dislodge Jekyll's personality from their mutual body; poor Jekyll falls into a doze and wakes to see his own hand ("professional in shape and size . . . large, firm, white and comely") replaced by the odious hand of Hyde ("lean, corded, knuckly, of a dusky pallor and thickly shaded with a swart growth of hair"). Yet Jekyll speaks helplessly of "ecstasy," "delirium," the "transportation of joy."

The inverted wonderland of the psyche, which Stevenson explores in such memorable fabulist images, is made to appeal to us, as readers and participants, as well. Loathsome as Hyde undoubtedly is to contemplate he is not loathsome to *be;* for as soon as one crosses over into Hyde one is freed of tiresome moral and professional obligations; one simply exists. Without Hyde there is very little life in Jekyll; without Hyde there would be no story. It seems inevitable that, as Jekyll weakens, Hyde grows stronger. "Jekyll" and "Hyde" eventually become autonomous personalities in a pattern known to modern psychiatry as the phenomenon of the split self, well documented in our time but only vaguely understood. (In fact, persons suffering from this curious psychopathology often accommodate far more "selves" than Jekyll does.) When Hyde is in power he plays "apelike" tricks on Jekyll; when Jekyll is in power he contemplates doing away with Hyde altogether.

The mysterious door in the wall leads to an accursed laboratory and, naturally, to death. But the very popular success of Stevenson's moral parable—like that of Mary Shelley's *Frankenstein*—has obscured for many persons (not "readers") the fact that the monster self, the demon, the horror, the inextricable "other"—is an image of ourselves, caged in our flesh.

H. G. Wells's comparatively unknown short story "The Door in the Wall" (published in 1911 in a special edition illustrated with extremely interesting photographs by Alvin Langdon Coburn, in collaboration with Wells) is also a moral parable couched in surrealist or fairy-tale terms. It is less melodramatic than Stevenson's novella but in its way more poignant, more disturbing; for here the mysterious door and the enchanted garden both are, and are not, vehicles of destruction. Like the nameless narrator who tells the tale, we are left ambivalent about the nature of the hero's experience: is he finally betrayed by his childhood vision, or is it the means of his salvation?

The door in the wall—"a real door leading through a real wall to immortal realities"—appears to the motherless Wallace when he is about five years old and wandering in his neighborhood in West Kensington. He happens upon a green door in a white wall; he enters it and finds himself in the mysterious garden that is to haunt him all his life. It is a child's garden, the very reverse of his life of emotional deprivation: there are playmates, many people who are "beautiful and kind," even tame panthers and a capuchin monkey ("very clean"). Unlike most enchanted regions it seems to the child familiar—entering it is "just like coming home"—a place of luminosity, exhilaration, a world with a "different quality," where the light itself is more penetrating and mellower; and where, in an instant of coming into it, "one was exquisitely glad." Though the vision granted Wallace by a "sombre dark woman" who shows him the book of his life is a painful one, he is to remember the garden, in fact to be haunted by it, until his death.

Inevitably, Wallace is expelled from the garden; he returns home and is punished by his father for lying about where he has been; as the years pass he sees, always by accident, the green door in the white wall but hasn't the opportunity of reentering. As a schoolboy, as an ambitious young man on his way to Oxford, as an adult caught up in a career in government, he seems to feel that other doors are more important: the door to his career, the door to his public self, the door to his "success." Past the midpoint of his life, however, he begins to lose interest in the external world that had been "so bright and interesting, [had] seemed so full of meaning and opportunity that the half-effaced charm of the garden was by comparison gentle and remote"; he finds no nourishment in his success, has no real friends, no wife. He feels that he "wants the garden badly" but has no way of finding it . . . until, not long after he has been named a cabinet minister, he steps through a door in a construction fence and dies by accident; or is it intention? The narrator of the story knows only the circumstances of Wallace's death, not the man's experience.

(It is an intriguing coincidence that Frances Hodgson Burnett's *The Secret Garden,* which features not one but two motherless children as well as an Edenic garden hidden behind a door in a wall, was published within a year of Wells's grim little fable; and that in both works of fiction the garden possesses a luminous, mystical quality, as if it compensated, in fantasy, for the painful absence of the mother.)

Obsessed with an idyllic memory out of childhood, Wells suggests, how does one cross over into the adult world; how can one be satisfied with the relatively superficial rewards of adult life? The garden is the place (warm, sequestered, maternal, "secret") where one is loved regardless of one's achievements, hence its irresistible attraction. Yet to succumb to its intoxicating spell is to abrogate the responsibilities of adulthood and be swallowed up in a malevolent narcissism, in Wallace's instance fatal. The subtlety of the story lies in its ambiguity—the reader cannot know whether Wallace is imagined as a tragic figure or whether he is simply deluded. Nor can one know with certitude whether Wallace sought his secret garden too late in life, thereby arousing the wrath of the denied "maternal" forces, or whether, all along, he has been under the sway of a crippling psychosis. Wells's narrator seems to share in his "vision" to some extent: "I am more than half convinced that he had, in truth, an abnormal gift, and a sense, something— I know not what—that in the guise of wall and door offered him an outlet, a secret and peculiar passage of escape into another and altogether more beautiful world," he concludes. Yet these are fin-de-siècle sentiments of an extremely pessimistic sort since, after all, the door in the wall is a doorway to death. The mysterious regenerating powers of the secret garden touch, it seems, only children, in the "golden hours" of life; forever afterward they are inaccessible. Or they return in a terrifying guise, as impulses that lead to disintegration and death.

In that bleakly comic parable of our century, Franz Kafka's *The Trial,* Joseph K., a condemned man, is told an enigmatic tale meant to reconcile him to his fate. It seems that a man from the country seeks admittance to the Law; is barred by a doorkeeper from entering; lives out his life waiting outside the door, never being admitted. As he dies he perceives in the darkness "a radiance that streams immortally" from the doorway. It occurs to him to ask why, in all these years, no one else has sought to enter the door except him, and the doorkeeper replies, "No one but you could gain admittance through this door, since this door was intended only for you. I am now going to shut it."

Is the doorkeeper just or unjust, is the man from the country deluded or within his rights, is one subordinate to the other, are all speculations about the Law futile? After a closely reasoned discussion between Joseph K. and the priest who has told him the story, it becomes clear that the riddle has no solution: just as the hapless man from the country waits out his life without being admitted to the Law, so will Joseph K. conduct his defense in vain, asking questions that have no answers. Guilt is a foregone conclusion in this odd region of the psyche; no crime committed by mortal man can be equal to it. Why the cruel terms of the parable?— why Joseph K.'s condemnation, when he is blameless of wrongdoing? The priest consoles him with the doubtful proposition that it is not necessary to accept everything pertaining to the Law as true, only as necessary; whereupon Joseph K. says that this is a melancholy conclusion: "It turns lying into a universal principle."

No vision of the malevolent inverted wonderlands of our century is more powerful than Kafka's. It is a measure of his prophetic genius—and of the great distance we have traveled since more innocent times—that an art that appeared modish and surrealist when it began to appear in the 1930s now has the air of psychological realism. Only the imagery of Kafka's surfaces is dreamlike; what lies beneath is history.

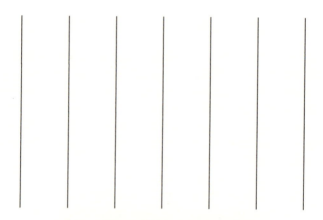

FRANKENSTEIN'S FALLEN ANGEL

*"Am I to be thought the only criminal,
when all human kind sinned against
me?"*

—Frankenstein's demon

Quite apart from its enduring celebrity, and its proliferation in numberless extraliterary forms, Mary Shelley's *Franken-stein; or, The Modern Prometheus* is a remarkable work: a novel sui generis—if a novel at all—and a unique blending of Gothic, fabulist, allegorical, and philosophical materials. Though certainly one of the most calculated and *willed* of fantasies, being in large part a kind of gloss upon or rejoinder to Milton's *Paradise Lost, Frankenstein* is fueled by the kind of grotesque, faintly absurd, and wildly inventive images that spring direct from the unconscious—the eight-foot creature designed to be "beautiful" who turns out almost indescribably repulsive (yellow-skinned, shriveled of countenance, with straight black lips and near-colorless eyes); the cherished cousin bride who *is* beautiful but, in the mind's dreaming, yields horrors ("as I imprinted the first kiss on her lips, they became livid with the hue of death; her features appeared to change, and I thought that I held the corpse of my dead mother in my arms; a shroud enveloped her form, and I saw the grave-worms crawling in the folds"); the mad dream of the Arctic as a country of "eternal light" that will prove, of course, only a place of endless ice, the appropriate landscape for Victor Frankenstein's death and his demon's self-immolation.

Central to *Frankenstein*—as it is central to a vastly different nineteenth-century romance, *Jane Eyre*—is a stroke of lightning that appears to issue in a dazzling "stream of fire" from a beautiful old oak tree ("so soon the light vanished, the oak had disappeared, and nothing remained but a blasted stump"): the literal stimulus for Frankenstein's subsequent discovery of the cause of generation and life. And according to Mary Shelley's account of the origin of her "ghost story," the very image of Frankenstein and his demon creature spring from a waking dream of extraordinary vividness:

> I did not sleep, nor could I be said to think. My imagination, unbidden, possessed and guided me, gifting the successive images that arose in my mind with a vividness far beyond the usual bound of reverie. I saw—with shut eyes, but acute mental vision—I saw the pale student of unhallowed arts kneeling beside the thing he had put together. I saw the hideous phantasm of a man stretched out, and then, on the working of some powerful engine, show signs of life, and stir with an uneasy, half-vital motion. . . . [The student] sleeps; but he is awakened; he opens his eyes: behold the horrid thing stands at his bedside, opening his cur-

tains, and looking on him with yellow, watery, but speculative eyes.

Hallucinatory and surrealist on its deepest level, *Frankenstein* is of course one of the most self-consciously literary "novels" ever written: its awkward form is the epistolary Gothic, its lyric descriptions of natural scenes (the grandiose Valley of Chamounix in particular) spring from Romantic sources, its speeches and monologues echo both Shakespeare and Milton, and, should the author's didactic intention not be clear enough, the demon creature educates himself by studying three books of symbolic significance—Goethe's *The Sorrows of Young Werther,* Plutarch's *Lives,* and Milton's *Paradise Lost.* (The last-named conveniently supplies him with a sense of his own predicament, as Mary Shelley hopes to dramatize it. He reads Milton's great epic as if it were a "true history" giving the picture of an omnipotent God warring with his creatures; he identifies himself with Adam except so far as Adam had come forth from God a "perfect creature, happy and prosperous." Finally, of course, he identifies with Satan: "I am thy creature: I ought to be thy Adam; but I am rather the fallen angel, whom thou drivest from joy for no misdeed. Everywhere I see bliss, from which I alone am irrevocably excluded. I was benevolent and good; misery made me a fiend. Make me happy, and I shall again be virtuous.")

The search of medieval alchemists for the legendary Philosopher's Stone (the talismanic process by which base metals might be transformed into gold or, in psychological terms, the means by which the individual might realize his destiny)—Faust's reckless defiance of human limitations and his willingness to barter his soul for knowledge; the fatal search for answers to the mysteries of their lives of such tragic figures as Oedipus and Hamlet—these are the archetypal dramas to which *Frankenstein* bears an obvious kinship. Yet, as one reads, as Frankenstein and his despised shadow self engage in one after another of the novel's many dialogues, it begins to seem as if the nineteen-year-old author is discovering these archetypal elements for the first time. Frankenstein "is" a demonic parody (or extension) of Milton's God; he "is" *Prometheus plasticator,* the creator of mankind; but at the same time, by his own account, he is totally unable to control the behavior of his demon (variously called "monster," "fiend," "wretch," but necessarily lacking a name). Surprisingly, it is not by way of the priggish and "self-devoted" young scientist that Mary Shelley discovers the great power of her narrative, but by way of the misshapen demon, with whom most readers identify: "My person was hideous, and my stature gigantic: what did this mean? Who was I? What was I? Whence did I come? What was my destination?" It is not simply the case that the demon—like Satan and Adam in *Paradise Lost*—has the most compelling speeches in the novel and is far wiser and more magnanimous than his creator: he is also the means by which a transcendent love—a romantically *unrequited* love—is expressed. Surely one of the secrets of *Frankenstein,* which helps to account for its abiding appeal, is the demon's patient, unquestioning, utterly faithful, and utterly *human* love for his irresponsible creator.

(For instance, when Frankenstein is tracking the demon into the Arctic regions, it is clearly the demon who is helping him in his search and even leaving food for him; but Frankenstein is so blind—in fact, so comically blind—he believes that "spirits" are responsible. "Yet still a spirit of good followed and directed my steps, and, when I most murmured, would suddenly extricate me from seemingly insurmountable difficulties. Sometimes, when nature, overcome by hunger, sunk under the exhaustion, a repast was prepared for me in the desert, that restored and inspirited me. . . . I may not doubt that it was set there by the spirits that I had invoked to aid me.")

By degrees, with the progression of the fable's unlikely plot, the inhuman creation becomes increasingly human while his creator becomes increasingly inhuman, frozen in a posture of rigorous denial. (He is blameless of any wrongdoing in terms of the demon; and even dares to tell Walton, literally with his dying breath, that another scientist might succeed where he had failed!—so that the lesson of the "Frankenstein monster" is revealed as totally lost on Frankenstein himself.) The demon is (sub)human consciousness-in-the-making, naturally benevolent as Milton's Satan is not, and received with horror and contempt solely because of his physical appearance. He is sired without a mother in defiance of nature but he is in one sense an infant—a comically monstrous eight-foot baby—whose progenitor rejects him immediately after creating him, in one of the most curious (and dreamlike) scenes in the novel:

> How can I describe my emotions at this catastrophe, or how delineate the wretch whom, with such infinite pains and care, I had endeavored to form? [says Victor Frankenstein]. . . . I had worked hard for nearly two years, for the sole purpose of infusing life into an inanimate body. For this I had deprived myself of rest and health. I had desired it with an ardor that far exceeded moderation; but now that I had finished, the beauty of the dream vanished, and breathless horror and disgust filled my heart. Unable to endure the aspect of the being I had created, I rushed out of the room, and continued a long time traversing my bed-chamber, unable to compose my mind to sleep.

Here follows the nightmare vision of Frankenstein's bride-to-be Elizabeth as a form of his dead mother, with "grave-worms crawling" in her shroud; and shortly afterward the "wretch" himself appears at Frankenstein's bed, drawing away the canopy as Mary Shelley had imagined. But Frankenstein is so cowardly he runs away again; and this time the demon is indeed abandoned, to reappear after the first of the "murders" of Frankenstein's kin. On the surface Frankenstein's behavior is preposterous, even idiotic, for he seems blind to the fact that is apparent to any reader: that he has loosed a fearful power into the world, whether it strikes his eye as aesthetically pleasing or not, and he *must* take responsibility for it. Except of course he does not: for, as he keeps telling himself, he is blameless of any wrongdoing apart from the act of creation itself. The emotions he catalogues for us—gloom, sorrow, misery, despair—are conventionally Romantic attitudes, mere luxuries in a context that requires action and not simply response.

By contrast the demon is all activity, all yearning, all hope: his love for his maker is unrequited and seems incapable of making any impression upon him, yet he never gives it up, even when he sounds most threatening. ("Beware," says the demon midway in the novel, "for I am fearless, and therefore powerful. I will watch with the wiliness of a snake, that I may sting with its venom. Man, you shall repent of the injuries you inflict.") His voice is very like his creator's—indeed, everyone in *Frankenstein* sounds alike—but his posture is always one of simple need; he requires love in order to become less monstrous, but, as he *is* a monster, love is denied him; and the man responsible for this comically tragic state of affairs says repeatedly that he is not to blame. (Frankenstein's typical response to the situation is: "I felt as if I had committed some great crime, the consciousness of which haunted me. I was guiltless, but I had indeed drawn a horrible curse upon my head, as mortal as that of crime.") But if Frankenstein is not to blame for the various deaths that occur, who is? Has he endowed his creation, as God endowed Adam in Milton's epic, with free will? Or is the demon psychologically his creature, committing the forbidden acts he wants committed—so long as he himself remains "guiltless"?

It is a measure of the subtlety of this moral parable that the demon strikes so many archetypal chords and suggests so many variant readings. He recapitulates in truncated form the history of consciousness of his race (learning to speak, read, write, etc., by closely watching the De Lacey family); he is an abandoned child, a parentless orphan; he takes on the voices of Adam, Satan ("Evil thenceforth became my good," he says, as Milton's fallen angel says, "Evil be thou my good"), even our "first mother" Eve. When the demon terrifies himself by seeing his reflection in a pool and grasping at once the nature of his own deformity, he is surely not mirroring Narcissus, as some commentators have suggested, but Milton's Eve in her surprised discovery of her own beauty, in Book IV of *Paradise Lost*.[1] He is Shakespeare's Edmund, though *unloved;* a shadow figure more tragic, because more "conscious," than the hero he represents. Most suggestively he has become by the novel's melodramatic conclusion a form of Christ: sinned against by all humankind, yet fundamentally blameless, and *yet* quite willing to die as a sacrifice. He speaks of his death as a "consummation"; he is going to burn himself on a funeral pyre some-

[1] The influence of Milton on *Frankenstein* is so general as to figure on nearly every page; and certainly the very conception of the monumental *Paradise Lost* stands behind the conception of Mary Shelley's "ghost story." According to Christopher Small's excellent *Ariel Like a Harpy: Shelley, Mary, and Frankenstein* (New York: Humanities Press, 1974), Mary Shelley's booklist notes *Paradise Regained* as read in 1815, and in 1816 she and Shelley were both reading *Paradise Lost* at intervals during the year. At one point Shelley read the long poem aloud to her, finishing it in a week in November of 1816.

where in the Arctic wastes. Unlikely, certainly, but a fitting end to a life conceived by way of lightning and electricity:

> "But soon," he cried with sad and solemn enthusiasm, "I shall die, and what I now feel be no longer felt. Soon these burning miseries will be extinct. I shall ascend my funeral pile triumphantly, and exult in the agony of the torturing flames. The light of that conflagration will fade away; my ashes will be swept into the sea by the winds. My spirit will sleep in peace; or, if it thinks, it will not surely think thus."

But the demon does not die within the confines of the novel, so perhaps he has not died after all. He is a "modern" species of shadow or doppelgänger—*the nightmare that is deliberately created by man's ingenuity* and not a mere supernatural being or fairy-tale remnant.

Frankenstein's double significance as a work of prose fiction and a cultural myth—as "novel" of 1818 and timeless "metaphor"—makes it a highly difficult story to read directly. A number of popular misconceptions obscure it for most readers: Frankenstein is of course not the monster but his creator; nor is he a mad scientist of genius—he is in fact a highly idealistic and naïve youth in the conventional Romantic mode (in Walton's admiring eyes "noble," "cultivated," a "celestial spirit" who has suffered "great and unparalleled misfortunes"), not unlike Mary Shelley's fated lover Shelley. Despite the fact that a number of catastrophes occur around him and indirectly because of him, Victor Frankenstein is well intentioned, gentlemanly, *good;* he is no sadist like H. G. Wells's exiled vivisectionist Dr. Moreau (who boasts, "You cannot imagine the strange colorless delight of these intellectual desires. The thing before you is no longer an animal, a fellow-creature, but a problem.")[2] Frankenstein's mission is selfless, even messianic:

> No one can conceive the variety of feelings which bore me onwards, like a hurricane, in the first enthusiasm of success. Life and death appeared to me ideal bounds, which I should first break through, and pour a torrent of light into our dark world. A new species would bless me as its creator and source; many happy and excellent natures would owe their being to me. No father could claim the gratitude of his child so completely as I should deserve theirs. . . . If I could bestow animation upon lifeless matter, I might in process of time . . . renew life where death had apparently devoted the body to corruption.

It is a measure of the novel's extraordinary fame that the very name "Frankenstein" has long since supplanted "Prometheus" in popular usage, and the "Frankenstein legend" retains a significance for our time as the "Prometheus legend" does not.

How many fictional characters after all have made the great leap from literature to mythology; how many creations of sheer language have stepped from the rhythms of their authors' unique voices into what might be called a collective cultural consciousness? Don Quixote, Dracula, Sherlock Holmes, Alice (in Wonderland), certain figures in the fairy tales of Hans Christian Andersen . . . and of course Fran-

---

[2] H. G. Wells's *The Island of Dr. Moreau* (1896) is a savage variant on the Frankenstein legend. Moreau experiments on living animals, trying to make them "human" or humanoid; he succeeds in creating a race of Beast Folk who eventually rise up against him and kill him. Moreau's beliefs strike a more chilling—and more contemporary—note than Frankenstein's idealism: "To this day I have never troubled about the ethics of the matter. The study of Nature makes a man at last as remorseless as Nature," boasts Moreau.

kenstein's "monster." Virtually millions of people who have never heard of the novel *Frankenstein,* let alone that a young Englishwoman named Mary Shelley (in fact, Godwin) wrote it at the age of nineteen, are well acquainted with the image of Frankenstein popularized by Boris Karloff in the 1930s; and understand at least intuitively the ethical implications of the metaphor. (As in the expression, particularly relevant for our time, "We have created a Frankenstein monster.") The more potent the archetype evoked by a work of literature, the more readily its specific form slips free of the time-bound *personal* work. On the level of cultural myth the figures of Dracula, Sherlock Holmes, Alice, and the rest are near-autonomous beings, linked to no specific books and no specific authors. They have become communal creations; they belong to us all. Hence the very real difficulty in reading Mary Shelley's novel for the first time. (Subsequent readings are far easier and yield greater rewards.)

Precisely because of this extraordinary fame, one should be reminded of how original and unique the novel was at the time of its publication. Can it even be read at the present time in a context hospitable to its specific allusions and assumptions—one conversant with the thorny glories of *Paradise Lost,* the sentimental ironies of Coleridge's "The Rime of the Ancient Mariner," the Gothic conventions of tales-within-tales, epistolary frames, and histrionic speeches delivered at length? In a more accomplished work, *Wuthering Heights,* the structural complexities of tales-within-tales are employed for artistic ends; the ostensible fracturing of time yields a rich poetic significance; characters grow and change like people whom we have come to know. In Mary Shelley's *Frankenstein* the strained conventions of the romance are mere structural devices to allow Victor Frankenstein and his demon their opposing—but intimately linked—

"voices." Thus abrupt transitions in space and time take place in a kind of rhetorical vacuum: all is summary, past history, exemplum.

But it is a mistake to wish to read *Frankenstein* as a modern novel of psychological realism, or as a "novel" at all. It contains no characters, only points of view; its concerns are pointedly moral and didactic; it makes no claims for verisimilitude of even a poetic Wordsworthian nature. (The Alpine landscapes are all self-consciously sublime and theatrical; Mont Blanc, for instance, suggests "another earth, the habitations of another race of beings.") If one were pressed to choose a literary antecedent for *Frankenstein* it might be, surprisingly, Samuel Johnson's *Rasselas,* rather than a popular Gothic like Mrs. Radcliffe's *Mysteries of Udolpho,* which allegedly had the power to frighten its readers. (A character in Jane Austen's *Northanger Abbey* says of this once-famous novel: "I remember finishing it in two days—my hair standing on end the whole time.") Though *Frankenstein* and *Dracula* are commonly linked, Bram Stoker's tour de force of 1897 is vastly different in tone, theme, and intention from Shelley's novel: its "monster" is not at all monstrous in appearance, only in behavior; and he is thoroughly and irremediably evil by nature. But no one in *Frankenstein* is evil—the universe is emptied of God and of theistic assumptions of "good" and "evil." Hence its modernity.

Tragedy does not arise spontaneous and unwilled in so "modern" a setting, it must be made—in fact, manufactured. The Fates are not to blame; there *are* no Fates, only the brash young scientist who boasts of never having feared the supernatural. ("In my education my father had taken the greatest precautions that my mind should be impressed with no supernatural horrors. I do not ever remember to have trembled at a tale of superstition, or to have feared the apparition of a spirit. . . . A churchyard was to me merely the receptacle of bodies deprived of life, which, from being the seat of beauty and strength, had become food for the worm.") Where *Dracula* and other conventional Gothic works are fantasies, with clear links to fairy tales and legends, and even popular ballads, *Frankenstein* has the theoretical and cautionary tone of science fiction. It is meant to prophesize, not to entertain.

Another aspect of *Frankenstein's* uniqueness lies in the curious bond between Frankenstein and his created demon. Where by tradition such beings as doubles, shadow-selves, "imps of the perverse," and classic doppelgängers (like poor Golyadkin's nemesis in Dostoyevski's "The Double," of 1846) spring full grown from supernatural origins—that is, from unacknowledged recesses of the human spirit—Frankenstein's demon is *natural* in origin: a manufactured nemesis. He is an abstract idea made flesh, a Platonic essence given a horrific (and certainly ludicrous) existence. Yet though he is meant to be Frankenstein's ideal, a man-made miracle that would "pour a torrent of light into our dark world," he is only a fragment of that ideal—which is to say, a mockery, a parody, a joke. The monsters we create by way of an advanced technological civilization "are" ourselves as we cannot hope to see ourselves—incomplete, blind, blighted, and, most of all, self-destructive. For it is the forbidden wish for death that dominates. (In intention it is customarily the deaths of others, "enemies"; in fact it may be our own deaths we plan.) Hence the tradition of recognizing Faustian pacts with the Devil as acts of aggression against the human self—the very "I" of the rational being.

Since Frankenstein's creature is made up of parts collected from charnel houses and graves, and his creator acknowledges that he "disturbed, with profane fingers, the tremendous secrets of the human frame," it is inevitable that he be a profane thing. He cannot be blessed or loved: he springs not from a natural union but has been forged in what Frankenstein calls a "workshop of filthy creation." One of the brilliant surrealist touches of the narrative is the fact that Frankenstein's shadow self is a giant; even the rationalization for this curious decision is ingenious. "As the minuteness of the parts formed a great hindrance to my speed," Frankenstein explains to Walton, "I resolved, contrary to my first intention, to make the being of a gigantic stature; that is to say, about eight feet in height, and proportionably large." A demon of mere human size would not have been nearly so compelling.

(The reader should keep in mind the fact that, in 1818, the notion that "life" might be galvanized in laboratory conditions was really not so farfetched; for the properties of electricity were not commonly understood and seem to have been bound up magically with what might be called metaphorically the "spark" of life.[3] Again, in our own time, the possibility of artificially induced life, human or otherwise, does not seem especially remote.)

Because in one sense the demon is Frankenstein's deepest self, the relationship between them is dreamlike, fraught with undefined emotion. Throughout the novel Frankenstein is susceptible to fainting fits, bouts of illness and exhaustion, and nightmares of romantic intensity, less a fully realized personality than a queer stunted half-self (rather like Roderick Usher, whose sister, Madeleine, *his* secret self, is buried alive). It is significant that as soon as Frankenstein induces life in his eight-foot monster he notices *for the first time* what he has created. "His limbs were in proportion,"

---

[3] In Thomas Hogg's *The Life of Percy Bysshe Shelley* (1858) Shelley's lifelong fascination with lightning, electricity, and galvanism is discussed at some length. As a boy he owned something called an "electrical machine" with which he amused himself with experiments; as a young man he was mesmerized by lightning and thunder and made it a point to "enjoy" electrical storms.

Frankenstein testifies, "and I had selected his features as beautiful." But something has clearly gone wrong:

> Beautiful! Great God! His yellow skin scarcely covered the work of muscles and arteries beneath; his hair was of a lustrous black, and flowing; his teeth of a pearly whiteness; but these luxuriances only formed a more horrid contrast with his watery eyes, that seemed almost of the same color as the dun white sockets in which they were set, his shrivelled complexion, and straight black lips.

Significant too is the fact that Frankenstein retreats from this vision and falls asleep—an unlikely response in naturalistic terms, but quite appropriate symbolically—so that, shortly afterward, his demon can arouse *him* from sleep:

> I started from my sleep with horror; a cold dew covered my forehead, my teeth chattered, and every limb became convulsed; when, by the dim and yellow light of the moon, as it forced its way through the window-shutters, I beheld the wretch, the miserable monster whom I had created. He held up the curtain of the bed; and his eyes, if eyes they may be called, were fixed on me. His jaws opened, and he muttered some inarticulate sounds, while a grin wrinkled his cheeks. . . .
>
> Oh! no mortal could support the horror of that countenance. A mummy again endued with animation could not be so hideous as that wretch. I had gazed on him while unfinished: he was ugly then; but when those muscles and joints were rendered capable of motion, it became a thing such as even Dante could not have conceived.

Frankenstein's superficial response to the "thing" he has created is solely in aesthetic terms, for his atheistic morality precludes all thoughts of transgression. (Considering the fact that the author of *Frankenstein* is a woman, a woman well acquainted with pregnancy and childbirth at a precocious age, it is curious that nowhere in the novel does anyone raise the issue of the demon's "unnatural" genesis: he is a monster son born of Man exclusively, a parody of the Word or the Idea made flesh.) Ethically, Frankenstein is "blameless"— though he is haunted by the suspicion throughout that he has committed a crime of some sort, with the very best of intentions.

Where the realistic novel presents characters in a more or less coherent "field," as part of a defined society, firmly established in time and place, romance does away with questions of verisimilitude and plausibility altogether and deals directly with the elements of narrative: it might be said to be an "easier" form psychologically, since it evokes archetypal responses on its primary level. No one expects of Victor Frankenstein that he behave plausibly when he is a near-allegorical figure; no one expects of his demon that he behave plausibly since he is a demonic presence, an outsized mirror image of his creator. When the demon warns Frankenstein (in traditional Gothic form, incidentally), "I shall be with you on your wedding-night," it seems only natural, granted Frankenstein's egocentricity, that he worry about his own safety and not his bride's; and that, despite the warning, Frankenstein allows Elizabeth to be murdered. His wish is his demon self's command, though he never acknowledges his complicity. Indeed, *Frankenstein* begins to read as an anti-romance, a merciless critique of Romantic attitudes—sorrow, misery, self-loathing, despair, paralysis, etc.—written, as it were, from the inside, by a young woman who had already lost a baby in infancy (in 1815, a girl); would lose another, also a girl, in 1817; and, in 1819, a third—named, oddly, William (the very name of the little boy murdered early on in the narrative by Frankenstein's demon).[4] Regardless of the sufferings of others, the romantically "self-devoted" hero responds solely in terms of his own emotions. He might be a lyric poet of the early 1800s, for all his preoccupation with self: everything refers tragically to him, everything is rendered in terms of *his* experience:

> Great God! why did I not then expire? Why am I here to relate the destruction of the best hope, and the purest creature of earth? [Elizabeth] was there, lifeless and inanimate, thrown across the bed, her head hanging down, and her pale and distorted features half covered by her hair. Everywhere I turn I see the same figure—her bloodless arms and relaxed form flung by the murderer on its bridal bier. Could I behold this, and live? (Alas, life is obstinate, and clings closest where it is most hated.) For a moment only, and I lost recollection: I fainted.

Frankenstein grapples with the complex moral issues raised by his demonic creation by "fainting" in one way or another throughout the novel. And in his abrogation of consciousness and responsibility, the demon naturally acts: for this is the Word, the secret wish for destruction, made Flesh.

The cruelest act of all is performed by Frankenstein

---

[4] The feminist critic Ellen Moers interprets *Frankenstein* solely in terms of a birth myth "that was lodged in the novelist's imagination . . . by the fact that she was herself a mother." Though her argument certainly aids in understanding some of the less evident motives for the composition of *Frankenstein*, it reduces a complex philosophical narrative to little more than a semiconscious fantasy, scarcely a *literary* work at all. Did Mary Shelley's womb, or her brain, write *Frankenstein?* In virtually a parody of feminist myth-making, Moers argues that Shelley's book is "most powerful" where it is "most feminine": "in the motif of revulsion against newborn life, and the drama of guilt, dread, and flight surrounding birth and its consequences." See Ellen Moers, "Female Gothic," in *Literary Women* (Garden City, N.Y.: Doubleday & Co., 1974).

before the very eyes of his demon: this is the sudden destruction of the partly assembled "bride." He makes the creature at the bidding of his demon, who has promised, most convincingly, to leave Europe with her and to live "virtuously," but, suddenly repulsed by the "filthy process" he has undertaken, Frankenstein destroys his work. ("The wretch saw me destroy the creature on whose future existence he depended for happiness, and, with a howl of devilish despair and revenge, withdrew.") Afterward he thinks, looking at the remains of the half-finished creature, that he has almost mangled the living flesh of a human being; but he never feels any remorse for what he has done and never considers that, in "mangling" the flesh of his demon's bride, he is murdering the pious and rather too perfect Elizabeth, the cousin bride whom he professes to love. "Am I to be thought the only criminal," the demon asks, "when all human kind sinned against me?" He might have said, as reasonably, *when all human kind conspired in my sin.*

While *Paradise Lost* is to Frankenstein's demon (and very likely to Mary Shelley as well) the picture of an "omnipotent God warring with his creatures," *Frankenstein* is the picture of a finite and flawed god at war with, and eventually overcome by, his creation. It is a parable for our time, an enduring prophecy, a remarkably acute diagnosis of the lethal nature of *denial:* denial of responsibility for one's actions, denial of the shadow self locked within consciousness. Even in the debased and sensational form in which Frankenstein's monster is known by most persons—as a kind of retarded giant, one might say, with electrodes in his neck—his archetypal significance rings true. "My form," he says eloquently, "is a filthy type of yours."

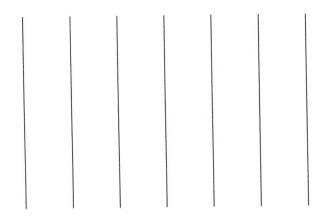

JANE EYRE:
AN INTRODUCTION

Reader, if you have yet to discover the unique voice of Charlotte Brontë's *Jane Eyre,* you have a special delight awaiting you.

For this most acclaimed of novels—"English," "Gothic," "romantic," "female"—is always a surprise, in the very authority, resonance, and inimitable voice of its heroine. "I resisted all the way," Jane Eyre states at the beginning of Chapter 2, and this attitude, this declaration of a unique and iconoclastic female rebelliousness, strikes the perfect note for the entire novel. That a woman will "resist" the terms of her destiny (social or spiritual) is not perhaps entirely new in English literature up to the publication of *Jane Eyre* in 1847: we have after all the willful heroines of certain of Shakespeare's plays, and those of Jane Austen's elegant comedies of manners. But Jane Eyre is a young woman wholly unprotected by social position, family, or independent wealth; she is without power; she is, as Charlotte Brontë judged herself, "small and plain and Quaker-like"— lacking the most superficial yet seemingly necessary qualities of femininity. ("You are not pretty any more than I am handsome," Rochester says bluntly.) Considered as a fictitious character and, in this instance, the vocal consciousness of a long and intricately plotted novel of considerable ambition, Jane Eyre was a risk for her young creator—had not Henry Fielding gambled, and lost, on the virtuous but impoverished and less than ravishingly beautiful heroine of his *Amelia,* of 1751, arousing the scorn of readers who had so applauded *Joseph Andrews* and *Tom Jones?* Jane Eyre, who seems to us, in retrospect, the very voice of highly educated but socially and economically disenfranchised gentility, as natural in her place in the literature of nineteenth-century England as Twain's Huckleberry Finn is in our literature, was unique for her time. She speaks with an apparent artlessness that strikes the ear as disturbingly forthright. (Compare the slow, clotted, indefatigably rhetorical prose of Mary Shelley's *Frankenstein,* of 1818; or the pious and exsanguine narrative of Esther Summerson of Charles Dickens's *Bleak House,* of 1853; and the melancholy, rather overdetermined self-consciousness of Brontë's Lucy Snowe, the heroine of *Villette,* of 1853: "If life be a war, it seemed my destiny to conduct it singlehanded. I pondered how to break up my winter-quarters—to leave an encampment where food and forage failed. Perhaps, to effect this change, another pitched battle must be fought with fortune; if so, I had a mind to the encounter: too poor to lose, God might destine me to gain. But what road was open?—what plan available?")

One of the reasons for Jane Eyre's authority over her own experience, and the confidence with which she assesses that experience, is that, as the romantically convoluted plot evolves, the reader learns that it is *history* rather than *story.* Jane Eyre, who is wife and mother in 1819, is recounting the events of 1799–1809 in a language that is unfailingly masterful precisely because it is after the fact: if the Romantic/Gothic novel be, in one sense, sheer wish, Jane's triumph (wife to Lord Rochester after all and mother to his son—as it scarcely needs be said) represents a wish fulfillment of extraordinary dimensions. The material of legends and fairy tales, perhaps; yet also, sometimes, *this* time at least, of life. For we are led to believe Jane Eyre's good fortune because we are led to believe her voice. It is, in its directness, its ruefulness and scarcely concealed rage, startlingly contemporary; and confirms the critical insight that all works of genius are contemporaneous both with their own times and with ours.

Jane Eyre was written under a pseudonym when Charlotte Brontë was thirty-one years old, a casualty, so to speak, of ten years of servitude as a governess. Though "Currer Bell" was an unknown author and of indeterminate sex, the novel was accepted almost immediately upon being offered to the publishing house of Smith, Elder; it was published within seven weeks and became an instant success. Like Brontë's romantic hero Lord Byron, the new author "awoke one morning to find [herself] famous."

That *Jane Eyre* sold so well should force us to reassess our custom of too casually dismissing the tastes and expectations of the large audience of "female" readers of the nineteenth century. For *Jane Eyre,* whatever its kinship to eighteenth-century Gothic and however melodramatic certain of its episodes (the one in which Rochester disguises himself as a gypsy is particularly strained), is nonetheless a work of stubbornly idiosyncratic intelligence; its strength lies as much in passages of introspective analysis as in conventionally dramatized scenes. Jane projects such rebellious undercurrents that some critics, including sympathetic readers, found the novel "coarse." Jane does not sentimentalize herself as an orphaned child any more than she sentimentalizes other children—in the scene in which she confronts Mrs. Reed her voice is "savage": "I am glad you are no relation of mine: I will never call you aunt again as long as I live. I will never come to see you when I am grown up; and if any one asks me how I liked you, and how you treated me, I will say the very thought of you makes me sick." During Jane's stay at Lowood, when so many of her classmates sicken and die, Jane voices no false piety in noting that spring is "unclouded" nonetheless. Not coarseness but an unfashionable realism provokes the child's insight: "My mind made its first earnest effort to comprehend what had been infused into it concerning heaven and hell: and for the first time it recoiled, baffled; and for the first time glancing behind, on each side, and before it, it saw all round an unfathomed gulf: it felt the one point where it stood—the present; all the rest was formless cloud and vacant depth: and it shuddered at the thought of tottering, and plunging amid that chaos." At a time when women were imagined as merely inhabiting bodies meant to bear children, but being, in other respects, chastely bodiless, Jane rejects the proffered love of the martyrish St. John Rivers because it is merely spiritual. Surely this suggests a "coarseness" very much at odds with Victorian ideals?

Like *Villette, Jane Eyre* is a story of hunger; unlike that more complex and perhaps more aesthetically "pure" novel, it is a story of hunger satisfied. That young Jane Eyre supplants the formerly exotic Bertha (the Creole heiress whom Rochester recklessly married in his youth) is not, given the terms of the novel's logic, a matter of moral ambiguity: for in her deranged and diseased state Bertha is no longer a human woman but sheer appetite, and therefore beyond the range of Jane's (and presumably the reader's) sympathy. Her laughter is "demonic"; her figure "hideous." Jane is necessarily repelled, for this is an *other* quite truly *other,* lacking even the intelligence and sense of moral proportion so artfully voiced by Dr. Frankenstein's doomed monster. When Jane first sees Rochester's lawfully wedded wife the reader is as shocked as she.

> In the deep shade, at the farther end of the room, a figure ran backwards and forwards. What it was, whether beast or human being, one could not, at first sight, tell: it grovelled, seemingly, on all fours; it snatched and growled like some strange wild animal: but it was covered with clothing; and a quantity of dark, grizzled hair, wild as a mane, hid its head and face.

This secret wife lacks even a gender. She is *it,* and animal: "the clothed hyena rose up, and stood tall on its hind feet." Rochester mockingly addresses Jane as a "young girl, who stands so grave and quiet at the mouth of hell, looking collectedly at the gambols of a demon." (Rochester confesses to having married Bertha, the daughter of a West India planter, in a trance of youthful "prurience" and to having discovered, after it was too late, that their natures were antithetical—her "pygmy intellect" was "common, low, narrow, and singularly incapable of being led to anything higher"; she was sexually promiscuous—"her vices sprang up fast and rank"; and diseased—"her excesses had prematurely developed the germs of insanity." That Bertha Mason suffers from atypical general paresis, the consequence of syphilitic infection, must be passed by in silence—since, in realistic terms, Rochester too would be syphilitic; and would infect Jane Eyre if she married him.)

Jane Eyre's hunger and that of Bertha Mason are not seen to overlap, for one is always qualified by intellectual scrupulosity and a fierce sense of integrity; the other is, and was, sheerly animal. Jane goes against the grain of her deepest wishes; she renounces emotional fulfillment in the service of an ideal that includes, as "Currer Bell" carefully notes in the preface to the novel's second edition, "the world-redeeming creed of Christ." Jane's self-banishment and the remarkably literal terms of her hunger—she comes close to starving after she flees Thornfield—identify her in fact as a kind of Christ: misunderstood, defiant, isolated, willing (almost) to die for her beliefs. The reiteration of "master" and "my master" in the narrative suggests Jane's ultimate if not immediate acknowledgement of her place in the hierarchy of a civilized cosmos; in this, she strikes a chord of willful submission not unlike that of Emily Dickinson, whose insistence upon "Master" as a force in her emotional life carried with it an air of obsessive conviction. How seemingly passive, how subtly aggressive! Jane Eyre is the ideal heroine as she is the ideal narrator of her romance.

It is interesting to note that the Brontë sisters—Charlotte, Emily, and Anne—began writing as children, creating a private mythology out of the exigencies of a motherless, isolated, and intensely private domestic life in Haworth Parsonage on the Yorkshire moor. In 1826, when Charlotte was ten, her father Patrick Brontë gave her brother, Branwell, a box of twelve wooden soldiers, which seemed to awaken a fervor of creativity in the children: they began making up stories in which the soldiers figured as characters. In time, they created plays, mimes, games, and serial stories transcribed in minute italic handwriting that mimics print; they were influenced by their father's storytelling and by their wide and promiscuous reading—among contemporaries, Scott, Byron, E. T. A. Hoffmann, and supernatural stories by James Hogg that appeared in serial form in *Blackwood's Magazine*. Out of the children's elaborate fantasizing grew two long-enduring partnerships between Emily and Anne (the "Gondal" sagas) and Charlotte and Branwell (the "Angrian" stories): Emily continued to live imaginatively in Gondal until she was at least twenty-seven years old, while Charlotte wrote her last Angrian story at the age of twenty-three. Emily Brontë's *Wuthering Heights* is more clearly an adult's rendering of incestuous childhood obsession than are any of Charlotte Brontë's novels, but the romantically dangerous Rochester is most likely a remnant of the children's sensational world, the poetic antithesis of all that was dull, dreary, routine, and circumscribed in the world of Haworth Parsonage. Here is Jane's first vision of the man she will adore:

> Something of daylight still lingered, and the moon was waxing bright; I could see him plainly. His figure was enveloped in a riding cloak, fur collared and steel clasped; its details were not apparent, but I traced the general points of middle height, and considerable breadth of chest. He had a dark face, with stern features and a heavy brow; his eyes and gathered eyebrows looked ireful and thwarted . . . ; he was past youth, but had not reached middle age.

Like Emily's Heathcliff, that Byronic, doomed hero; yet unlike Heathcliff—who after all starves himself to death in his deranged attachment to the past—since, by the novel's end, after he goes blind, Rochester does become domesticated. The Gothic has become tamed, and redeemed, by ordinary marital love. However unlikely for Brontë's time, or for ours, *Jane Eyre* ends upon a note of conjugal bliss:

> I am my husband's life as fully as he is mine. No woman was ever nearer to her mate than I am: ever more absolutely bone of his bone and flesh of his flesh. I know no weariness of my Edward's society: he knows none of mine, any more than we each do of the pulsation of the heart that beats in our separate bosoms; consequently, we are ever together. . . . We talk, I believe, all day long: to talk to each other is but a more animated and an audible thinking.

The orphan Jane is no longer "resisting all the way"; no longer, at this point, required to be Jane. The novel's passionate energies consume themselves as the apocalyptic fire at Thornfield consumes unregenerate Bertha.

Much of the power of *Jane Eyre* derives from a dialectic the author unobtrusively pursues on several structural levels. For instance, in the largest, most spacious sense the novel is about character stimulated into growth—truly remarkable growth—by place: Jane Eyre, orphaned and presumably defenseless, and a mere girl, discovers the strength of her personality by way of the challenges of several contrasting environments—the Reed household, in which she is despised; Lowood School, where she discovers a model in Miss Temple and a spiritual sister in Helen Burns; Thornfield, where she cultivates, with agreeable naturalness, a measure of sexual power; Whitcross, where, at last, she acquires the semblance of a family; and Ferndean, Rochester's retreat, a manor house of "considerable antiquity . . . deep buried in a wood," where she is at last wed.

Just as these carefully rendered places differ greatly from one another, so Jane differs greatly in them; one has the sense of a soul in ceaseless evolution. As a child in the Reed household, rebuking Mrs. Reed, Jane feels a sense of precocious triumph: "Ere I had finished this reply, my soul began to expand, to exult, with the strangest sense of freedom, of triumph, I ever felt. It seemed as if an invisible bond had burst, and that I had struggled out into unhoped-for liberty." Brontë's sense of human personality is that it is pliant, fluid, and living, in immediate (and often defiant) response to its surroundings; not that it is stable and determined, as if sculpted in marble. *Jane Eyre* is no portrait of a lady but the story of a young woman in a "heroic" mold, as susceptible as any man to restlessness and ennui when opposition fails to provide a cause against which to struggle. Grown bored at Thornfield, for instance, before the arrival of the master, Jane longs for a power of vision that might overpass the limits of her sequestered life, pastoral as it is. Very like the nameless governess of Henry James's *The Turn of the Screw,*[1] Jane walks agitatedly about, alone, "safe in the silence and solitude," and eager for adventure: which is to say, romance.

Women are supposed to be calm, Jane says, but women feel precisely as men do, requiring exercise for their faculties and suffering from stagnation. On the third floor of Thornfield she paces about, not unlike the captive Bertha

---

[1] Henry James's fated governess has visions of "a castle of romance . . . such a place as would somehow, for diversion of the young idea, take all color out of story-books and fairy tales. Wasn't it just a story-book over which I had fallen adoze and adream?" Just before her initial encounter with the sinister Peter Quint, she thinks "that it would be as charming as a charming story suddenly to meet someone. Someone would appear there at the turn of a path and would stand before me and smile and approve." Jane Eyre's romantic imagination summons forth, as it were, her "master" Fairfax Rochester; James's governess, wishing for her "master," initiates disaster.

in *her* backward-and-forward movements, allowing "my mind's eye to dwell upon whatever bright visions rose before it—and, certainly, they were many and glowing; to let my heart be heaved by the exultant movement, which, while it swelled it in trouble, expanded it with life; and, best of all, to open my inward ear to a tale that was never ended—a tale my imagination created, and narrated continuously; quickened with all of incident, life, fire, feeling, that I desired and had not in my actual existence." Jane is Charlotte Brontë telling us of the mesmerizing psychological experience of the writing of *Jane Eyre*. (It was written in five months.)

In recounting her story, Jane typically introduces a situation meant to provoke conventional associations on the part of the reader (to whom, as to a friend, Jane speaks candidly) and then, within a paragraph or two, deftly qualifies or refutes it. The narrative's dialectic, it might be said, constitutes a plot motion of its own, quite distinct from Jane's activities. A thesis of sorts is presented; but, should we respond to it, the narrator will set us right: for she is always in control of her narrative. We learn, with Jane, that what *seems to be* rarely *is;* even when Rochester disguises himself as a fortune-telling gypsy, improbably fooling his guests, Jane is keen enough to suspect "something of a masquerade."

The novel begins with a blunt statement: "There was no possibility of taking a walk that day." The shrubbery is leafless; the winter sky overcast; the rain penetrating; Eliza, John, and Georgiana, and the despised orphan, Jane, are cooped up together in the house. But, should the reader be tempted to respond automatically to this privation, Jane immediately declares, "I was glad of it; I never liked long walks." Excluded from Christmas celebrations in the Reed household, Jane describes the festivities and exchanges of gifts she missed; then says, "To speak the truth, I had not the least wish to go into company." Given what is known of

Charlotte's grief at the deaths of her two elder sisters at school, when she was a very small child, the dialectic of Chapter 9 is all the more surprising: for here the typhus epidemic at Lowood Orphan Asylum is set against an unusually idyllic spring, and while disease, death, gloom, hospital smells, and the "effluvia of mortality" predominate, Jane, untouched by the disease, is frank about her enjoyment of the situation. Forty-five out of eighty girls are affected; some go home to die (as Charlotte's sisters did, from the Cowan Bridge School), and some die at school, like Helen Burns, and are buried "quietly and quickly"; but the ten-year-old Jane, clearly no kin to child heroines in works of George Eliot or Charles Dickens, responds instinctively to the bright May sunshine and the "majestic life" that is being restored to Nature. She delights in her freedom to ramble in the woods and to eat as much as she likes, for the first time in her life: with very little Victorian delicacy, but with a refreshing air of truthfulness, Jane notes that her breakfast basin is "better filled" because the sick lack appetite. Even the death of Helen Burns is sparely treated; and Jane's close questioning of Helen's religious convictions does not appear resolved: "Again I questioned; but this time only in thought. Where is [Heaven]? Does it exist?"

Jane Eyre is remarkable for its forthright declaration of its heroine's passions and appetites. Unlike Lucy Snowe, with whom she bears a family kinship, Jane hardly needs to work at cultivating a "healthy hunger": she is ravenous with appetite at Lowood, and, in fleeing Thornfield, in the brilliantly sustained nightmare of Chapter 28, she is in danger of literally starving to death. In the latter scene, Jane responds at first like any romantic heroine, imagining a Wordsworthian solace in the moorland: "Not a tie holds me to human society at this moment—not a charm or hope calls me where my fellow-creatures are—none that saw me would have a kind thought or good wish for me. I have no relative but the universal mother, Nature: I will seek her breast and ask repose." Outcast that she is from human society, Jane knows herself loved by Nature, to which she clings with an ingenuous "filial fondness": "Tonight, at least, I would be her guest, as I was her child: my mother would lodge me without money and without price. I had one more morsel of bread. . . . My hunger, sharp before, was, if not satisfied, appeased by this hermit's meal." As her reverie continues Jane speculates about God, a *He* set beside Nature's *She:* "We know that God is everywhere; but certainly we feel His presence most when His works are on the grandest scale spread out before us: and it is in the unclouded night sky, where His worlds wheel their silent course, that we read clearest His infinitude."

Jane's awakening next morning is to a bitter revelation: she begins to experience genuine hunger and to suffer the humiliation, mounting very nearly to physical terror, of near-starvation. Piety rapidly vanishes; romantic rhetoric is dropped. Brontë renders this painful interlude with such exactitude that one cannot doubt she wrote from first-hand experience, as her earliest biographer Mrs. Gaskell suggests.[2] Few scenes in English literature are so harrowing as those in which Jane overcomes her pride to beg for food and is given a crust of bread, or food meant for hogs, or rebuffed altogether. ("I blamed none of those who repulsed me. I felt it was what was to be expected.") Hunger has become real to Jane in a way that the platitudes of "Nature"

[2] Gaskell discusses in detail the meager diet—consisting mainly of potatoes—which the Brontë children were given at home and at the infamous Cowan Bridge School, the model for Lowood. Even in adulthood Charlotte Brontë seems to have fasted intermittently, and was so malnourished at the time of her final illness that she begged constantly for food. "A wren would have starved on what she ate during those last six weeks," one observer is quoted. (See E. C. Gaskell, *The Life of Charlotte Brontë* [Edinburgh: John Grant, 1905].)

and "God" are not. (One is reminded of the "thin, haggard, and hollow-eyed" Lucy Snowe, who, confronted with a Renoir-like portrait of a voluptuous female, ostensibly Cleopatra, responds with startling violence. Indeed, Brontë herself is so incensed by this "enormous piece of claptrap" that, for some paragraphs, the fastidiously subdued prose of *Villette* is enlivened by a genuine passion: "I calculated that this lady . . . would infallibly turn from fourteen to sixteen stone. She was, indeed, extremely well fed: very much butcher's meat—to say nothing of bread, vegetables, and liquids—must she have consumed to attain that breadth and height, that wealth of muscle, that affluence of flesh. . . . She had no business to lounge away the noon on a sofa. She ought likewise to have worn decent garments; a gown covering her properly." Lucy Snowe is an older and embittered Jane Eyre, recoiling from the very emblem of flesh.)

The plot of *Jane Eyre* is increasingly contrived and melodramatic—the novel is after all a late-Romantic, early Victorian form of the "manufactured fiction" of which Henry James spoke, in terms of Dickens, with some disdain—and, so far as "story" is concerned, the tensions of an interior dialectic sometimes lack subtlety. No aura of mystery or exoticism accrues to Rochester's visitor from the West Indies, Richard Mason: in Jane's sharp eyes he is sallow and unmanly, with something in his face that fails to please. "His features were regular, but too relaxed; his eye was large and well cut, but the life looking out of it was a tame, vacant life." When, later, Jane is brought into Bertha Mason's presence and mockingly introduced to Rochester's wife, she is naturally revulsed—she feels no kinship with *this* creature. And though Jane charges Rochester with cruelty in so despising and exhibiting his mad wife, claiming that Bertha cannot help her condition, Jane cannot really identify with the woman; and rather too readily forgives Rochester his curious (and ungentlemanly) behavior.[3] That Rochester had intended to dishonestly marry her, and, in the most fundamental sense, "deflower" her, matters less to Jane than the reader anticipates. But the legitimate Mrs. Rochester, along with Thornfield Hall itself and all it represents of a diseased past, will soon be destroyed in a refining fire.

Numerous readers have felt that the long Whitcross section, consisting as it does of nearly one hundred pages, is an awkward digression in *Jane Eyre;* and one is nudged to recall that the publishing firm of Smith, Elder had rejected Charlotte Brontë's earlier novel, *The Professor,* as "undersized." (But if Currer Bell would write a full-scale, three-volume novel for them, they would be "most interested.") Still, the carefully transcribed section is required for symmetry's sake. Brontë's authorial strategy is to balance one kind of temptation with its obverse (if Rochester is all romantic passion, urging her to succumb to emotional excess, St. John Rivers is all Christian ambition, urging her to attempt a spiritual asceticism of which she knows herself incapable): is not *Jane Eyre* an orchestrated novel of ideas, closer in temperament to the fiction of George Eliot than to that

[3] For a very different account, from a Modernist perspective, of the doomed love of the West Indies heiress and her English husband, Rochester, see Jean Rhys's haunting and hallucinatory prose poem of a novel, *Wide Sargasso Sea* (New York: W. W. Norton & Co., 1966). Rhys's novel is the first-person account of the very Mrs. Rochester whom Jane Eyre supplants: a re-vision of the great Victorian classic. It is an evocation, by means of a highly compressed and elliptical language, of the authentic experience of madness—more precisely, of being driven into madness; it constitutes a brilliantly sustained anti-romance, a reverse mirror image of Charlotte Brontë's England. Where *Jane Eyre* is triumphant nineteenth-century romance, *Wide Sargasso Sea* is twentieth-century tragedy: the appropriation, colonization, exploitation, and destruction of a pastoral tropical world by a wholly alien English sensibility. When Rhys's heroine at last catches a glimpse of the young Englishwoman who will succeed her as Rochester's wife, she sees her as a "ghost" with streaming hair: "She was surrounded by a gilt frame, but I knew her." Inhabiting contrary and mutually exclusive worlds, Womankind split in two, the one is a savage to the other; the other, a ghost.

of Emily Brontë? The miraculously realized "family" of Diana, Mary, and Rivers himself strikes us as a benign adumbration of the novel's original household, in which Jane was despised by Eliza, Georgiana, and the spectacularly loathsome John Reed. Rochester, following the novel's design, must be altered too in some respect, but it is probably incorrect to read his blinding as a species of castration—as that perennial cliché of Brontë criticism would have it. Not only is the blind and crippled Rochester no less masculine than before, but, more significantly, it was never the case that Jane Eyre, for all her inexperience, shrank from either her master's passion or her own: the issue was not Jane's sexual timidity but her shrewd understanding that, should she become his mistress, she would lose Rochester's respect. One might say, *inevitably* lose his respect. These were the hardly secret terms of Victorian mores, and Jane Eyre would have to have been a very naïve young woman, as self-deluded as George Eliot's Hetty, to have believed otherwise. And Jane is anything but naïve.

"Reader, I married him," Jane announces boldly in the novel's final chapter. The tacit message is that *I* married *him*—not that *he* married *me*. What greater triumph for the orphan, the governess, the small, plain, and "Quaker-like" virgin? The novel ends with a curious aside to St. John Rivers, away in India "laboring for his race" and anticipating, with a martyr's greed, his "incorruptible crown." It is St. John's grim and exultant language that rounds the story off, however ironically: " 'Amen; even so, come, Lord Jesus!' " But those who have love have no need of this particular Lord Jesus.

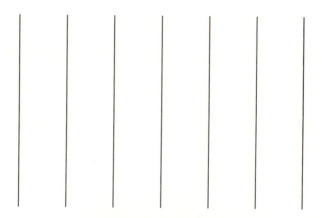

MOBY DICK: AN AMERICAN BOOK OF WONDERS

Why is it that *Moby Dick,* our greatest native work of prose fiction, strikes us as so uniquely American?—the product of a successful young writer at the peak of his somewhat precocious powers (Melville was only thirty-two years old at the time of its publication in 1851); a tour de force of brilliantly sustained metaphor, in which an albino whale and his fanatic pursuers enact a tragic drama as old as the race; the most sympathetic and unsentimental exploration of monomania in our literature; a novel of ideas—many ideas—imposed upon an epic adventure of the high seas; a compendium of data on whales, whaling vessels, and the men who made up their crews; a prodigious assemblage of humor, and philosophizing, and prose poetry, and monologues reminiscent of the great soliloquies of Shakespeare; a work that reveals on virtually every page its youthful author's exuberance, as, daringly, sometimes recklessly, he addresses the reader in defiance of authorial decorum? Herman Melville is not content merely to tell his baroque tale, he must guide our reading of it, stepping forward at will (in the chapter titled "The Affidavit," for instance) to interrupt his melodramatic narrative with an amplification of whale lore and an insistence upon the literal reality of "the whole story of the White Whale." Granted that the novel *Moby Dick* is very much a fable, an allegory, a work rich (if not occasionally over-rich) with symbolic meanings, it is urgent that the reader be assured that the White Whale himself exists—that he is, for all his supranatural powers, no "monstrous fable, or still worse and more detestable, a hideous and intolerable allegory."

Which is to say, *Moby Dick; or, The Whale,* while as self-consciously and as elaborately *written* as anything in our language, and as intercalated with portents and omens as any Gothic work of fiction, is nevertheless a "real" story, fundamentally, and must be approached in that spirit. The chapters provide us with information and then conclude, usually, with the author's—or Ishmael's—commentary on it; a typical chapter, "The Mast-Head," for instance, consists of pages of documentary data, then ends with a description of what it feels like to be on duty high on the mast: the growing ennui, the hypnotic lull, the "opium-like listlessness of vacant, unconscious reverie" that steals from the sailor his identity, so that he begins to take the ocean below him for the image of "that deep, blue, bottomless soul, pervading mankind and nature." So enchanted, the man high on the masthead is in danger of losing his sense of self completely and of falling to his death. The language in which Melville speaks in the chapter's concluding paragraphs is very different from his "documentary" language, but rises quite naturally from it. And the warning to Pantheists who would confuse the outer world with their interior worlds, abrupt as it is, also emerges without strain from Ishmael's commentary: "While this sleep, this dream is on ye, move your foot or hand an inch; slip your hold at all; and your identity comes back in horror. And . . . at mid-day, in the fairest weather, with one half-throttled shriek you drop through that transparent air into the summer sea, no more to rise forever. Heed it well, ye Pantheists!"

Like all great works of art, *Moby Dick* will support many readings, many interpretations. Yet, chapter by chapter, its meanings are not at all obscure; if Fedallah and the other members of Ahab's "shadow crew" have a symbolic significance, for instance, Ishmael will tell us what it is, just as he will tell us what Pip's terrible madness means, and how it relates to us all. Indeed, repeated readings of *Moby Dick* confirm one's sense of Ishmael/Melville as a voice of remarkable subtlety, intelligence, and variety; and though it has often been charged against Melville that his narrator "disappears" into the narration, one might argue that the novel's innumerable voices (in the dramatized sections, for instance) are but ingenious manifestations, recollected after the fact, of the novel's central voice. (By which I mean that, as Ishmael has escaped the catastrophe and is, indeed, the sole survivor, the "authentic" chronicle he tells us is purely *his*.)

A distinctly American voice, ambitious, daring, endlessly resourceful; perhaps rather outrageous, set beside the high-toned dignity of Hawthorne and Emerson; and certainly boastful, as if Herman Melville could have known he was writing a "great book." Such high spirits—such brashness—will depart from Melville forever after the publication (and commercial failure) of *Moby Dick,* to return in bitter transmogrified form in the prosy, clotted, heavily ironic *Pierre* and in the mysterious but finally lifeless *The Confidence Man,* a "novel" of ideas in which the physical world scarcely appears. But in 1850 young Melville sensed himself at the height of his powers, moving with ease from the straightforward (but frequently quite lyric) prose of *White-Jacket; or, The World in a Man-of-War,* to the exuberance of *Moby Dick.* Consider this remarkable outburst, in the chapter titled "The Fossil Whale":

> One often hears of writers that rise and swell with their subject, though it may seem but an ordinary one. How, then, with me, writing of this Leviathan? Unconsciously my chirography expands into placard capitals. Give me a condor's quill! Give me Vesuvius' crater for an inkstand! Friends, hold my arms! For in the mere act of penning my thoughts of this Leviathan, they weary me, and make me faint with their outreaching comprehensiveness of sweep, as if to include the whole circle of the sciences, and all the generations of whales, and men, and mastodons, past, present, and to come, with all the revolving panoramas of empire on earth, and throughout the whole universe. . . . Such, and so magnifying, is the virtue of a large and liberal theme! We expand to its bulk. To produce a mighty book, you must choose a mighty theme. No great and enduring volume can ever be written on the flea, though many there be who have tried it.

This is the voice of a writer in whom raw energy freely burns, consuming itself even as it illuminates; the voice of an Ishmael who has survived, in triumph, but who will, before long, be writing to his friend Nathaniel Hawthorne, whom he admired above all men and to whom "in admiration of his genius" he dedicated *Moby Dick:*

> Until I was 25 I had no development at all. From my 25th year I date my life. Three weeks have scarcely passed, at any time between now and then, that I have not unfolded within myself. But I feel that I am now come to the inmost leaf of the bulb, and that shortly the flower must fall to the mould.

Moby Dick, the product of the "inmost leaf of the bulb," would not have been written (as a tragic epic of Hawthornean and Shakespearean subtlety) without the example of Hawthorne's allegorical fiction. Melville's reading of the *Twice-Told Tales* in 1850 virtually changed his life, inspiring him to recast his "romance of the whale fisheries" into a work of high seriousness and dignity. (Consequently the reader should be forewarned that the novel's tone changes considerably as it progresses: the opening section is brisk, chatty, funny, engaging, but relatively slight when set beside the magisterial chapters to come—from approximately "Ahab" onward.) Melville's irony on the subject of Transcendentalism and Pantheism (at the conclusion of "The Mast-Head" in particular) is in response to the writings of Emerson and his circle—which could not have failed to strike the young man, with his arduous seafaring experience, as the products of a bookish life. (Emerson's *Essays, First Series,* were published in 1841; the *Second Series* in 1844; *Representative Men* in 1850.) And one should bear in mind the achievements of this extraordinary era in general—Poe's *The Raven and Other Poems* (1845) and *Tales* (1845); Hawthorne's *The Scarlet Letter* (1850); Harriet Beecher Stowe's *Uncle Tom's Cabin* (1852); Henry David Thoreau's *Walden* (1854); Longfellow's *Hia-*

watha (1855); Walt Whitman's *Leaves of Grass* (first edition, 1855). (Though Emily Dickinson began writing her poems in the early fifties they were not to be assembled and published until 1890.)

Moby Dick; or, The Whale, a novel like no other before or since, is nonetheless a product of its era; and Herman Melville, the best-selling author of *Typee; or, A Peep at Polynesian Life* (1846) and *Omoo* (1847)—good-natured "travel/adventure" romances of no special literary or intellectual distinction—realized his genius by way of his fellow writers.

Herman Melville was born in 1819, died in 1891 (virtually forgotten, as melancholy legend would have it), and wrote his most brilliantly sustained work long before the midpoint of his career. His successes *Typee* and *Omoo* were never to be repeated, though *Redburn* (1849) and *White-Jacket* (1850), each cast in the popular mode of first-person accounts of the sea, sold well; and when Melville began writing *Moby Dick* in 1850 there was every reason for the optimistic young writer to believe that greater success lay immediately before him. The novel's composition took place in cramped and impoverished circumstances (for the most part in a farmhouse near Pittsfield, Massachusetts), but Melville's mood was robust, often euphoric; he set himself the task of recalling his seafaring experiences of 1841, when, desperate for work, he had signed on the whaling ship *Acushnet,* with near-disastrous results. (Melville deserted, in the Marquesas Islands, in the summer of 1842.) Consequently he was able to write for long feverish stretches at a time, confident of his powers, fired with an exuberance that is communicated to the reader in the novel's every line. The *Pequod* and its crew are doomed—all save Ishmael, who alone has escaped to tell us:

. . . liberated by reason of its cunning spring, and, owing to its great buoyancy, rising with great force, the coffin life-buoy shot lengthwise from the sea, fell over, and floated by my side. Buoyed up by that coffin, for almost one whole day and night, I floated on a soft and dirge-like main. The unharming sharks, they glided by as if with padlocks on their mouths; the savage sea-hawks sailed with sheated sheathed beaks. On the second day, a sail drew near, nearer, and picked me up at last.

Ishmael, speaking for Melville, instructs us through-out in the reading of *Moby Dick*. Even when he seems to disappear from the narrative for long periods (when, for in-stance, we are privileged to overhear Ahab's eloquent solil-oquies, or those of his mates, or to be told in tireless detail of the history and nature of whales), it is Melville's intention that Ishmael remain our central, guiding consciousness, an absolutely reliable witness. His voice undergoes a change once the *Pequod* sets sail and Captain Ahab appears, but the novel's primary theme of man's comic helplessness in the face of "Providence" is struck at once; and Ishmael explains to us, succinctly and poetically, the ineffable power of the sea:

. . . still deeper [is] the meaning of that story of Narcis-sus, who because he could not grasp the tormenting, mild image he saw in the fountain, plunged into it and was drowned. But that same image, we ourselves see in all riv-ers and oceans. It is the image of the ungraspable phantom of life; and this is the key to it all.

Ishmael also confides in us that seafaring for him is a way of thwarting the "damp, drizzly November in his soul" that urges him to suicide; he tells us that it is the "over-whelming idea of the great whale itself"—the "grand hooded phantom, like a snow hill in the air"—that draws him to a whaling vessel. Most significantly he instructs us in the eerie "whiteness of the whale" in the famous chapter (XLII) of that title, a rhapsodic prose poem of nine pages that seeks to explore the symbolic meaning of the *albino* whale, in spiritual terms:

> Is it that by its indefiniteness it shadows forth the heartless voids and immensities of the universe, and thus stabs us from behind with the thought of annihilation, when beholding the white depths of the milky way? Or is it, that as in essence whiteness is not so much a color as the visible absence of color; and at the same time the concrete of all colors; is it for these reasons that there is such a dumb blankness, full of meaning, as in a wide landscape of snows— a colorless all-color of atheism from which we shrink? [Colors] are but subtle deceits, not actually inherent in substances, but only laid on from without; so that all deified Nature absolutely paints like a harlot, whose allurements cover nothing but the charnel-house within; and when we proceed further and consider that the mystical cosmetic which produces every one of her hues, the great principle of light, for ever remains white or colorless in itself . . . pondering all this, the palsied universe lies before us like a leper; and like wilful travelers in Lapland, who refuse to wear colored . . . glasses upon their eyes, so the wretched infidel gazes himself blind at the monumental white shroud that wraps all the prospect around him. And of all these things the Albino whale was the symbol. Wonder ye then at the fiery hunt?

In this extraordinary passage Ishmael's and Ahab's voices seem to blend. While in many of its aspects, says Ishmael, the visible world seems formed in love, "the invisible spheres were formed in fright."

Herman Melville was clearly one of those figures of the mid- and late nineteenth century who suffered the absence of God with as much passion as his Puritan and Calvinist predecessors suffered God's probable wrath. The will to believe, to *have faith,* is so poignant a motive in Melville's major works—*Pierre, The Confidence Man,* and *Billy Budd,* in addition to *Moby Dick*—that it is no exaggeration to say that it informs their very conceptions. The white whale is the most celebrated (and, in literary terms, the most inspired) of the images of an unknowable God; the spirit made flesh, so to speak; a creature called a "dumb beast" by Starbuck, but granted a demonic and highly intelligent will by Ahab and, later, Ishmael. (Moby Dick is also believed by superstitious sailors to be both ubiquitous and immortal—an "unearthly conceit" that nearly grants him Godhead.) In Ahab's grandiloquent cosmology, in which the phenomenal world is but a pasteboard mask cloaking God (or God's maddening absence), one must, in seeking revenge, "strike through the mask"—one must take vengeance upon God by way of God's creatures. In tones worthy of Shakespearean tragedy, Ahab declares ("The Quarter-Deck"):

> [The white whale] tasks me; he heaps me; I see in him outrageous strength, with an inscrutable malice sinewing it. That inscrutable thing is chiefly what I hate; and be the white whale agent, or be the white whale principal, I will wreak that hate upon him. Talk to me not of blasphemy, man; I'd strike the sun if it insulted me.

Ahab is not an atheist but an anti-theist, one who would destroy God, had he the means (like Satan, perhaps): the diabolism which gives him such furious energy is the very passion that underlies *Moby Dick* as a work of imaginative fiction. Melville and Ahab are not one—the differences between them are considerable—but Ahab's rebelliousness in language is certainly akin to Melville's. In brooding upon the nature of tragic "greatness," Ishmael concludes that morbidness, even disease, underlie it ("The Ship"), sentiments that echo Melville's own; Ahab boasts that he never thinks, "he only feels, feels, feels; *that's* tingling enough for mortal man" ("The Chase—Third Day"), just as Herman Melville, in a letter to Hawthorne of June 1852, declared, "I stand for the heart. To the dogs with the head!"

Though Captain Ahab is fifty-eight years old he is fired with a passionate, seemingly indefatigable energy; Ishmael calls him a monomaniac and a lunatic—but admires him nonetheless. It is clear that Melville wishes to align him with the greatest rebel of all in our tradition, Satan, as Milton imagined him: "I am darkness leaping out of light," Ahab proclaims. Only late in the voyage ("The Symphony") does Ahab confess to Starbuck that he is, in truth, exhausted, as though he were Adam, "staggering beneath the piled centuries since Paradise."

> God! God! God!—crack my heart!—stave my brain!—mockery!—mockery! Bitter, biting mockery of grey hairs, have I lived enough joy to weary ye; and seem and feel thus intolerably old?

No Romantic figure of Byronic or Faustian excess, Ahab reveals himself in such rare passages as a human being exiled from his species by the accident (or was it design?) of the white whale's "malevolence." He knows, yet seems not to know, that, in giving chase to Moby Dick, he must die, as the fulfillment of a prophecy; yet it is not possible for him to turn back. His character bears a remarkable resemblance to Melville's own, as Hawthorne sketched it in his notebook for 1854, when, in Hawthorne's judgment, he was suffering from "constant literary occupation, pursued without much success." His late writings seemed to Hawthorne to indicate a "morbid state of mind."

> Melville, as he always does, began to reason of Providence and futurity, and of everything that lies beyond human ken, and informed me that he had "pretty much made up his mind to be annihilated"; but still he does not seem to rest in that anticipation; and, I think, will never rest until he gets hold of a definite belief. It is strange how he persists— and has persisted ever since I knew him, and probably long before—in wandering to-and-fro over these deserts, as dismal and monotonous as the sand hills amid which we were sitting. He can never believe, nor be comfortable in his unbelief; and he is too honest and courageous not to try to do one or the other. If he were a religious man, he would be one of the most truly religious and reverential; he has a very high and noble nature, and better worth immortality than most of us.

(A portrait, for all its admiration, of a lonely, brooding, obsessive man, confirmed in his bitterness, with the passage of time, by the failure of his most ambitious books.)

In his *Studies in Classic American Literature,* D. H. Lawrence reads *Moby Dick* as a peculiarly American work. The *Pequod,* containing "many races, many peoples, many nations, under the Stars and Stripes," is the ship of America's soul; it can be no accident that the ship is governed by a mad captain embarked upon a fanatic's hunt. Moby Dick is the "deepest blood-being of the white race," hunted by the "maniacal fanaticism of our white mental consciousness." Being a whale, a mammal, he is hot-blooded; hunted by monomaniacs of the Idea; incapable finally of being destroyed, but capable of wreaking great havoc upon his pursuers.

Lawrence's famous reading is biased, impulsive, rather slapdash, like much of his most perceptive criticism, yet it seems to me a wholly legitimate and convincing interpretation. He might have discussed the amplifying fact that the pursuit of the white whale—the pursuit of whales generally—was a commercial venture primarily: an assemblage, whether "democratic" or merely representative of humanity, of men bent upon exploiting Nature because, in order to live, they must do so. Were the whales themselves carnivores, the reader might feel less sympathy for them, but Melville is unsparing in his delineation of what actually happens in whaling—what is killed, how it is killed, and who the killers are. Moby Dick may enjoy the invulnerability of a creature of legend, but his kin, pursued by harpooners, are not so fortunate. Consider the powerful descriptive passages in such chapters as "The Virgin," in which Melville sets aside his allegorical philosophizing in order to write as succinctly, and as brilliantly, as he can:

> It was a terrible, most pitiable, and maddening sight. The whale was now going head out, and sending his spout before him in a continued tormented jet; while his one poor fin beat his side in an agony of fright. Now to this hand, now to that, he yawed in his faltering flight, and still at every billow that he broke, he spasmodically sank in the sea, or sideways rolled toward the sky his one beating fin. So I have seen a bird with clipped wing, making affrighted broken circles in the air, vainly striving to escape the piratical hawks. But the bird has a voice, and with plaintive cries will make known her fear; but the fear of this vast dumb brute of the sea, was chained up and enchanted in him; he had no voice, save that choking respiration through

his spiracle, and this made the sight of him unspeakably pitiable.

It is discovered that the whale is blind, that bulblike growths protrude from his eyes; but the harpooners have no pity for him. "For all his old age, and his one arm, and his blind eyes," says Ishmael, "he must die the death and be murdered, in order to light the gay bridals and other merrymakings of men, and also to illuminate the solemn churches that preach unconditional inoffensiveness by all to all." It is the Christian's pursuit of the helpless dumb beast in order to reduce him to mere material, mere whale oil (to be used in lamps): a diabolism of rampaging Man, without pity and without compassion. And it may well be true, as Lawrence argues, that Man, in hunting down animals, hunts down his own "blood consciousness"; and that, in systematically destroying Nature, he destroys himself. Could any vision be contemporary and more terrifying? "Doom! Doom! Doom! something seems to whisper it in the very dark trees of America," says Lawrence.

But the splendid white whale Moby Dick does escape. Provoked to both savagery and cunning by the *Pequod*'s three-day chase, he destroys the ship, kills everyone but Ishmael, disappears. And, for a brief moment, we are privileged to see Nature emptied of Man, as if Man had never been:

> Now small fowls flew screaming over the yet yawning gulf; a sullen white surf beat against its steep sides; then all collapsed, and the great shroud of the sea rolled on as it rolled five thousand years ago.

Moby Dick is so powerful a work of prose fiction because it allows us to feel, for ourselves, this extraordinary prophetic vision; to read it is a profound experience, scarcely to be suggested by way of critical commentary. Like Thoreau's *Walden* it is in part a cautionary work, warning that the wages of sin (our plundering of Nature) is death for our own species. Like *Walden* it is composed of numberless elements, a mosaic of sorts containing the diverse ideas, impressions, recollections, insights, moments of humor and satire, and above all the incomparable observations of the physical world, that strike the writer, without necessary regard for the old conventions of "unity" and "coherence"— even, in Melville's case, of probability.

Moby Dick is our most daring and our most thoroughly American work of prose fiction, a book of wonders yet to be—like its enigmatic whale—thoroughly comprehended.

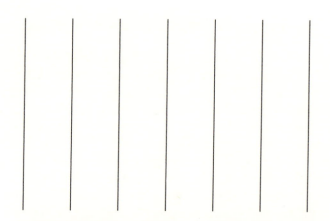

LOOKING FOR THOREAU

*I stand in awe of my body, this matter
to which I am bound has become so
strange to me. I fear not spirits, ghosts,
of which I am one . . . but I fear bodies, I tremble to meet them. What is this
Titan that has possession of me? Talk
of mysteries!—Think of our life in nature,—daily to be shown matter, to come
into contact with it,—rocks, trees, wind
on our cheeks! the solid earth! the actual world! the common sense! Contact! Contact! Who are we? where are
we?*

—Thoreau, "Ktaadn and the Maine
Woods," 1848

Of our classic American writers Henry David Thoreau is
the supreme poet of doubleness, of evasion and mystery.
Who is he? Where does he stand? Is he to be defined even
by his own words, deliberately and fastidiously chosen as
they are, and famously much revised? The facts of his life,
available in any Thoreau "chronology," seem more detached

from the man himself than such facts commonly do: Thoreau warns us that the outward aspect of his life may be "no more I than it is you." He boasts of having the capacity to stand as remote from himself as from another. He is both actor and spectator. He views himself as a participant in Time as if he were a kind of fiction—"a work of the imagination only." We know with certainty of the historical man, born 12 July 1817, Concord, Massachusetts, and who died 6 May 1862, Concord, Massachusetts; what lies between is a mystery.

Perhaps for these reasons, and because of the redoubtable tone of Thoreau's voice, he is the most controversial of American writers. Whether he writes with oneiric precision of thawing earth, or a ferocious war between red and black ants, or the primeval beauty of Mt. Katahdin in Maine, or in angry defense of the martyred John Brown ("I do not wish to kill or be killed but I can foresee circumstances in which both of these things would be by me unavoidable"), he asserts himself with such force that the reader is compelled to react: what compromise is possible? Always Thoreau tells us, *You must change your life.* Where his fellow Transcendentalists spoke of self-reliance as a virtue Thoreau actively practiced it, and gloried in it—"Sometimes, when I compare myself with other men, it seems as if I were more favored by the gods than they"; where most writers secretly feel superior to their contemporaries Thoreau is blunt, provoking—"The greater part of what my neighbors call good I believe in my soul to be bad." Yet his own position is frequently ambiguous, and even what he meant by Nature is something of a puzzle. Who is the omniscient "I" of *Walden?*

So intimately bound up with my imaginative life is the Henry David Thoreau of *Walden,* first read when I was fifteen, that it is difficult for me to speak of him with any pretense of objectivity. Any number of his pithy remarks have sunk so deep in my consciousness as to have assumed a sort of autonomy: *As if you could kill time without injuring eternity. Be it life or death we crave only reality. God himself culminates in the present moment, and will never be more divine in the lapse of all the ages. Why so seeming fast, but deadly slow?* So close to my heart is *Beware of all enterprises that require new clothes* I might delude myself it is my invention. Eventually I would read other works of Thoreau's and even teach *Walden* numberless times (in startling but always fruitful juxtaposition with, among other texts, Freud's *Civilization and Its Discontents,* Nietzsche's *Zarathustra,* Upton Sinclair's *The Jungle,* Lewis Carroll's *Alice* books and *The Hunting of the Snark*), but it is the *Walden* of my adolescence I remember most vividly—suffused with the powerfully intense, romantic energies of adolescence, the sense that life is boundless, experimental, provisional, ever-fluid, and unpredictable; the conviction that, whatever the accident of the outer self, the truest self is inward, secret, inviolable. "I love to be alone," says Thoreau. "I never found the companion that was so companionable as solitude." The celebrant of earthly, and of earthy, mysteries, Thoreau is also a celebrant of the human spirit in contradistinction to what might be called the social being—the public identities with which we are specified at birth and which through our lifetimes we labor to assert in a context of other social beings similarly hypnotized by the mystery of their own identities. But "self" to Thoreau appears to be but the lens through which the world is perceived, and as the world shifts on its axis, as season yields to season, place to place, one enigmatic form of matter to another, the prismatic lens itself shifts. "Daily to be shown matter"—what does it mean? If there is a self it must be this very shifting of perspective, this ceaseless transformation and metamorphosis. If in 1854, the very year of

Walden's publication, Thoreau could note in his journal, "We soon get through with Nature. She excites an expectation which she cannot satisfy," the testament of *Walden* is otherwise. What more radical perspective: "Shall I not have intelligence with the earth? Am I not partly leaves and vegetable mould myself?"

Thoreau's appeal is to that instinct in us—adolescent, perhaps, but not merely adolescent—that resists our own gravitation toward the outer, larger, fiercely competitive world of responsibility, false courage, and "reputation." It is an appeal as readily described as existential, as Transcendentalist; its voice is unique, individual, skeptical, rebellious. The greatest good for the greatest number—the sense that we might owe something to the state—the possibility that life is fulfilled, not handicapped, by human relationships: these are moral positions not to be considered. "I have lived some thirty years on this planet," Thoreau says boldly, "and I have yet to hear the first syllable of valuable or even earnest advice from my seniors. They have told me nothing, and probably cannot tell me anything, to the purpose."

Can it be true, or is it a useful fiction, that the cosmos is created anew in the individual?—that one can, by way of a defiant act of self-begetting, transcend the fate of the species, the nation, the community, the family, and—for a woman—the socially determined parameters of gender? Surely it is doubtful that Nature is a single entity, a noun congenial to capitalization:

> The indescribable innocence and beneficence of Nature,—
> of sun and wind and rain, of summer and winter,—such
> health, such cheer, they afford forever! and such sympathy
> have they ever with our race, that all Nature would be af-
> fected, and the sun's brightness fade, and the winds would
> sigh humanely, and the clouds rain tears, and the woods

shed their leaves and put on mourning in midsummer, if any man should ever for a just cause grieve.

(How to reconcile this Nature with the Nature of lockjaw and tuberculosis, of agonizing deaths and prolonged griefs? Thoreau himself was to die young, aged forty-four, of consumption.) Yet these fictions, these willed metaphors, very nearly convince within the total argument of *Walden*. We believe even while disbelieving, even as we cannot entirely believe, but do—or wish to—in what Thoreau tells us repeatedly of the autonomy of the human soul. Quite apart from his mastery of the English language—and certainly no American has ever written more beautiful, vigorous, supple prose—Thoreau's peculiar triumph as a stylist is to transform reality itself by way of his perception of it: *his* language. What is the motive for metaphor in any poet—in any poetic sensibility—but the ceaseless defining of the self and of the world by way of language? In his journal for 6 May 1854 Thoreau writes: "All that a man has to say or do that can possibly concern mankind, is in some shape or other to tell the story of his love,—to sing; and, if he is fortunate and keeps alive, he will be forever in love. This alone is to be alive to the extremities."

To read Thoreau in adolescence is to read him at a time when such statements carry the weight, the promise, of prophecy; "to be alive to the extremities," with no fixed or even definable object for one's love, seems not merely possible but inevitable, and desirable. As existence precedes essence, so emotion precedes and helps to create its object. If the human world disappoints us—as in adolescence it so frequently does, not only in falling short of its ideals but in failing to grant us the value we wish for ourselves—we have the privilege of repudiating it forever in exchange for the certainty of a far different kind of romance, or religious mission. "We should be blessed if we lived in the present always, and took advantage of every accident that befell us," Thoreau says, but such vigilance is possible only if one has broken free of human restraints and obligations—plans for the future, let's say, or remorse over one's past acts; only if the object of one's love is not another human being. Thoreau proposed marriage to a young woman named Ellen Sewall in 1840, was rejected, and forever afterward seems to have turned his energies—his "love"—inward to the mysterious self and outward to an equally mysterious Nature. "I have never felt lonesome, or in the least oppressed by a sense of solitude, but once . . . but I was at the same time conscious of a slight insanity in my mood, and seemed to foresee my recovery," Thoreau says in that most eloquent of chapters, "Solitude." Here aloneness is so natural, so right, lonesomeness itself is a slight insanity. Even Nietzsche's celibate prophet Zarathustra, that most alone of men, admits to being lonely; and does not shrink from saying "I love man," though his love is not returned.

But all art is a matter of exclusions, rejections. To write of one subject is to ignore all others. To live one life passionately—to drive it into a corner, reduce it to its lowest terms, see whether it be "mean or sublime"—is necessarily to detach oneself from other lives. If Henry David Thoreau is an emblematic and even a heroic figure for many writers it is partly because the "Henry David Thoreau" of *Walden* is so triumphant a literary creation—a fiction, surely, metaphorical rather than human, pieced together as we now know by slow painstaking labor out of the journals of many years. (At the time of his death Thoreau left behind an extraordinary record—thirty-nine manuscript volumes containing nearly two million words, a journal religiously kept from his twentieth year until his death.) But so superb a stylist is Thoreau we always have the sense as we read of a mind flying brilliantly before us, throwing off sparks, dazzling and iridescent and seemingly effortless as a butterfly in flight: What an eye, we are moved to think—what an ear! what spontaneity! In fact *Walden* is mosaic rather than narrative, a carefully orchestrated symbolic fiction and not a forthright account of a man's sojourn in the woods. More important still, we should understand Thoreau's "I" to be a calculated literary invention, a fictitious character set in a naturalistic but fictitious world. Surely the bodiless and seemingly nameless persona who brags for humanity rather than for himself had no historical existence and might be set beside Hawthorne's Hester Prynne, Melville's Ahab, and Twain's Huckleberry Finn as one of the great literary creations of the nineteenth century. Like his Transcendentalist companions Thoreau scorned the art of fiction ("One world at a time," he might have said wittily in this context too), while not acknowledging that the art of fiction takes many guises, just as telling the truth requires many forms.

Certainly the meticulous craftsmanship of *Walden*—reminiscent of the obsessive, fanatic, inspired craftsmanship of Joyce's *Ulysses* and *Finnegans Wake*—gives the book another dimension, another angle of appeal, of particular interest to writers. Writing is not after all merely the record of having lived but an aspect of living itself. And if there are those to whom living is a preparation for writing—why not? Only a sensibility hostile to the act of writing, or doubtful of writing's validity to life, would wish to criticize—as, oddly, many critics have criticized Thoreau for the very precision of his prose!—as if writing poorly were a measure of sincerity. (Alfred Kazin, for instance, in *An American Procession,* speaks slightingly of Thoreau as having written rather than "achieved" ecstasy: "Whatever the moment was, his expression of it was forged, fabricated, worked over, soldered from fragmentary responses, to make those single sentences that created Thoreau's reputation as an aphorist and fostered the myth that in such cleverness a man could live." But in such art a man *did* live. And, in any case, the most difficult experiences to record are those we have actually experienced: we toil to express what we have felt without premeditation.)

Thoreau is, as I have suggested, the quintessential poet of evasion, paradox, mystery. If like Walt Whitman he contradicts himself—very well, he contradicts himself. A foolish consistency is the hobgoblin of small minds, but disparity itself may well lie in the mind of the beholder.

Who are we?—*where* are we? Thoreau repeatedly asks. He confesses or brags that he knows not the first letter of the alphabet, and is not so wise now as the day he was born. Though the voice of *Walden* is the voice of Thoreau's other works, one is hard put to characterize the self behind it. And even the object of his ecstatic love, Nature, is elusive, teasingly undefined. Is there Nature, or merely nature? Richer and more palpable in every respect than Emerson's Nature—as how could it fail to be—Thoreau's Nature is at times airily Platonic, at other times minute, graphic, gritty, unsparing. It is Transcendentalist and sentimental, Puritan and "obscene," existential and amoral, by turns. All we know with certainty is that it is mute: "Nature puts no question and answers none which we mortals ask."

In one of the didactic chapters of *Walden,* "Higher Laws," Thoreau speaks of an unsettling experience:

> As I came home through the woods . . . I caught a glimpse of a woodchuck stealing across my path, and felt a strange thrill of savage delight, and was strongly tempted to seize and devour him raw; not that I was hungry then, except for the wildness which he represented. [At another time] I found

myself ranging the woods, like a half-starved hound, with a
strange abandonment, seeking some kind of venison which
I might devour, and no morsel would have been too savage
for me. The wildest scenes had become unaccountably familiar.

Thoreau tells us he finds in himself an instinct toward the
higher, or spiritual, life; and another toward a primitive and
savage one. He reverences them both: "I love the wild no
less than the good." For *wildness* and *goodness* must ever be
separate. As the chapter develops, however, Thoreau repu-
diates the physical life with the astounding statement—in
Walden of all books—"Nature is hard to be overcome but
she must be overcome." In this new context it appears that
Nature is abruptly aligned with the feminine, the carnivo-
rous, and the carnal; though a man's spiritual life is "startlingly moral" one is nonetheless susceptible to temptations
from the merely physical, or feminine; urges to indulge in a
"slimy beastly life" of eating, drinking, and undifferentiated
sensuality. Thoreau speaks as a man to other men, in the
hectoring tone of a Puritan preacher, warning his readers
not against damnation (in which he cannot believe—he is
too canny, too Yankee) but against succumbing to their own
lower natures: "We are conscious of an animal in us, which
awakens in proportion as our higher nature slumbers." Sensuality takes many forms but it is all one—one vice. All purity is one. Though sexuality of any kind is foreign to *Walden,* chastity is evoked as a value, and a chapter which began
with an extravagant paean to wildness concludes with a de-
nunciation of the unnamed sexual instincts. ("I hesitate to
say these things, but it is not because of the subject,—I care
not how obscene my *words* are,—but because I cannot speak
of them without betraying my impurity. We discourse freely
without shame of one form of sensuality, and are silent about
another.")

Did Woman exist for Thoreau except as a projection of his own celibate soul, to be "transcended"? Though a radical thinker in so many other regards, Thoreau is profoundly conservative in these matters, as his conventional trope of Nature as "she" suggests. In the chapter "Reading," for instance, he differentiates between spoken and written languages, the language we hear and the language we read. The insight is profound, the expression crude and unexamined:

> The one is commonly transitory, a sound, a tongue, a dialect merely, almost brutish, and we learn it unconsciously, like the brutes, of our mothers. The other is the maturity and experience of that; if that is our mother tongue, this is our father tongue, a reserved and select expression, too significant to be heard by the ear, which we must be born again in order to speak.

The expression "born again" suggests the fundamentally religious bias of this classic misogyny.

Elsewhere Thoreau's Nature is unsentimental, existentialist. In "Brute Neighbors," for instance, Thoreau observes an ant war of nearly Homeric proportions and examines two maimed soldier ants under a microscope; the analogue with the human world is too obvious to be emphasized. In the rhapsodic passage with which "Spring" ends, wildness and Nature are again evoked as good, necessary for our spiritual wholeness. We need to witness our own limits transgressed: "We are cheered when we observe the vulture feeding on the carrion which disgusts and disheartens us and deriving health and strength from the repast." The impression made on a wise man is that of universal innocence. And we have no doubt who the "wise man" is.

Similarly unsentimental but cast in a Transcendentalist mode is the long and brilliantly sustained passage in

"Spring" in which Thoreau studies the hieroglyphic forms of thawing sand and clay on the side of a railroad embankment. In this extraordinary prose poem Thoreau observes so minutely and with such stark precision that the reader experiences the phenomenon far more vividly than he might ever hope to in life. As the earth thaws, numberless little streams are formed to overlap and interlace with one another, taking on the quality of leaves and vines and resembling "the laciniated lobed and imbricated thalluses of lichens"—or do they rather evoke coral, leopards' paws, birds' feet? brains or lungs or bowels? excrements of all kinds? The grotesque vegetation possesses such beauty Thoreau imagines himself in the very presence of the Artist who made the world and himself: "I feel as if I were nearer to the vitals of the globe, for this sandy overflow is something such a foliaceous mass as the vitals of the animal body." In Nature all forms mimic one another. The tree is but a single leaf—rivers are leaves whose pulp is intervening earth—towns and cities are the ova of insects in their axils!

Where in later life Thoreau would become obsessed with facts, data, matter ("the *solid* earth! the *actual* world!"), here he argues for so compelling a correspondence between man and the fantastical designs on the embankment we are led to see how mysticism is science, science mysticism, poetry merely common sense. The earth is not a fragment of dead history, "stratum upon stratum like the leaves of a book," but living poetry like the leaves of a tree; not a fossil earth but a living earth. In these lines Thoreau is writing at the very peak of his inimitable powers, yet the result, the elaborate metaphor in sand and clay, reads smoothly, "naturally."

The universe is after all wider than our views of it.

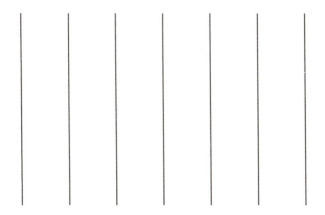

"SOUL AT THE WHITE HEAT": THE ROMANCE OF EMILY DICKINSON'S POETRY

Emily Dickinson is the most paradoxical of poets: the very poet of paradox. By way of voluminous biographical material, not to mention the extraordinary intimacy of her poetry, it would seem that we know everything about her: yet the common experience of reading her work, particularly if the poems are read sequentially, is that we come away seeming to know nothing. We would recognize her inimitable voice anywhere—in the "prose" of her letters no less than in her poetry—yet it is a voice of the most deliberate, the most teasing anonymity. "I'm Nobody!" is a proclamation to be interpreted in the most literal of ways. Like no other poet before her and like very few after her—Rilke comes most readily to mind, and, perhaps, Yeats and Lawrence—Dickinson exposes her heart's most subtle secrets; she confesses the very sentiments that, in society, would have embarrassed her dog (to paraphrase a remark of Dickinson's to Thomas Wentworth Higginson, explaining her aversion for the company of most people, whose prattle of "Hallowed things" offended her). Yet who is this "I" at the center of experience? In her astonishing body of 1,775 poems Dickinson records what is surely one of the most meticulous examinations of the phenomenon of human "consciousness" ever undertaken. The poet's persona—the tantalizing "I"—seems, in nearly every poem, to be addressing us directly with perceptions that are ours as well as hers. (Or his: these "Representatives of the Verse," though speaking in Dickinson's voice, are not restricted to the female gender.) The poems' refusal to be rhetorical, their daunting intimacy, suggests the self-evident in the way that certain Zen koans and riddles suggest the self-evident while being indecipherable. But what is challenged is, perhaps, "meaning" itself:

> Wonder — is not precisely Knowing
> And not precisely Knowing not —
> A beautiful but bleak condition
> He has not lived who has not felt —
>
> Suspense — is his maturer Sister —
> Whether Adult Delight is Pain
> Or of itself a new misgiving —
> This is the Gnat that mangles men —
> (1331, ca. 1874)[1]

[1] *The Complete Poems of Emily Dickinson*, edited by Thomas H. Johnson (Boston: Little, Brown & Co., 1960). Subsequent references in the text to the poems will cite the Johnson number and the date assigned by Johnson to each poem.

In this wonder there is a tone of the purest anonymity, as if the poet, speaking out of her "beautiful but bleak condition," were speaking of our condition as well. Dickinson's idiom has the startling ring of contemporaneity, like much of Shakespeare's; she speaks from the interior of a life as we might imagine ourselves speaking, gifted with genius's audacity and shorn of the merely local and time-bound. If anonymity is the soul's essential voice—its seductive, mesmerizing, fatal voice—then Emily Dickinson is our poet of the soul: our most endlessly fascinating American poet. As Whitman so powerfully addresses the exterior of American life, so Dickinson addresses—or has she helped create?—its unknowable interior.

No one who has read even a few of Dickinson's extraordinary poems can fail to sense the heroic nature of this poet's quest. It is riddlesome, obsessive, haunting, very often frustrating (to the poet no less than to the reader), but above all heroic; a romance of epic proportions. For the "poetic enterprise" is nothing less than the attempt to realize the soul. And the attempt to realize the soul (in its muteness, its perfection) is nothing less than the attempt to create a poetry of transcendence—the kind that outlives its human habitation and its name.

> *Dare you see a Soul at the White Heat?*
> *Then crouch within the door —*
> *Red — is the Fire's common tint —*
> *But when the vivid Ore*
> *Has vanquished Flame's conditions,*
> *It quivers from the Forge*
> *Without a color, but the light*
> *Of unanointed Blaze.*
> *Least Village has its Blacksmith*
> *Whose Anvil's even ring*

Stands symbol for the finger Forge
That soundless tugs – within –
Refining these impatient Ores
With Hammer, and with Blaze
Until the Designated Light
Repudiate the Forge –

(365, ca. 1862)

Only the soul "at the white heat" achieves the light of "un-anointed Blaze"—colorless, soundless, transcendent. This is the triumph of art as well as the triumph of personality, but it is not readily achieved.

Very often the "self" is set in opposition to the soul. The personality is mysteriously split, warring: "Of Consciousness, her awful Mate/ The Soul cannot be rid –" And: "Me from Myself – to banish –/ Had I Art –" A successful work of art is a consequence of the integration of conscious and unconscious elements; a balance of what is known and not quite known held in an exquisite tension. Art *is* tension, and poetry of the kind Emily Dickinson wrote is an art of strain, of nerves strung brilliantly tight. It is compact, dense, coiled in upon itself very nearly to the point of pain: like one of those stellar bodies whose gravity is so condensed it is on the point of disappearing altogether. How tight, how violent, this syntax!—making the reader's heart beat quickly, at times, in sympathy with the poet's heart. By way of Dickinson's radically experimental verse—and, not least, her employment of dashes as punctuation—the drama of the split self is made palpable. One is not merely told of it, one is made to experience it.

Anything less demanding would not be poetry, but prose—the kind of prose written by other people. Though Dickinson was an assured writer of prose herself, "prose" for her assumes a pejorative tone: see the famously rebellious poem in which the predicament of the female (artist? or simply "female"?) is dramatized—

> *They shut me up in Prose –*
> *As when a little Girl*
> *They put me in the Closet –*
> *Because they liked me "still" –*
>
> *Still! Could themself have peeped –*
> *And seen my Brain – go round –*
> *They might as wise have lodged a Bird*
> *For Treason – in the Pound –*
>
> *Himself has but to will*
> *And easy as a Star*
> *Abolish his Captivity –*
> *And laugh – No more have I –*
> (613, ca. 1862)

Prose—it might be speculated—is discourse; poetry ellipsis. Prose is spoken aloud; poetry overheard. The one is presumably articulate and social, a shared language, the voice of "communication"; the other is private, allusive, teasing, sly, idiosyncratic as the spider's delicate web, a kind of witchcraft unfathomable to ordinary minds. Poetry, paraphrased, is something other than poetry, while prose *is* paraphrase. Consequently the difficulty of much of Dickinson's poetry, its necessary strategies, for the act of writing is invariably an act of rebellion, a way of (secretly, subversively) "abolishing" captivity:

> *Tell all the Truth but tell it slant –*
> *Success in Circuit lies*
> *Too bright for our infirm Delight*
> *The Truth's superb surprise*
> *As Lightning to the Children eased*

JOYCE CAROL OATES

With explanation kind
The Truth must dazzle gradually
Or every man be blind –
                    (1129, ca. 1868)

Surely there is a witty irony behind the notion that lightning
can be domesticated by way of "kind explanations" told to
children; that the dazzle of Truth might be gradual and not
blinding. The "superb surprise" of which the poet speaks is
too much for mankind to bear head-on—like the Medusa it
can be glimpsed only indirectly, through the subtly distort-
ing mirror of art.

    Elsewhere, in a later poem, the poet suggests a radi-
cal distinction between two species of consciousness. Two
species of human being?—

Best Witchcraft is Geometry
To the magician's mind –
His ordinary acts are feats
To thinking of mankind.
                    (1158, ca. 1870)

The "witchcraft" of art is (mere) geometry to the practitioner: by which is meant that it is orderly, natural, obedient
to its own rules of logic; an ordinary event. What constitutes
the "feat" is the relative ignorance of others—non-magi-
cians. It is a measure of the poet's modesty that, in this poem
and in others, she excludes herself from the practice of
witchcraft, even as she brilliantly practices it. Dickinson is
most herself when she stands, like us, in awe of her remarkable powers as if sensing how little she controls them; how
little, finally, the mute and unknowable Soul has to do with
the restless, ever-improvising voice. "Silence," says the poet,

"is all we dread./ There's Ransom in a Voice —/ But Silence is Infinity./ Himself have not a face" (1251, ca. 1873).

Is the poet's anonymity in her art a conscious decision, or does this voice require a paring back of all that is presumably superfluous and distracting? (Which is to say, most of the world: the Civil War, it has been frequently noted, is not once named in Dickinson's poetry, though the poet wrote no less than a poem a day in the terrible years 1862–63.) Like Emerson in his terse, elliptical poems of "transcendence"—which Dickinson had read—the poet refines herself of the close-at-hand, the local, in order to meditate upon the universal: one would not know she was a daughter of Amherst, Massachusetts, an articulate citizen of a specific society. "I hide myself within my flower," the poet says in an enigmatic little poem of 1864, "That fading from your Vase,/ You, unsuspecting, feel for me —/ Almost a loneliness" (903). How perfectly the romance of Dickinson's poetry is suggested here, with what tenderness the poet anticipates our longing to know her: our loneliness (which is surely Dickinson's loneliness as well) in our relationship to her. Poetry of such precision excludes even the poet—consumes his heart away, as Yeats observed. Is this self-love, or the doomed love of Narcissus, that most misunderstood of mythological figures, for the seductive image he could not have known was his own? It would be a rare artist who does not fall under the enchantment of the unconscious, in the white heat of the enterprise we call "creative." The artist willingly effaces the merely personal self in the service of what can feel like an impersonal force, an interior Vesuvius or a still calm "disseminating" light—

> *The Poets light but Lamps —*
> *Themselves — go out —*

The Wicks they stimulate —
If vital Light

Inhere as do the Suns —
Each Age a Lens
Disseminating their
Circumference —

(883, ca. 1864)

But should the poet be tempted to step forward and declare herself, should she truly lay bare her heart (as Poe suggested the most courageous of writers might attempt), here is a pithy little warning:

A Charm invests a face
Imperfectly beheld —
The Lady dare not lift her Veil
For fear it be dispelled —

But peers beyond her mesh —
And wishes — and denies —
Lest Interview — annul a want
That Image — satisfies.

(421, ca. 1862)

One should keep in mind that this witty poem was written by a woman called "eccentric"—"partially cracked"—even, unfairly, "insane." A woman who chose in her maturity to live cloistered in her father's house and to withdraw from the presence of most visitors; a woman who chose, rather like Melville's stubborn Bartleby the Scrivener, *not* to play the game as others conspicuously played it, yet arranged some of her household appearances as theatrical events, costumed in white and carrying flowers. Dickinson's awkward relationship with the perplexed Higginson suggests the soundness of her judgment in stating that "Interview [may] annul a want/ That Image – satisfies." She understood that Emily Dickinson in her person could not be equal to Emily Dickinson in her poetry. The "self" and the "Soul" are too radically adverse.

In a later poem the bold statement is made:

> *A Counterfeit – (a Plated Person) –*
> *I would not be –*
> *Whatever strata of Iniquity*
> *My Nature underlie –*
> *Truth is good Health – and Safety, and the Sky.*
> *How meagre, what an Exile – is a Lie,*
> *And Vocal – when we die –*
>
> (1453, ca. 1879)

How much wiser, after all, the poet's anonymity.

Readers generally accept literature's subjects as given and inevitable. But the writer knows how permeable is the "self" of early years, how chancy influences—influences that may last a lifetime, or in fact define a lifetime; how what is random and arbitrary and merely luck (that there was an actor capable of playing Falstaff, for instance; that James Joyce's perpetually indebted father scraped up enough money to send his eldest son to the Jesuits, and not out to learn a useful trade) is read, in retrospect, romantically, as Fate. What is to be done with accident except transform it—romantically—into Fate? For most writers the desire to write—or the need, or the lust—precedes its subject; one reaches out for a subject so that one's "voice" will be given a coherent form, and lifted, and refined, and again refined, out of the inchoate passions of the unconscious. To say that the creative impulse predates its expression is to say something so very simple—that the singer must be able to breathe before singing, for instance, or that we must walk before we can run—that it is invariably misunderstood. Form and content are usually gracefully matched, in a successful work of art, yet "form" surely brings "content" into being—indeed, it makes "content" possible. Just as the brain filters out the blooming buzz of confusion of the world so that we can undertake the various processes called thinking, so the artist's expectations in terms of form (which is to say: what has been done before, and how can I alter it?) bring content into focus.

We are speaking of the artist's presumed "egocentricity"—that pejorative but surely misunderstood word. To be centered upon one's own ego is no more unnatural—no less a necessity—than to be centered in one's own brain, in one's own body. Who will nourish you, if not you? Who can spin in orbit about that kernel of yourself that both is, yet is not, you—the "soul"? To say that the kingdom of God is within is, in one sense, to speak simply in metaphor, and very simply. To say that most people are very rarely interested in the kingdom of God (at least as it lies within, and not without) is to speak the most obvious truth: left to oneself, with no companions, no distractions, nothing to do but "create," the average person would very likely go mad. Not other people, as Sartre said, but the absence of other people constitutes Hell. Is there a psychological equivalent of the neurophysiological phenomenon called the "ganzfeld," a completely patternless visual field which, when contemplated for some twenty minutes, generates the eerie sensation of blindness of "blank-out"? (Without image and especially without movement, the mechanism for seeing seems to evaporate: you don't know if your eyes are open or closed, and can't control your eyes' muscular movements.) If the artist is considered more egocentric than most people, it is perhaps because the prolonged contemplation of interior worlds does not evoke terror, or boredom; the ego is porous enough to be mesmerized by unconscious contents, yet strong enough not to be overwhelmed by them. And who among us can resist the unconscious when it is most potent, most turbulent, at white heat, flooding consciousness with its unsought images, phrases, near-audible voices?

Picasso, speaking of the motive for art, has said:

> I paint the way some people write their autobiography. The paintings, finished or not, are the pages of my journal, and as such they are valid. The future will choose the pages it prefers. It's not up to me to make the choice. I have the impression that time is speeding on past me more and more rapidly. I'm like a river that rolls on, dragging with it the trees that grow too close to its banks. . . . I carry all that along with me and go on. It's the movement of painting that interests me, the dramatic movement from one effort to the next. . . . I have less and less time, and yet I have more and more to say, and what I have to say is, increasingly, something about what goes on in the movement of my thought. I've reached the moment, you see, when the movement of my thought interests me more than the thought itself.[2]

This is an expression of the most supreme confidence; a manifesto of the artist's absolute authority. Not all art is self-referential—not all art is autobiography-in-progress—but all art springs from the artist's fascination with the "movement of thought" of which Picasso speaks. Otherwise there would be no art, for out of what would it spring? The external world possesses no soul.

[2] Quoted in *Life with Picasso,* by Françoise Gilot and Carlton Lake (New York: Penguin Books, 1965), p. 121.

The motive for Emily Dickinson's poetry is very likely a motive close to Picasso's, for clearly it is the poet's interior experience that fascinates. Improvisation and impersonation, submitted to a rigorous method of revision; the braiding together of disparate fragments jotted down over a period of time—even years: the task is to make of the finite, infinity; and of the self's dying, immortality. In her most euphoric states it is not uncommon for the poet to feel queenly: "Title divine – is mine!/ The Wife – without the Sign!/ Acute Degree – conferred on me –/ Empress of Calvary!" Yet the practice of her craft is generally a homely one, performed with unfailing skill, in the secrecy of her room:

> *A Spider sewed at Night*
> *Without a Light*
> *Upon an Arc of White.*
>
> *If Ruff it was of Dame*
> *Or Shroud of Gnome*
> *Himself himself inform.*
>
> *Of Immortality*
> *His Strategy*
> *Was Physiognomy.*
> (1138, ca. 1869)

The activity is ceaseless; as much a part of oneself as one's very face. "Immortality" is language for the poet—what must be fended off is silence. Yet Dickinson is well aware of the dangers of self-consumption:

> *The Mind lives on the Heart*
> *Like any Parasite –*
> *If that is full of Meat*
> *The Mind is fat.*

> *But if the Heart omit*
> *Emaciate the Wit —*
> *The Aliment of it*
> *So absolute.*
>
> (1355, ca. 1876)

The relationship between the conscious ego (mind) and the unconscious self or soul (heart) has never been more succinctly or forcefully argued. What is remarkable about Dickinson's career is the fact that, living so fierce an interior life as Dickinson did, with virtually no stimulus apart from human relationships of a domestic and social kind, and what she might have read, or heard, of the larger world, she did not burn herself out as so many lyric poets have done. Nor did she reach the point of repudiating her "masterful images" like the elder Yeats, who says so poignantly in "The Circus Animals' Desertion" that, now his ladder's gone, "I must lie down where all the ladders start/ In the foul rag and bone shop of the heart." There is a diminution in the number of poems Dickinson wrote in the years beyond 1862–63 but hardly a diminution in quality, as some critics have suggested.

"Winter under cultivation," says the poet in a late, undated, two-line poem, "Is as arable as Spring."

It has frequently been observed that most women are deprived of experiences in the "great" world of politics, history, combat, and that their vision, if not their art, has suffered as a consequence. But it is not often observed that the woman artist who stays close to home, in a protective—and even claustral—atmosphere, has many advantages inaccessible to men. She moves with instinctive certainty in a private, domestic, scaled-down world her masculine equivalent can only attempt to imagine; if, like Emily Dickinson, she remains unmarried and enjoys a certain level of economic freedom, she can spend a good deal of her time looking inward, contemplating what in another era would be called the soul and the soul's relationship to God. The traditional goal of the religious contemplative—the realization of God— is not precisely the poet's goal, but the means are nearly identical. If Emily Dickinson is the single American poet who most closely resembles Rilke in her obsessive preoccupation with states of consciousness and in the astonishing refinements of her perceptions, it is surely because the presumed limitations of her sex and her social position allowed her the sanctity of this kind of freedom. The routine of household tasks—numbing, or oddly comforting?—the cyclical nature of domestic employment—the sense that one has a place, a role, that is given by birth, and not to be challenged: these provide an ideal foreground for the woman of genius to contemplate her art. In her peculiar family situation Emily Dickinson must be seen as singularly fortunate. What other life would have yielded, for her, such riches? Like Emily Brontë, whom she much admired, Dickinson had no need to leave home, for the soul's passions are as readily at hand at home, as elsewhere.

> *The Brain — is wider than the Sky —*
> *For — put them side by side —*
> *The one the other will contain*
> *With ease — and You — beside —*
>
> *The Brain is deeper than the sea —*
> *For — hold them — Blue to Blue —*
> *The one the other will absorb —*
> *As Sponges — Buckets — do —*
>
> *The Brain is just the weight of God —*
> *For — Heft them — Pound for Pound —*

THE ROMANCE OF EMILY DICKINSON'S POETRY

And they will differ — if they do —
As Syllable from Sound —
                              (632, ca. 1862)

Flannery O'Connor, an involuntary recluse (she was confined for most of her adult life to her mother's house in Milledgeville, Georgia, a sufferer from the incurable wasting disease lupus), once noted with characteristic irony that her life would be of no possible interest to biographers, limited, as it was, to a space circumscribed by house, dairy barn, and chicken coop. Yet O'Connor too must have been nourished by her environment: how else can we account for the highly original and idiosyncratic body of fiction she produced?—and the leisure that allowed her to spend six weeks on a single short story? Even Alice James, the younger sister of William and Henry, managed, while confined to her invalid's couch, to write a diary of exceptional worth, in language that, page for page, paragraph for paragraph, challenges that of her famous brothers. And we are well aware of the many precautions Leonard Woolf was obliged to take, to provide for Virginia Woolf the domestic tranquillity she required in order to write. Vulnerable as Leonard seems to feminist charges in recent years, it does remain an indisputable fact that Virginia *did* write her books, after all.

The life of a man or woman of genius must be seen as the necessary complement of the art. One has no more right to speak condescendingly of the life as of the art, for it is the life that makes the art possible: we live the lives we live in order to produce the art of which we believe ourselves capable. How absurd then to label Emily Dickinson a madwoman (an agoraphobiac) simply because she declined to participate in the conventional life of her time and place. She knew the society she was denying herself, after all; and in refusing to see those individuals (like Samuel Bowles) for whom she felt intense emotion, she was hoarding her energies, asserting *her* control. (As Dickinson's editor, Mabel Loomis Todd, observed, "Emily was more interested in her poems than in any man.") In withdrawing from society in her distinctly female way she was setting her boundaries very much as Henry David Thoreau had done in his characteristically masculine way, yet no one has ever suggested that Thoreau was mad. (Thoreau set his boundaries with enviable precision, in absolutely straightforward prose: "The greater part of what my neighbors call good I believe in my soul to be bad.")

Because Dickinson never left her father's house (as she was inclined to call it) for very long and, in later years, did not leave it at all, the energies out of which she writes are inclined to be romantically adolescent and rebellious. The air of deprivation that so much characterizes the angrier of the poems is really self-deprivation, though attributed to other sources. Hunger—literal? sexual? a hunger for freedom and power?—is a familiar motif of the poetry, set forth in brilliantly compact images:

> It would have starved a Gnat
> To live so small as I –
> And yet I was a living Child –
> With Food's necessity
>
> Upon me – like a Claw –
> I could no more remove
> Than I could coax a Leech away –
> Or make a Dragon – move
>
> Nor like the Gnat – had I –
> The privilege to fly
> And seek a Dinner for myself –
> How mightier He – than I –

> *Nor like Himself — the Art*
> *Upon the Window Pane*
> *To gad my little Being out —*
> *And not begin — again —*
> (612, ca. 1862)

It is one of the marvels of Dickinson's poetry that, fueled by such impotence, poems of great passion emerge, "breathless" in the characteristically Dickinsonian manner, yet finely honed, cool, even icy—

> *I'm ceded — I've stopped being Theirs —*
> *The name They dropped upon my face*
> *With water, in the country church*
> *Is finished using, now,*
> *And They can put it with my Dolls,*
> *My childhood, and the string of spools,*
> *I've finished threading — too —*

—with two stanzas to follow in which the poet claims a second, and higher, baptism: "Crowned — Crowing — on my Father's breast —/ A half-unconscious Queen —" (508, ca. 1862). And there is the famous declaration of the self's supreme independence:

> *Much Madness is divinest Sense —*
> *To a discerning Eye —*
> *Much sense — the starkest Madness —*
> *'Tis the Majority*
> *In this, as All, prevail —*
> *Assent — and you are sane —*
> *Demur — you're straightway dangerous —*
> *And handled with a Chain —*
> (435, ca. 1862)

If one were obliged to say what Emily Dickinson's poems as a whole are about, the answer must be ambiguous. The poems are in one sense about the creation of the self capable of creating in turn this very body of poetry. For poetry does not "write itself"—the mind may feed on the heart, but the heart is mute, and requires not only being fed upon but being scrupulously tamed. Like virtually all poets of genius, Emily Dickinson worked hard at her craft. Passion comes unbidden—poetry's flashes of great good luck come unbidden—but the structures into which such flashes are put must be intellectually interesting. For the wisdom of the heart is after all ahistorical—it is always the same wisdom, one might say, across centuries. But human beings live in time, not simply in Time. The historical evolution of one's craft cannot be ignored: in creating art one is always, in a sense, vying for space with preexisting art. Emily Dickinson is perhaps our greatest American poet not because she felt more deeply and more profoundly than other people, or even that she "distilled amazing sense from ordinary Meanings," but that she wrote so well.

Dickinson discovered, early on, her distinctive voice—it is evident in letters written when she was a girl—and worked all her life to make it ever more distinctive. She was the spider, sometimes working at night in the secrecy of her room, unwinding a "Yarn of Pearl" unperceived by others and plying "from Nought to Nought/ In unsubstantial Trade —" but she was far more than merely the spider: she is the presence, never directly cited, or even hinted at, who intends to dazzle the world with her genius. Literary fame is not precisely a goal, but it *is* a subject to which the poet has given some thought: "Some – Work for Immortality –/ the Chiefer part, for Time –/ "He – Compensates – immediately –/ The former – Checks – on Fame –" And, more eloquently in these late, undated poems that might have been written by an elder poet who had in fact enjoyed public acclaim:

> *Fame is a bee.*
> *It has a song –*
> *It has a sting –*
> *Ah, too, it has a*
> *wing.*
>
> (1763)

And:

> *Fame is a fickle food*
> *Upon a shifting plate*
> *Whose table once a*
> *Guest but not*
> *The second time is set.*
>
> *Whose crumbs the crows inspect*
> *And with ironic caw*
> *Flap past it to the*
> *Farmer's Corn –*
> *Men eat of it and die.*
>
> (1659)

Dickinson's specific practice as a writer might strike most people as haphazard, if not wasteful, but clearly it was the practice most suited to her temperament and her domestic situation. During the day, while working at household tasks, she jotted down sentences or fragments of sentences as they occurred to her, scribbling on any handy scrap of paper (which suggests the improvised, unplanned nature of the process). Later, in her room, she added these scraps to her scrapbasket collection of phrases, to be "used" when she wrote poetry or letters. Both Dickinson's poetry and prose, reading as if they were quickly—breathlessly—imagined, are the consequence of any number of drafts and revisions. As biographers have noted, a word or a phrase or a striking image might be worked into a poem or a letter years after it was first written down: the motive even in the private correspondence is to create a persona, not to speak spontaneously. And surely, after a point, it was not possible for Dickinson to speak except by way of a persona. She addresses posterity—in fact, us, her admiring readers—over the shoulder, so to speak, of her unsuspecting correspondents. "Master," feeling the weight of a lonely woman's fantasy of passion and submission, could not have guessed how he was codified, a character in a drama not of his own devising.

In any case, the result is a body of poetry like no other. Its silences are no less potent than its speech. Slant meaning and slant rhyme contribute to the poems' suggestion of dramatic situations of the most teasing subtlety—here is a life that is a "Loaded Gun," yet writ so small it can fit into a woman's sewing basket, along with other scraps of material. From time to time there emerge mysterious "Representatives of the Verse"—"supposed persons"—an "I" that may be an attitude rather than a specific person—but, so far as literal meaning is concerned, one poem will cancel out another. It is perhaps this very drama that constitutes the poems' true subject: the self's preoccupation with the Soul, and the anguish and delight of its roles. The method is diaristic in practice, the scrupulous recording of the "unremitting Bass/ And Blue Monotony" of daily domestic life, even as it analyzes those terrible times (moments? hours? days? entire seasons?) in which the heart turns "convulsive" in learning "That Calm is but a Wall/ Of unattempted Gauze/ An instant's Push demolishes/ A Questioning – dissolves" (928, ca. 1864). The quest is no less epistemological than personal and emotional. It is at that point of juncture that the quest becomes our own as well as the poet's.

If Emily Dickinson suffered a breakdown of some kind, as a number of the poems vividly suggest, the experience is brilliantly translated into art. Indeed, these poems of disintegration and halting reintegration are among her most powerful, making her the unwitting precursor of any number of contemporary poets:

> *There is a pain — so utter —*
> *It swallows substance up —*
> *Then covers the Abyss with Trance —*
> *So Memory can step*
> *Around — across — upon it —*
> *As one within a Swoon —*
> *Goes safely — where an open eye —*
> *Would drop Him — Bone by Bone.*
>   (599, ca. 1862)

And:

> *I felt a Cleaving in my Mind —*
> *As if my Brain had split —*
> *I tried to match it — Seam by Seam —*
> *Bu could not make them fit.*
>
> *The thought behind, I strove to join*
> *Unto the thought before —*
> *But Sequence ravelled out of Sound*
> *Like Balls — upon a Floor.*
>   (937, ca. 1864)

And what is perhaps the most terrifying poem on this subject by any poet:

The first Day's Night had come —
And grateful that a thing
So terrible — had been endured —
I told my Soul to sing —

She said her Strings were snapt —
Her Bow — to Atoms blown —
And so to mend her — gave me work
Until another Morn —

And then — a Day as huge —
As Yesterdays in pairs,
Unrolled its horror in my face —
Until it blocked my eyes —

My Brain — begun to laugh —
I mumbled — like a fool —
And tho' 'tis Years ago — that Day —
My Brain keeps giggling — still.

And Something's odd — within —
That person that I was —
And this One — do not feel the same —
Could it be Madness — this?
                              (410, ca. 1862)

In this extraordinary poem the speaker not only succumbs to the unspecified "terrible thing" but suffers a violent and seemingly irreparable splitting of the self. The Soul cannot sing; poetry is not possible as a means of articulating grief; yet—and here is the poet's triumphant irony—madness *becomes* poetry in its very expression of paralysis. The brilliance of the poem betrays its origins, for here, as elsewhere, the poet's stubborn self survives, altered, stronger:

After great pain, a formal feeling comes —
The Nerves sit ceremonious, like Tombs —
The stiff Heart questions was it He, that bore,
And Yesterday, or Centuries before?

The Feet, mechanical, go round —
Of Ground, or Air, or Ought —
A Wooden way
Regardless grown,
A Quartz contentment, like a stone —

This is the Hour of Lead —
Remembered, if outlived,
As Freezing persons, recollect the Snow —
First — Chill — then Stupor — then the letting go —
                                        (341, ca. 1862)

Dickinson's greatness as a poet, however, lies in the amplitude of her poetry. She is the celebrant not only of hazardous states of the psyche but of the psyche's possible wholeness, that mysterious integration of the personality that has its theological analogue in the concept of grace. As the work of art most succeeds when a delicate balance is struck between that which is known, and conscious, and that which is not yet known, and unconscious, so the psyche seems to be at its fullest when contradictory forces are held in suspension. This mystical state is frequently the subject of lyric poetry because it is so notoriously difficult to describe except in the briefest of spaces. As a state of mind rather than an arid intellectual concept it is evanescent, though its power to transform the entire personality has been documented (by, among others, William James in his classic of American psychology, *The Varieties of Religious Experience*). If the mystical experience is attached to an external source it tends to have a public character, often aggressively so: one is converted, saved, born again. One becomes then a proselyte for the new belief. If the mystical experience is a consequence of the individual's own efforts—bound up, perhaps, with the intense but initially undefined desire to create art—it tends to have a deeply introspective and private character; and if there is any significant "external" object it is likely to be nature. The mystical impulse is to transcend time—and nature, unlike human beings, does not appear to age.

There are numerous poems that suggest that Emily Dickinson realized, at various points in her life, such states of wholeness and integration. If these poems are not among her most memorable, it is primarily because "ecstasy" and "bliss" are not readily exportable experiences: it is tragedy, as Yeats observed, that breaks down the dikes between human beings. But one cannot doubt the poems' sincerity:

> *You'll know it – as you know 'tis Noon –*
> *By Glory –*
> *As you do the Sun –*
> *By Glory –*
> *As you will in Heaven –*
> *Know God the Father – and the Son.*
>
> *By intuition, Mightiest Things*
> *Assert themselves – and not by terms –*
> *"I'm Midnight" – need the Midnight say –*
> *"I'm Sunrise" – Need the Majesty?*
>
> *Omnipotence – had not a Tongue –*
> *His lisp – is Lightning – and the Sun –*
> *His Conversation – with the Sea –*
> *"How shall you know"?*
> *Consult your Eye!*
>
> (420, ca. 1862)

And even more explicit still, this poem of more than twenty years later:

> *Take all away from me, but leave me Ecstasy,*
> *And I am richer then than all my Fellow Men –*
> *Ill it becometh me to dwell so wealthily*
> *When at my very Door are those possessing more,*
> *In abject poverty –*
>
> (1640, ca. 1885)

On the whole, however, Emily Dickinson's naturally skeptical imagination—her "Sweet Skepticism," as she calls it—saves the great body of her work from the dogma of mere statement. The self-righteous, hectoring, frequently insufferable smugness of most religious (and "mystical") verse is contrary to her temperament:

> *Of Paradise' existence*
> *All we know*
> *Is the uncertain certainty —*
> *But its vicinity infer,*
> *By its Bisecting*
> *Messenger —*
> (1411, ca. 1877)

Though "God" is frequently evoked in the poetry, one is never quite certain what "God" means to Dickinson. A presence? an experience? an outdated tradition? In these late undated poems the poet takes a heretic's playful stance:

> *God is indeed a jealous God —*
> *He cannot bear to see*
> *That we had rather not with Him*
> *But with each other play.*
> (1719)

And:

> *A Letter is a joy of Earth —*
> *It is denied the Gods —*
> (1639)

Death—that obsessive theme of the poetry!—did not intimidate Dickinson at the end. Her final letter, written on her deathbed to her cousins Loo and Fanny Norcross, is a perfect little poem, typically Dickinson, a gesture of the gentlest irony:

> *Little Cousins,*
> *Called back –*
> *Emily.*
> (May 1885)

An early poem by William Carlos Williams in honor of Emily Dickinson is both an imaginative commentary on Dickinson's life and an attempt to wed Dickinson's voice with the poet's own. It is a curious work, a not entirely successful experiment—

TO AN ELDER POET

> *To be able*
> *and not to do it*
>
> *Still as a flower*
>
> *No flame,*
> *a flower spent*
> *with heat –*
>
> *lovely flower*
>   *hanging*
> *in the rain*
>
>   *Never!*
>
> *Soberly*
>
> *Whiter than day*
>
> *Wait forever*
> *shaken by the rain*
>   *forever*

But Williams cannot approximate Dickinson; the poem merely suggests her life (as it merely suggests her art).

Dickinson of course has no heirs or heiresses. In the minuteness of their perceptions and the precision of their images one might think of Marianne Moore, Elizabeth Bishop, the early Anne Sexton, and, certainly, Sylvia Plath, but so far as the development of American poetry is concerned, Emily Dickinson really leads nowhere since she herself is the highest embodiment of the experimental method she developed. Genius of her kind is simply inimitable. In this too Dickinson is Whitman's opposite: Whitman's heirs are ubiquitous. Whitman transformed American poetry forever, Dickinson sets an aesthetic standard no other poet dares approach. She is perfection, an end stop, as perhaps she anticipated: "Nobody!" as the emblem of the absolutely inviolable, incomparable self.

What one absorbs from Dickinson's poetry is something more valuable than an artistic method—a quality of personality and vision unlike any other; a heightened sense of the mind's uncharted possibilities; a triumphant sense that the solitary soul, confronted with the irrefutable fact of mortality, can nonetheless define its own "Superior instants." Here is an American artist of words as inexhaustible as Shakespeare, as ingeniously skillful in her craft as Yeats, a poet whom we can set with confidence beside the greatest poets of modern times. Out of hunger, pain, anguish, powerlessness—the paradoxical abundance of art.

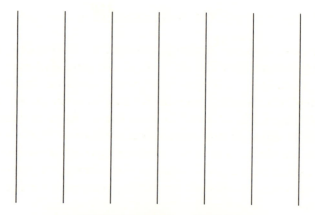

PLEASURE, DUTY, REDEMPTION THEN AND NOW: SUSAN WARNER'S *DIANA*

The Lady's Vase, The Lady's Wreath, Letters to Young Ladies, The Gentle Art of Pleasing, The Lady's Guide to Perfect Gentility, The Physical Life of Woman: Advice to the Maiden, Wife, and Mother by the pious physician Dr. George N. Naphey . . . such best-selling novels as *St. Elmo* by Mrs. Augusta Jane Evans, *The Gates Ajar* by Mrs. Elizabeth Stuart Phelps Ward, *The Discarded Daughter* by Mrs. E. D. E. N. Southworth, *Tempest and Sunshine* by Mary Jane Holmes, *The Wide, Wide World* and *Diana* by Susan Warner . . . these are a few of the titles enormously popular in the second half of nineteenth-century America, when both the etiquette book (for Christian ladies anxious to please God *and* man) and the "romance" (the genre practiced by those "scribbling women" who aroused such uncharacteristic outrage and envy in Nathaniel Hawthorne) were in vogue. Reading them today is a sobering and instructive experience, not least because we really cannot *read* them, whatever our intentions. We examine them, analyze them, exclaim over them, isolate passages here and there to quote in amusement or alarm, or both—

> Dependence is in itself an easy and pleasant thing: dependence upon one we love perhaps the very sweetest thing in the world. To resign oneself totally and contentedly into the hand of another; to have no longer any need of asserting one's rights or one's personality . . . how delicious this all is.*

—but we are incapable of reading these books with the suspension of disbelief and skepticism required if we are to understand them as they were intended—emotionally. Academics approach them as "texts" (that most sinister of terms); they were written as urgent human documents.

Contemporary feminist criticism of nineteenth-century women's literature is handicapped, to a degree, by its secular and humanist perspective. Confronted with religious convictions of a traditional sort, often expressed in the most banal and shopworn of terms, the feminist is inclined to see the author as misguided, or self-deluded, or (what seems to us more attractive) *ironic:* love of God and Christ and one's fellowman, the sacrifice of the self, an elevation of duty over

---

*From "A Woman's Thoughts About Women," in *Chambers' Journal,* 1857. Quoted in Jennie Calder, *Women and Marriage in Victorian Fiction* (New York: Oxford University Press, 1976), p. 59.

all human activities—are these not clever authorial strategies for the indirect expression of hostility and anger? For
if *we* employed them, assuredly they would be.

Our assumptions about virtually everything have
changed irrevocably since the mid- and late nineteenth century. Few of us believe that society, the strife of nations, the
very phenomenon of chronological historical time itself, must
be interpreted in the context of a God- or Christ-centered
universe; we don't, can't, believe that suffering is finite but
the bliss of Heaven infinite. That Christ died for our sins is
not a notion that inspires very many contemporary writers
to create complex works of fiction. We can analyze our
ancestors' stated beliefs, and the philosophical, sociological,
political, and psychological foundations of those beliefs, but
it is virtually impossible for us to *believe:* we read their musical notations but we can't hear them. We presumably share
a common language with our ancestors, but much of our
vocabulary—such words as "soul," "eternity," "subservience," "dependence"—even "lady"; even "sin"—is irrevocably altered. Hamlet is our contemporary, Emma Bovary is
our contemporary, even Swift's Gulliver is our contemporary, but what of the numberless heroines of the best-selling
novels of 1850 to 1900? We are prone to the anthropolo-
gist's occupational hazard—the imposition of unconscious
and unexamined cultural prejudices upon the subject to be
studied.

Of virtually no interest to the formalist critic, the
popular-sentimental romance—frequently selling in the
hundreds of thousands of copies—yields its occasional riches
to those with other expectations from literature. Since the
plot of the typical romance, along with its numerous digres-
sions and melodramatic reversals, appears to be a given, it
is in *parts,* and rarely in structural *wholes,* that we find evidence of fresh insights and imaginative writing: descriptions

of female domestic life, including conversations between women (with no men present); descriptions of church activities, quilting bees, blackberry-picking excursions; passages of rigorous self-examination and prayer. In the foreground the romances are "realistic"; in other respects they are sheer fantasy—fairy tales populated by stereotypical characters, set in a wholly recognizable America.

"There is no pleasure apart from duty . . . God's will is happiness" is the grim lesson finally absorbed by Diana Starling, one of the most independent of all the heroines of the popular-sentimental genre. The tragic curve of Susan Warner's best-selling *Diana* (1888) is its remorseless catheterizing of Diana's youthful passion: in 388 pages we witness the transformation of an impulsive, courageous, strong-willed young woman—a feminist heroine in embryo—into her temperamental opposite. Though Susan Warner seems wholly sympathetic to her heroine and well aware of the hypocrisy of many of her elders (including Diana's "ugly" meddlesome mother), it is nonetheless her intention to squeeze Diana's rebellious blood from her drop by drop until, at the novel's end, she stands before us, a minister's "selfless" wife, a portrait of Christian womanhood. Unlike Henry James's Isabel Archer—the "lady" of another, more famous nineteenth-century portrait—Diana expresses no ambivalence about her fate. The secret message of *Diana* is not that there is no pleasure apart from duty but that there is no pleasure.

Yet this is a rich, complex, psychologically satisfying novel, at least until the point at which its didactic spirit takes over and it becomes rather suddenly yet another cautionary tale or handbook for female (i.e., feminine) behavior. Warner's special gift is for the meticulous, intimate examination of inner states—the "nervous breakdown" (as we might call it) Diana suffers, and her subsequent healing. One is reminded of similar introspective passages in George Eliot and of the obsessive intensity with which D. H. Lawrence describes Ursula Brangwen's wildly fluctuating states of mind in *The Rainbow* and *Women in Love.* Warner's treatment of the aftermath of extreme psychic violence gives the novel a resonance shared by few others of its genre.

In the beginning Diana is presented as an attractive, forceful young woman driven by "nervous energy" and an uncommon "power of will"; virtually alone among the colorfully drawn inhabitants of her New England community—Pleasant Valley!—she is a religious skeptic. Told that Christianity reveals the meaning of life, Diana replies, "No, it doesn't—to me." She sees no purpose in life, or why people live, "what it amounts to." She rejects commonplace pieties about God, Christ, religion; she has no illusions about human destiny or human relations; her feeling for her widowed mother is thoroughly unsentimental.

Yet Diana has her romance, Diana loses her lover (as a consequence of melodramatic complications), Diana suffers a collapse and a "death" of sorts, sympathetically rendered. It is this destruction of Diana's romantic sensibility that constitutes the novel's heart; and when Diana convalesces, marries a good-hearted but rather pallid minister, and, over a period of years, comes finally to love him by way of her awakened love for Christ, Warner's writing becomes increasingly perfunctory and predictable. The contemporary reader "loses" Diana: where she was stubborn, doubting, even arrogant, a plain dealer in the midst of the insipid pieties of "Pleasant Valley," she becomes priggish, complacent, narrow, self-righteous. Her cynicism and anger are completely obliterated in the denial (Warner would see it as the transcendence) of the self. How ironic, for us at least, that the Christian platitudes Diana scorns in her youth turn out to be the truths of her mature life: yet more ironic is the scene in which, a married woman, she exults in condemning her former lover for his "weakness" in still loving her. For passion *is* weakness in the Christian romance, just as it is redemptive in the romances of D. H. Lawrence; denial of passion is strength. One may read Warner's message as the eunuch's scorn or as a deeply felt and altogether sincere attempt to render, in prose fiction, the experience of conversion to a selfless, in this case Christian, mode of consciousness. We lose Diana as her ostensible "modern" attitudes are revealed, in nineteenth-century terms, as merely shallow and adolescent . . . the fancies of the unconverted.

"I cannot think of anything lovelier than to see . . . faces change with the knowledge of Christ," Diana says when, at the novel's conclusion, she and her saintly husband move to a dreary mill town in order to bring the Word to both mill workers and mill owners. The novel's final vision:

> And you may think of them as happy, with both hands full of work. They live in a house just a little bit out of town, where there is plenty of room for gardens, and the air is not poisoned with smoke or vapor. Roses and honeysuckles flourish . . . banks of violets and beds of lilies, and, in the spring-time, crocuses and primroses and hyacinths and snowdrops. . . . For even Diana's flowers are not for herself alone, nor even for her children alone, whose special connection with them is to make nosegays for sick and poor people, and to cultivate garden plots in order to have more to give away. . . . It is as [Diana's husband] meant it to be, and knew it would be. It is as it always is; when the box is broken at Christ's feet, the house is filled with the odour of the ointment.

The feminist response to so painfully "happy" an ending is to view Diana as a self-deluded, broken woman, whose life really ended with her marriage; the victim of a sanctimonious partriarchal religion in which the ideal of humility, meekness, and subservience is best practiced by women—and by lowly mill workers who will learn from Christ how to accept their lot. Diana, so animated once, has now become a function, a role. The postmodernist response might be to dismiss both Diana and Susan Warner as contemptible, unworthy of our serious critical interest, for where there is no irony or ambiguity, where words lack stylistic resonance, and fiction does not alter our ways of perceiving the world but merely confirms the most tedious of platitudes—there there *is* no literature: *Diana* falls off the map, to sink in the uncharted waters with *St. Elmo,* and *Fern Leaves from Fanny's Portfolio,* and *Haunted Hearts,* and *The Hidden Hand,* and *The Mother's Trial.*

Today, for most of us, a novel like Warner's *Diana* is examined rather than read; if we are able to contemplate its primary ethical and psychological issues at all, it is only through the clinical prismatic lens of irony. How, or why, a writer of Susan Warner's gifts would want to systematically destroy the individuality of her heroine is a mystery; and why end a work of idiosyncratic vigor with the most crushingly familiar of visions? Yet *Diana* is not a romance written for us; it is no less representative of its era than Doris Lessing's *The Golden Notebook* is of ours. The Christian romance demands the sacrifice of the self *as a liberation;* in this distant region of the soul, piety is not contrived but utterly natural.

In contemplating the heroines of nineteenth-century fiction—those who have survived, like Dorothea Casaubon of *Middlemarch;* those who have perished, like Warner's Diana—we are moved to wonder: Can irony and faith inhabit the same sensibility? Is it inevitable that one drive the other out? The anachronistic fallacy might be defined as a predilection for those who live *now* to feel automatically

condescending to those who lived *then;* we imagine ourselves superior to our ancestors because they are not us. As
a novelist of the 1980s my vision is postmodernist, and
therefore predisposed to irony; as a woman, however, an
inhabitant of the 1980s, I don't feel at all superior to these
puzzling heroines of a bygone world. I simply feel different.
Very different.

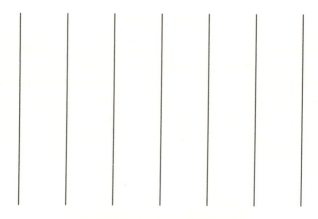

JEKYLL/HYDE

Like such mythopoetic figures as Frankenstein, Dracula, and even Alice (in Wonderland), Dr.-Jekyll-and-Mr.-Hyde has become, in the century following the publication of Robert Louis Stevenson's famous novella, what might be called an autonomous creation. That is, people who have never read the novella—people who do not in fact "read" at all—know by way of popular culture who Jekyll-Hyde is. (Though they are apt to speak of him, not altogether accurately, as two disparate beings: *Dr.* Jekyll, *Mr.* Hyde.) A character out of prose fiction, Jekyll-Hyde seems nonetheless autogenetic in the way that vampires and werewolves and (more benignly) fairies seem autogenetic: surely he has always existed in the collective imagination or, like Jack the Ripper, in actual history? (As "Dracula" is both the specific creation of the novelist Bram Stoker and a nightmare figure out of middle European history.) It is ironic that, in being so effaced, Robert Louis Stevenson has become immortalized by way of his private fantasy—which came to him, by his own testimony, unbidden, in a dream.

The Strange Case of Dr. Jekyll and Mr. Hyde (1886) will strike contemporary readers as a characteristically Victorian moral parable, not nearly so sensational (nor so piously lurid) as Stoker's *Dracula;* in the tradition, perhaps, of Mary Shelley's *Frankenstein,* in which a horrific tale is conscientiously subordinated to the author's didactic intention. Though melodramatic in conception, it is not melodramatic in execution since virtually all its scenes are narrated and summarized after the fact. There is no ironic ambiguity, no Wildean subtlety, in the doomed Dr. Jekyll's confession: he presents himself to the reader as a congenital "double dealer" who has nonetheless "an almost morbid sense of shame" and who, in typically Victorian middle-class fashion, must act to dissociate "himself" (i.e., his reputation as a highly regarded physician) from his baser instincts. He can no longer bear to suppress them and it is impossible to eradicate them. His discovery that "Man is not truly one, but two" is seen to be a scientific fact, not a cause for despair. (And, in time, it may be revealed that man is "a mere polity of multifarious, incongruous, and independent denizens"—which is to say that the ego contains multitudes: multiple personalities inhabit us all. It cannot be incidental that Robert Louis Stevenson was himself a man enamored of consciously playing roles and assuming personae: his friend Arthur Symons said of him that he was "never really himself except when he was in some fantastic disguise.")

Thus Dr. Jekyll's uncivilized self, to which he gives the symbolic name Hyde, is at once the consequence of a scientific experiment (as the creation of Frankenstein's monster was a scientific experiment) and a shameless indulgence of appetites that cannot be assimilated into the propriety of everyday Victorian life. There is a sense in which Hyde, for all his monstrosity, is but an addiction like alcohol, nicotine, drugs: "The moment I choose," Dr. Jekyll says, "I can be rid of him." Hyde must be hidden not simply because he is wicked but because Dr. Jekyll is a willfully good man—an example to others, like the much-admired lawyer Mr. Utterson, who is "lean, long, dusty, dreary and yet somehow [improbably?] lovable." Had the Victorian ideal been less hypocritically ideal or had Dr. Jekyll been content with a less perfect public reputation, his tragedy would not have occurred. (As Wilde's Basil Hallward says in *The Picture of Dorian Gray,* "We in our madness have separated the two [body and soul] and have invented a realism that is vulgar, and an ideality that is void." The key term here is surely "madness.")

Dr. Jekyll's initial experience, however, approaches ecstasy, as if he were, indeed, discovering the kingdom of God that lies within. The magic drug causes nausea and a grinding in the bones and a "horror of the spirit that cannot be exceeded at the hour of birth or death." Then:

> I came to myself as if out of a great sickness. There was something strange in my sensations, something indescribably new and, from its very novelty, incredibly sweet. I felt younger, lighter, happier in body; within I was conscious of a heady recklessness, a current of disordered sensual im-

ages running like a mill race in my fancy, a solution of the bonds of obligation, an unknown but not an innocent freedom of the soul. I knew myself, at the first breath of this new life, to be more wicked, tenfold more wicked, sold a slave to my original evil; and the thought, in that moment, braced and delighted in me like wine.

Unlike Frankenstein's monster, who is nearly twice the size of an average man, Jekyll's monster is dwarfed: "less robust and less developed" than the good self since Jekyll's rigorously suppressed life has been the consequence of unrelenting "effort, virtue, and control." (Stevenson's anatomy of the human psyche is as grim as Freud's—virtually all a "good" man's waking energies are required in beating back and denying the "badness" in him!) That Hyde's frenzied pleasures are even in part specifically sexual is never confirmed, given the Victorian cast of the narrative itself, but, to extrapolate from an incident recounted by an eyewitness, one is led to suspect they are: Hyde is observed running down a ten-year-old girl in the street and calmly trampling her body. Much is made subsequently of the girl's "screaming" and of the fact that money is paid to her family as recompense for her violation.

Viewed from without, Hyde is detestable in the abstract: "I never saw a man I so disliked," the lawyer Enfield says, "and yet I scarce know why. He must be deformed somewhere." Another witness testifies to his mysteriously intangible deformity "without any nameable malformation." But when Jekyll looks in the mirror he is conscious of no repugnance, "rather of a leap of welcome. This, too, was myself. It seemed natural and human." When Jekyll returns to himself after having been Hyde, he is plunged into wonder rather than remorse at his "vicarious depravity." The creature summoned out of his soul and sent forth to do his pleasure is a being "inherently malign and villainous; his every act and thought centered on self; drinking pleasure with bestial avidity from any degree of torture to another; relentless like a man of stone." Yet Hyde is safely *other*—"It was Hyde, after all, and Hyde alone, that was guilty."

Oscar Wilde's equally didactic but far more suggestive and poetic *The Picture of Dorian Gray* (1891) makes the disturbing point that Dorian Gray, the *unblemished* paragon of evil, "is the type of which the age is searching for, and what it is afraid it has found." (Just as Wilde's Lord Henry defends insincerity "as a method by which we can multiply our personalities.") By contrast, Jekyll's Hyde is a very nearly Bosch-like creature, proclaiming his wickedness to the naked eye as if, in Utterson's words, he is a troglodyte, "the radiance of a foul soul that thus transpires through, and transfigures, its clay continent." One is reminded of nineteenth-century theories of criminology advanced by Cesare Lombroso and Henry Maudsley, among others, who argued that outward physical defects and deformities are the visible signs of inward and invisible faults: the criminal is a type that can be easily identified by experts. Dr. Jekyll is the more reprehensible in his infatuation with Hyde in that, as a well-trained physician, he should have recognized at once the telltale symptoms of mental and moral degeneracy in his alter ego's very face.

By degrees, like any addict, Jekyll surrenders his autonomy. His ego ceases being "I" and splits into two distinct and eventually warring selves, which share memory as they share a common body. Only after Hyde commits murder does Jekyll make the effort to regain control; but by this time, of course, it is too late. What had been "Jekyll"—that precarious cuticle of a self, that field of tensions in perpetual opposition to desire—has irrevocably split. It is significant that the narrator of Jekyll's confession speaks of both Jekyll and Hyde as if from the outside—and with a passionate eloquence otherwise absent from Stevenson's prose:

> The powers of Hyde seemed to have grown with the sickliness of Jekyll. And certainly the hate that now divided them was equal on each side. With Jekyll, it was a thing of vital instinct. He had now seen the full deformity of that creature that shared with him some of the phenomena of consciousness, and was co-heir with him to death: and beyond these links of community, which in themselves made the most poignant part of his distress, he thought of Hyde, for all his energy of life, as of something not only hellish but inorganic. This was the shocking thing; that the slime of the pit seemed to utter cries and voices; that the amorphous dust gesticulated and sinned; that what was dead, and had no shape, should usurp the offices of life. And this again, that that insurgent horror was knit to him closer than a wife, closer than an eye; lay caged in his flesh, where he heard it mutter and felt it struggle to be born; and at every hour of weakness, and in the confidence of slumber, prevailed against him, and deposed him out of life.

"Think of it," Jekyll had gloated at the start, "—I did not even exist!" And the purely metaphorical becomes literally true.

The Strange Case of Dr. Jekyll and Mr. Hyde, though stimulated by a dream, is not without its literary antecedents: among them Edgar Allan Poe's "William Wilson" (1839), in which, paradoxically, the "evil" self is the narrator and the "good" self, or conscience, the double; and Charles Dickens's uncompleted *The Mystery of Edwin Drood* (1870), in which Choirmaster Jack Jasper, an opium addict, oscillates between "good" and "evil" impulses in his personality with an anguish so convincingly calibrated as to suggest that, had

Dickens lived to complete the novel, it would have been one of his masterpieces—and would have made *The Strange Case of Dr. Jekyll and Mr. Hyde* redundant. Cautionary tales of malevolent, often diabolical doubles abound in folklore and oral tradition; in Plato's *Symposium* it was whimsically suggested that each human being has a double to whom he was once *physically* attached—a bond of Eros that constituted in fact a third, and higher, sex in which male and female were conjoined.

The visionary starkness of *The Strange Case of Dr. Jekyll and Mr. Hyde* anticipates that of Freud in such late melancholy meditations as *Civilization and Its Discontents* (1929–30): there is a split in man's psyche between ego and instinct, between civilization and "nature," and the split can never be healed. Freud saw ethics as a reluctant concession of the individual to the group, veneer of a sort overlaid upon an unregenerate primordial self. The various stratagems of culture—including, not incidentally, the "sublimation" of raw aggression by way of art and science—are ultimately powerless to contain the discontent, which must erupt at certain periodic times, on a collective scale, as war. Stevenson's quintessentially Victorian parable is unique in that the protagonist initiates his tragedy of doubleness out of a fully lucid sensibility—one might say a scientific sensibility. Dr. Jekyll knows what he is doing, and why he is doing it, though he cannot, of course, know how it will turn out. What is not questioned throughout the narrative, by either Jekyll or his circle of friends, is mankind's fallen nature: sin is *original,* and *irremediable.* For Hyde, though hidden, will not remain so. And when Jekyll finally destroys him he must destroy Jekyll too.

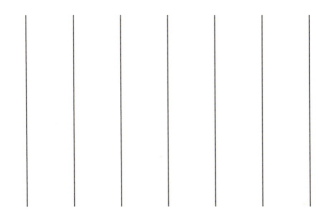

KAFKA
AS STORYTELLER

It would be an illuminating if arduous task to tabulate how frequently, and in what surprising contexts, one encounters the adjective "Kafkan" or "Kafkaesque" in the space of a single year—words that entered our language, presumably, only since the forties, when Kafka's translated works began to find their public. One always knows immediately what the words mean (as one always knows what Franz Kafka himself "means"), but how to explain to another person?— how to make clear that which is frankly cloudy, mysterious, inexplicable? As Kafka wittily observed in "On Parables":

"All these parables really set out to say merely that the incomprehensible is incomprehensible, and we know that already. But the cares we have to struggle with every day: that is a different matter."

Though the words "Kafkan" and "Kafkaesque" invariably point to paradox and human frustration and suggest childhood memories of terrifying disproportion, it is the case nonetheless that Franz Kafka's stories and parables are not at all difficult to read and to understand. (To explain—that is another matter: but a peripheral one.) In fact, one might claim that alone among the greatest twentieth-century writers Kafka is immediately accessible. His unique yet powerfully familiar world can be entered by any reader and comprehended *feelingly* at once, regardless of background or literary training. (In fact, unsophisticated—which is to say unprejudiced—readers respond to Kafka most directly, as he would have wished. Perceptive teenagers love him not because he is "one of the great moderns" but because he speaks their private language by speaking so boldly in his own.) Kafka is no more difficult than any riddle, or fairy tale, or biblical parable, though of course he can be made to seem so by persons intent on claiming him for their own.

To open to virtually any of Kafka's stories or parables, however, is to discover a marvelously direct and uncluttered language. The voice is frequently meditative, ruminative, quibbling, comically obsessed with minutiae; it ponders, it broods, it attempts to explain that which *can* be explained—while in the background the Incomprehensible looms ("and we know that already"). Kafka is a master of opening sentences, frontal attacks that have left their enduring marks upon our general cultural sensibility; for many admirers of Kafka their admiration—indeed, their capitulation to his genius—began with a first reading of those classic first sentences:

As Gregor Samsa awoke one morning from uneasy dreams he found himself transformed in his bed into a gigantic insect.[1]

("The Metamorphosis")

"It's a remarkable piece of apparatus," said the officer to the explorer.

("In the Penal Colony")

I was in great perplexity: I had to start on an urgent journey; a seriously ill patient was waiting for me in a village ten miles off; a thick blizzard of snow filled all the wide spaces between him and me; I had a gig, a light gig with big wheels, exactly right for our country roads; muffled in furs, my bag of instruments in my hand, I was in the courtyard all ready for the journey; but there was no horse to be had, no horse.

("A Country Doctor")

Someone must have been telling lies about Joseph K., for without having done anything wrong he was arrested one fine morning.

(*The Trial*)

Honored members of the Academy!
You have done me the honor of inviting me to give your Academy an account of the life I formerly led as an ape.

("A Report to an Academy")

I have completed the construction of my burrow and it seems to be successful.

("The Burrow")

It is characteristic of Kafka's nightmare logic that everything follows swiftly and inevitably from these remarkable first premises. The reader, like the Kafka protagonist, is drawn

[1] All passages from Kafka cited in this essay are from *Franz Kafka: The Complete Stories* (New York: Schocken Books, 1971) and *Parables and Paradoxes* (New York: Schocken Books, 1975).

irresistibly along by a subterranean coherence. (Is there "free will" in Kafka's universe? Must one deserve his fate? As the priest informs Joseph K. in the melancholy penultimate chapter of *The Trial:* "It is not necessary to accept everything as true, one must only accept it as necessary.")

Kafka's famous short stories, though they have proven alarmingly fertile for every sort of exegesis, are primarily tales—genuine tales—in which things happen. Dreamlike in tone, they are not whimsically haphazard or aleatory in their development: Gregor Samsa really has metamorphosed into a dung-beetle; the officer of the penal colony will sacrifice his very life in the service of his "apparatus"; the doomed country doctor will have his adventure tending a wounded boy, after which he will wander forever exposed to "the frost of this most unhappy of ages." And in "A Hunger Artist" the dying "artist" of fasting confesses that he is not superior to other human beings after all—he fasts only because he has never found the food he liked.

In other works of Kafka's, the parables and certain longer pieces like "The Great Wall of China" and "Investigations of a Dog," plot is subordinate to what one might call the dialectic or discursive voice. These tales, though less compelling on the superficial level than those cited first, exert by degrees a remarkable inner power. With no introduction one is plunged into an interior obsessive landscape and carried along by the sheer flow of thought of an alien—but oddly sympathetic—consciousness. ("This is too much for the human mind to grasp," Einstein is said to have remarked to Thomas Mann, regarding Kafka's short prose pieces.)

The parables or shorter stories resemble Zen koans in their teasing simplicity, but they are unmistakably Jewish—even lawyerly—in the mock-formal nature of their language. (See "The Animal in the Synagogue," "Abraham,"

"Before the Law," etc.) These are ingenious arguments or mimicries of argument; anecdotes so undetermined by history and locality that they come to possess the beauty (and the impersonal cruelty) of folk ballads or fairy tales. Their wisdom is childlike yet as old as the race, pruned of all sentiment and illusion: they may be "tragic" in their content but they are hardly lacking in humor. In "Prometheus," for instance, four legends are briefly considered, with equal emphasis, whereupon "the gods grew weary, the eagles grew weary, the wound closed wearily." But there remained, still, the "inexplicable" mass of rock: "The legend tried to explain the inexplicable. As it came out of a substratum of truth it had in turn to end in the inexplicable." Which is to say—the legend, or the riddle, simply outlives its principal figures.

The famous parables "Before the Law" and "An Imperial Message" provide an illuminating contrast with each other and seem to have been written in response to an identical motive. In the first (which is incorporated in *The Trial*), a "man from the country" is denied admittance to the Law despite the fact that he submits himself to its authority. He is faithful, he is indefatigable, he even follows tradition of a sort in attempting to bribe his Doorkeeper—all to no avail. The radiance that streams "inextinguishably" from the gateway of the Law never includes him: he dies unredeemed. The gateway *is* the means of salvation, yet it is also inaccessible.

Is the Law an expression of God?—any projected form of the Divine?—of order, coherence, collective or personal salvation? Is the Law merely a private obsession that has shaded into madness? Can one in fact believe the Doorkeeper?—or the parable itself? It might be said that the hapless "man from the country" has been waiting for admittance to his own life, which, as a consequence of his obsession, he has failed to live. Or, conversely, it might be argued that the Law represents his own soul, the "kingdom of God" that lies within. Even in wholly secular terms, the man in his single-minded quest may have failed to realize the fullest flowering of his personality: his relationship to all humanity has been, in fact, only by way of the intrepid Doorkeeper. (So Kafka's emblematic Hunger Artist dies unredeemed—indeed, unnamed—as a consequence of his wholly selfish immersion in his art. Kafka on his own interior obsession, his failure, as he sees it, to be normal, happy, undivided, *human:* "I do not envy particular married couples, I simply envy all married couples together; and even when I do envy one couple only, it is the happiness of married life in general, in all its infinite variety, that I envy—the happiness to be found in any one marriage, even in the unlikeliest case, would probably plunge me into despair. I don't believe people exist whose inner plight resembles mine; still, it is possible for me to imagine such people—but that the secret raven forever flaps about their heads as it does about mine, even to imagine that is impossible."[2])

By contrast, the companion parable "An Imperial Message" offers an unexpected revelation. The Emperor has sent a message to you but the messenger is impeded by the vast multitudes between the two of you—"if he could reach the open fields how fast he would fly!"—he wears out his strength in his effort, it is soon clear that the entire mission is hopeless, and the Emperor himself has long since died. A familiar Kafkan predicament, except for this puzzling final line: "But you sit at your window when evening falls and dream [the message] to yourself." So the Emperor's wisdom, after all, lies within. (One is reminded of a diary entry

[2] Franz Kafka, *Diaries 1914–1923,* edited by Max Brod (New York: Schocken Books, 1965), pp. 194–195.

of Kafka's for 19 January 1922: "Evil does not exist; once you have crossed the threshold, all is good. Once in another world, you must hold your tongue." Truth—the mystic's inner certitude—is associated not with art or writing or speaking or *telling* but with silence.[3])

Kafka's mysticism assured him that salvation was possible, even inevitable, though *he* was to be excluded: his sense of personal guilt precedes all action. That in his father's eyes he was contemptible, that his writing counted for very little, that his personal misfortune (his tubercular condition, for instance) was related in some mysterious way to his own will, his own secret *wish*—all these factors set Franz Kafka apart from what he chose to think of as the happiness of normal life: the effortless salvation of those who live without questioning the basic premises of their lives. The "man from the country" is both hero and victim, saint and fool, but he is certainly isolated, and his petition has come to nothing: the bitterest irony being that, perhaps, the Law lay with him all along; he might have dreamt it to himself.

Kafka reports having been filled with "endless astonishment" at simply seeing a group of people cheerfully assembled together: his intense self-consciousness and self-absorption made such exchanges impossible.[4] The way of the artist is lonely, stubborn, arrogant, pitiable—yet innocent. For one does not choose one's condition. Consider this brief gemlike parable, quoted here in its entirety:

[3] *Diaries,* p. 205. Elsewhere I have written at some length of the nature of Kafka's mysticism and its evident relationship to Taoism. See "Kafka's Paradise," in *New Heaven, New Earth: The Visionary Experience in Literature* (New York: Vanguard Press, 1974).

[4] *Diaries,* p. 214. The artist imagines himself as a sort of adversary/voyeur. Writing is both his means of salvation (however inadequate) and the sign of his probable damnation: "The strange, mysterious, perhaps dangerous, perhaps saving comfort that there is in writing: it is a leap out of murderers' row; *it is a seeing of what is really taking place*" (italics mine). See the diary for 27 January 1922.

The Sirens

> These are the seductive voices of the night; the Sirens, too, sang that way. It would be doing them an injustice to think that they wanted to seduce; they knew they had claws and sterile wombs, and they lamented this aloud. They could not help it if their laments sounded so beautiful.

So with the author of these extraordinary prose pieces: though he suspected that his art necessitated a private damnation, he seems to have known, in any case, that it contained beauty. And that it was seductive.

James Joyce claimed that anyone could understand *Finnegans Wake* if it were simply read aloud: a claim that, for all its attractiveness, must be dismissed as unlikely. Much of Kafka's prose, however, read aloud, not only yields layers of meaning but suggests a rare and subtle humor as well. (Indeed, Max Brod said that when Kafka read his stories aloud, in his subdued, lightly ironic voice, his listeners invariably responded with laughter.)

Of course Kafka's humor is deadpan, surrealistic, sometimes rather sadomasochistic: a highly sophisticated kind of comedy that might be missed by even an attentive reader. There is a danger in taking Kafka too seriously—too grimly—simply because he has attained the stature of a twentieth-century classic. (It might be argued that Kafka's wicked sense of humor is ultimately more painful to absorb than his sense of tragedy. For it is nearly always humor directed against the victim self, the very protagonist for whom the reader wishes to feel sympathy.) Consider the emaciated, dying, self-ordained martyr, the hunger artist, who not only insists upon his fasting but seems to imagine that the world should honor it. It is not a religious ideal; it is in the service of no Godhead but the hunger artist himself. ("Why should he be cheated of the fame he would get for fasting longer . . . for beating his own record by a performance beyond human imagination, since he felt that there were no limits to his capacity for fasting?") He seems never to have realized that he is simply—irremediably—committing suicide, and that the ostensible "admiration" of his public is only an expression of fleeting curiosity. Nowhere in the story does Kafka imply that the hunger artist is a failure in ordinary human terms, *hence* his success in the art of starvation, but the reader is meant to see the artist in terms other than those in which the artist so myopically sees himself:

> The impresario . . . grasped him about the emaciated waist, with exaggerated caution, so that the frail condition he was in might be appreciated; and committed him to the care of the blenching ladies, not without secretly giving him a shaking so that his legs and body tottered and swayed. The artist now submitted completely; his head lolled on his breast as if it had landed there by chance; his body was hollowed out; his legs in a spasm of self-preservation clung close to each other at the knees . . . ; and the whole weight of his body, a featherweight after all, relapsed onto one of the ladies, who, looking around for help and panting a little— this post of honor was not at all what she had expected it to be—first stretched her neck as far as she could to keep her face at least free from contact with the artist, then finding this impossible, and her more fortunate companion not coming to her aid but merely holding extended in her own trembling hand the little bunch of knucklebones that was the artist's, to the great delight of the spectators burst into tears and had to be replaced.

And, at the story's conclusion, as the dying artist lies in the dirty straw in his cage, forgotten until now:

They poked into the straw with sticks and found him in it. "Are you still fasting?" asked the overseer, "when on earth do you mean to stop?" "Forgive me, everybody," whispered the hunger artist. . . . "Of course," said the overseer, and tapped his forehead with a finger to let the attendants know what state the man was in, "we forgive you." "I always wanted you to admire my fasting," said the hunger artist. "We do admire it," said the overseer, affably. "But you shouldn't admire it," said the hunger artist. "Well then we don't admire it," said the overseer, "but why shouldn't we admire it?" "Because I have to fast, I can't help it," said the hunger artist. "What a fellow you are," said the overseer, "and why can't you help it?" "Because," said the hunger artist, lifting his head a little and speaking, with his lips pursed, as if for a kiss, right into the overseer's ear, so that no syllable might be lost, "because I couldn't find the food I liked. If I had found it, believe me, I would have made no fuss and stuffed myself like you or anyone else." These were his last words, but in his dimming eyes remained the firm though no longer proud persuasion that he was still continuing to fast. "Well, clear this out now!" said the overseer, and they buried the hunger artist, straw and all.

And into his cage they put a sleek young panther, suffused with a noble physical strength, the "joy of life" streaming with ardent passion from this throat: the onlookers, who had grown bored with the hunger artist, now crowded about the panther "and did not ever want to move away." So Kafka passes the cruelest judgment upon himself—upon, perhaps, the very Franz Kafka who is writing this most brilliant of allegories. The judgment is unfair, but comedy of this sort is always unfair. The savagery of its death sentence against the self is masked, if not muted, by the tone of understatement throughout.

There is something luridly comical about Georg Bendemann's father in the early story, "The Judgment," a nightmare invalid who leaps from his bed after his son naïvely believes he has tucked him in. ("Am I well covered up?" the old man asks. "Don't worry," says Georg, "you're well covered up.") So suffused with sudden strength is he, Georg's father gives a mocking speech to his astonished son, cavorts lewdly about the bed, and delivers, finally, "in an offhand manner," an extraordinary sentence of death: "An innocent child, yes, that you were, truly, but still more truly have you been a devilish human being!—And therefore take note: I sentence you now to death by drowning."

And Georg feels himself urged from the room and driven toward the water:

> Already he was grasping at the railings as a starving man clutches at food. He swung himself over, like the distinguished gymnast he had once been in his youth, to his parents' pride. With weakening grip he was still holding on when he spied between the railings a motor-bus coming which would easily cover the noise of his fall, called in a low voice: "Dear parents, I have always loved you, all the same," and let himself drop. At this moment an unending stream of traffic was just going over the bridge.

Kafka's essentially comic vision—dark and pitiless as it is—always insists upon the restoration of what might be called supremely ordinary life, after the individual's private tragedy runs its course. The hunger artist is replaced by a panther; an "unending stream of traffic" covers the meager noise of Georg Bendemann's death; Gregor Samsa's younger sister, Grete, seems to have undergone a metamorphosis of her own during the long weeks of her brother's passion, to emerge triumphant in life:

It struck both Mr. and Mrs. Samsa, almost at the same moment, as they became aware of their daughter's increasing vivacity, that in spite of all the sorrow of recent times, which had made her cheeks pale, she had bloomed into a pretty girl with a good figure. They grew quieter and half unconsciously exchanged glances of complete agreement, having come to the conclusion that it would soon be time to find a good husband for her. And it was like a confirmation of their new dreams and excellent intentions that at the end of their journey their daughter sprang to her feet first and stretched her young body.

Poor Gregor!—already he seems to have been forgotten, despite his numerous sacrifices for his family. In fact he is swept away and disposed of like any repulsive dung-beetle. ("Oh," said the charwoman, giggling so amiably that she could not at once continue, "just this, you don't need to bother about how to get rid of the thing next door. It's been seen to already.")

The ape in evening dress of "A Report to an Academy" is a comical figure, a surrealist cartoon, who convinces us by degrees of his humanity. Captured on the Gold Coast of Africa, caged and bound for Europe on a steamer, he soon realizes that to find a "way out" of his cage is his only hope for survival. The zoological garden or the variety stage?—a life as a penned animal or a life—of sorts—as a mock-human being? Our ape is clever enough to choose the latter. "It was so easy to imitate these people," he boasts. "I learned to spit in the very first days. We used to spit in each other's faces; the only difference was that I licked my face clean afterwards and they did not." He learns also to smoke a pipe and drink schnapps. Eventually he breaks into human speech. And, in Europe, trained by several teachers at once, he becomes a phenomenon: he manages to reach "the cultural level of an average European." Of course he must pay a heavy price—his "ape nature" flees out of him forever. In the end he is neither animal nor man, like many of Kafka's tortured protagonists. (The impetuous narrator of "Investigations of a Dog" asks himself, "How long will you be able to endure the fact that the world of dogs, as your researches make more and more evident, is pledged to silence and always will be? How long will you be able to endure it?")

It is frequently remarked that Kafka's language is remarkably forceful and direct, stripped clean of self-conscious figures of speech. In fact there are at least two "voices" in Kafka: that of the omniscient narrator (the strategy by which most of the famous stories are told), and that of the obsessed, perhaps mad protagonist who tells his tale in the first person ("The Burrow," for example—perhaps the most terrifying of Kafka's fables). Metaphorical language is unnecessary in Kafka's fiction because each story, each parable, each novel is a complete and often outrageous metaphor in itself: smaller units of metaphor would be redundant. Consider the marvelous imaginative leap that gives us such images as "The Great Wall of China" ("So vast is our land that no fable could do justice to its vastness, the heavens can scarcely span it—and Peking is only a dot in it, and the imperial palace less than a dot"), the monstrous machine of "transcendent" pain of "In the Penal Colony" ("Can you follow it? The Harrow is beginning to write; when it finishes the first draft of the inscription on the man's back, the layer of cotton wool begins to roll and slowly turns the body over, to give the Harrow fresh space for writing. Meanwhile the raw part that has been written on lies on the cotton wool, which is specially prepared to staunch the bleeding and so makes all ready for a new deepening of the script"), the stricken humanity of the legendary Hunter Gracchus, who can neither live nor die, yet seems blameless ("I am here, more than that I do not know, further than that I cannot go. My ship has no rudder, and it is driven by the wind that blows in the undermost regions of death").

The great conceit of *The Castle* is—simply and horribly—that one cannot get to the castle, no matter one's ingenuity; the conceit of *The Trial,* that Joseph K. is on trial for his life whether he consents to the authority of the court or not, and whether, in fact, he is guilty of any crime (when the hapless defendant protests his innocence he is informed that that is what "guilty men" always say). In the curious and altogether uncharacteristic playlet "The Warden of the Tomb," the fabulist setting is, as the Prince says, the frontier between the Human and the Other—where naturally he wishes to post a guard; in the brief yet suspenseful story "The Refusal" it is a small anonymous town presided over by a colonel who is really a tax collector. "The Burrow," not one of Kafka's more popular tales, is nonetheless a harrowing and brilliant investigation of anxiety—anxiety as it shades into madness—made unforgettable by way of its conceit of the Burrow itself: the defensive strategies that doom a man (one assumes that the narrator is a man—of sorts) to paranoia and dissolution, even as he believes himself protected from his enemies. The "I" seems to be addressing the reader but is in fact only talking to himself, rationalizing, debating, sifting through possibilities, trying to resist breakdown, trying—with what mad heroic calm!—to forestall disaster. His voice is hypnotic, seductive as any siren of the night, for it is our own voice, diminished, secretive, hardly raised to a whisper.

> Lying in my heap of earth I can naturally dream of all sorts of things, even of an understanding with the [imagined] beast, though I know well enough that no such thing can happen, and that at the instant when we see each other,

more, at the moment when we merely guess at each other's presence, we shall both blindly bare our claws and teeth . . . both of us filled with a new and different hunger. . . . Now actually the beast seems to be a great distance away; if it would only withdraw a little farther the noise too would probably disappear; perhaps in that case everything would be peaceful again as in the old days; all this would then become a painful but salutary lesson, spurring me on to make the most diverse improvements on the burrow; if I have peace, and danger does not threaten me, I am still quite fit for all sorts of hard work; perhaps, considering the enormous possibilities which its powers of work open before it, the beast has given up the idea of extending its burrow in my direction, and is compensating itself for that in some other one. That consummation also cannot, of course, be brought about by negotiation, but only by the beast itself, or by some compulsion exercised from my side.

In these artful cadences we hear the mimicry of reason, the parodied echoes of sanity. Human logic has become burrow logic. Human consciousness has become burrow consciousness. The image is a classic metaphor for one facet of the human condition, limned in prose so compelling it is an unnerving experience to read. And how perfect the terse concluding statement—"All remained unchanged"—after the long, long sentences in their obdurate paragraphs, as difficult to transverse as the burrower's labyrinthine hiding place. That it is also a grave—that his claustrophobic maneuvers assure his eventual death—is a realization he cannot make: we alone can make it for him.

Kafka noted in a diary entry for 25 September 1917 that happiness for him consisted in raising the world "into the pure, the true, and the immutable."[5] His dark prophetic art—

[5] *Diaries,* p. 187.

Aesopian fables, religious allegories, inverted romances—
suggested a future in which bureaucratic hells and "final so-
lutions" are not improbable: an increasingly dehumanized
future of a sort Joseph K. has already endured when, after
his struggle to acquit himself of guilt, he is executed and
dies "like a dog." This is a literature, admittedly, of symbolist extremes, in which the part must serve for the whole;
the dream or nightmare image must suggest the totality of
experience. In Kafka we never encounter persons, or personalities: we are always in the presence of souls—humanity
peeled to its essence and denuded of the camouflage of external circumstance. We see no faces or features—we experience no bodies—we become mere figures, abbreviations,
ciphers: participants in a vast, timeless, and, indeed, indecipherable drama. This is an art in which the social sphere
matters not at all, and even the "human" sphere becomes
by degrees irrelevant. Kafka is a realist of mystical perspective, resolutely unsentimental, even rather pitiless in his
tracking of our numerous delusions. But he is primarily a
superb storyteller, and a poet of matchless sensibility. Hear
him address us frankly in "At Night," quoted here in its
entirety:

At Night

Deeply lost in the night. Just as one sometimes lowers one's
head to reflect, thus to be utterly lost in the night. All around
people are asleep. It's just play acting, an innocent self-
deception, that they sleep in houses, in safe beds, under a
safe roof, stretched out or curled up on mattresses, in sheets,
under blankets; in reality they have flocked together as they
had once upon a time and again later in a deserted region,
a camp in the open, a countless number of men, an army,
a people, under a cold sky on cold earth, collapsed where
once they had stood, forehead pressed on the arm, face to

the ground, breathing quietly. And you are watching, are one of the watchmen, you find the next one by brandishing a burning stick from the brushwood pile beside you. Why are you watching? Someone must watch, it is said. Someone must be there.

3

IN THE RING

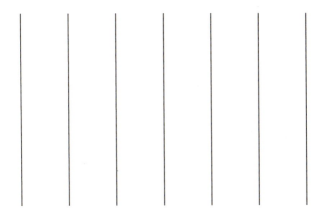

MIKE TYSON

22 November 1986. When twenty-year-old Mike Tyson enters the packed arena of the Las Vegas Hilton Convention Center, it is through a deafening wall of noise. A neutral observer would wonder: Is this young man already a champion?—a *great* champion? Of the nearly nine thousand people jammed into the arena—in seats as costly as $1,000 at ringside—virtually everyone has come in expectation of seeing not merely a heavyweight title fight that promises to be unusually dramatic but boxing history itself. If Tyson takes away the World Boxing Council heavyweight title held by thirty-three-year-old Trevor Berbick, as he has promised to do, he will become the youngest heavyweight champion in the sport's recorded history. He will fulfill the prophecy made by the late Cus D'Amato, his boxing trainer, mentor, and guardian, that he would one day break the record of another of D'Amato's heavyweight prodigies, Floyd Patterson, who won the title shortly before his twenty-second birthday in 1956.

Mike Tyson, a boy warrior, has become legendary, in a sense, before there is a legend to define him. And never has the collective will of a crowd—the very nearly palpable *wish* of a crowd—been more powerfully expressed than it is tonight in Las Vegas. With his much-publicized 27–0 record as a professional boxer, of which twenty-five victories are knockouts (fifteen in the first round, several within sixty seconds), with so much expectation centered upon him as the "new hope" of heavyweight boxing, Tyson recalls the young Jack Dempsey, who fought his most spectacular fights before winning the heavyweight title. Like Dempsey in the upward trajectory of his career, Tyson suggests a savagery only symbolically contained within the brightly illuminated elevated ring, with its referee, its resident physician, its scrupulously observed rules, regulations, customs, and rituals. Like Dempsey he has the power to galvanize crowds as if awakening in them the instinct not merely for raw aggression and the mysterious will to do hurt that resides, for better or worse, in the human soul, but for suggesting the incontestable *justice* of such an instinct: his is not the image of the Establishment-approved Olympic Gold Medalist, like Muhammad Ali or Sugar Ray Leonard (indeed, it is said in boxing circles that Tyson was cheated of a gold medal at the 1984 Summer Olympic Games by way of the politics of amateur boxing), but the image of the outsider, the psychic outlaw, the hungry young black contender for all that white America can give. In a weight division in which hard punching is the point, Tyson has acquired a reputation for being an awesome fighter, as much admired and feared among his coevals as Sonny Liston, George Foreman, and Rocky Marciano were in their times: he has been called a "tank," a "young bull," a "killer," a "block of granite"; a force primitive and irresistible as nature. As one observer noted, there is something of a comic-book quality about Tyson's fights—the violence is so exaggerated it has a surrealist air. Opponents are propelled across the ring, fall insensible into the ropes, or, fully conscious, lose muscular control in their legs; they lie without moving for what seems a very long time. The violence may appear primitive and surrealist but it is thoughtfully administered: the result, as Tyson explains carefully in his soft, earnest, boyish voice, of punches thrown with a "bad intention in a vital area." Cus D'Amato was, among other things, a "master of anatomy."

Tyson himself has spoken of the phenomenon of Mike Tyson in gladiatorial terms: the warrior's vow to fight to the death if necessary precludes and makes irrelevant all merely personal motives, all conventional rationalizations for what he does. Boxing is his life, his vocation; his calling. The Roman boast of *munera sine missione* in the gladiatorial games— no mercy shown—would be perfectly logical to him. And so mesmerizing has the young boxer become in his scant eighteen months as a professional, his appearance in the ring tonight in Las Vegas, his mere physical *presence,* captivates the crowd's attention to the degree that the entrance of reigning WBC champion Trevor Berbick goes virtually unnoticed. Even the blazoning recorded music is abruptly and mysteriously silenced.

Mike Tyson—"Kid Dynamite" as he has lately been billed—exudes an air of tension, control, fierce concentration. At five feet eleven inches, he is short for a heavyweight and strikes the eye as shorter still; his 222¼-pound body is so sculpted in muscle it looks foreshortened, brutally compact. (Berbick, at 218½ pounds, stands six feet two inches—not a large man by today's heavyweight standards—and will have a daunting seven-inch reach advantage.) Indeed, Tyson is so muscular as to resemble a bodybuilder rather than a boxer, for whom upper-body flexibility is crucial; his neck measures an extraordinary nineteen inches—larger than any heavyweight champion's since the circus strongman Primo Carnera. His hair is trimmed savagely short, Dempsey-style, along the back and sides, as if it were done with a razor; he wears not a robe but a crude white terrycloth pullover that looks as if he might have made it himself and, as usual, no socks—"I feel more like a warrior this way"; and though his managers Jim Jacobs and Bill Cayton will be fined $5,000 by the Nevada State Athletic Commission for the privilege, Tyson is wearing the black trunks that have become his trademark. (Trevor Berbick, who usually wears white, preempted black for *his* trunks—very likely because he resents the extraordinary prefight publicity Tyson has engendered and the humiliating fact that, though the young challenger has never met an opponent of Berbick's stature, he is a 3-to-1 favorite to win tonight.) Tyson remains the object of the crowd's rapt attention. He is pumped up, covered in sweat, ready to fight. Though this is the hour—the very moment—to which the past six years of his life have been subordinated, he gives no sign of nerves and will say, afterward, that he was "calm" and "relaxed" in the knowledge that he could not fail.

As he gives Tyson final instructions, his trainer, Kevin Rooney—himself a D'Amato protégé—touches foreheads with him and kisses him lightly on the cheek. (Strangers to boxing's eerie combination of violence and childlike affection are invariably startled by such gestures, as by the abruptness with which, after the final bell, boxers often embrace each other in mutual gratitude for the fight. But such behavior, as spontaneous as it is traditional, and as natural as it is apparently contradictory, lies at the very heart of boxing.) As soon as the bell sounds, opening round one, Tyson rushes out of his corner to bring the fight to Berbick. In these quicksilver seconds, when far more happens than the eye, let alone the verbalizing consciousness, can absorb, it is clear that Tyson is the stronger of the two, the more dominant; willful. He pushes forward unmindful of Berbick's greater age and experience; the fight is to be *his* fight. If boxing is as much a contest of psyches as of physical prowess, it is soon clear that Tyson, on the attack, throwing beautifully controlled punches, is the superior boxer; and he is fast—unexpectedly fast. "This kid don't let you do what you want to do," Berbick's trainer Angelo Dundee will say after the fight. "He created the pressure and my guy didn't react to the pressure. . . . He throws combinations I never saw before. When have you seen a guy throw a right hand to the kidney, come up the middle with an uppercut, then throw a left hook. He throws punches . . . like a trigger." (This in significant contrast to Tyson's less effective performances against José Ribalta in August 1986 and James "Quick" Tillis in May: the improvement, in so brief a period of time, is remarkable.) For those of us who have been watching preliminary bouts for the past two and a half hours, including a perfectly controlled but lackluster if not contemptuous performance by former WBC champion Pinklon Thomas, the quality of Tyson's fighting—one might say Tyson's *being*— is profound. The impact of certain of his body blows is felt in the farthest corners of the arena; the intensity of his fighting is without parallel. As an observer notes, Tyson's punches even sound different from other boxers' punches. In the ring, in the terrible intensity of action, Tyson is both sui generis and as stylized as the heraldic, struggling figures painted by George Bellows in such famous oils as "Stag at Sharkey's" and "Dempsey and Firpo." It seems suddenly possible that, as Cus D'Amato predicted, Tyson differs not merely in degree but in kind from his fellow boxers.

Early in the second round, Tyson knocks Berbick to the canvas with a powerful combination of blows, including a left hook; when Berbick manages to get gamely to his feet he is knocked down a second time with a left hook to the head—to be precise, to the right temple, a "vital area." (As Tyson will say afterward, he had come to "destroy" the champion: "Every punch had a murderous intention.") Accompanied by the wild clamor of the crowd as by an exotic sort of music, Berbick struggles to his feet, his expression glazed like that of a man trapped in a dream; he lurches across the ring on wobbly legs, falls another time, onto the ropes; as if by a sheer effort of will gets up, staggers across the ring in the opposite direction, is precariously on his feet when the referee, Mills Lane, stops the fight. No more than nine seconds have passed since Tyson's blow but the sequence, in slow motion, has seemed much longer. . . . The nightmare image of a man struggling to retain consciousness and physical control before nine thousand witnesses is likely to linger in the memory: it is an image as inevitable in boxing as that of the ecstatic boxer with his gloved hands raised in triumph.

At two minutes thirty-five seconds of the second round, the fight is over and twenty-year-old Mike Tyson is the new WBC champion. "I am the heavyweight champion of the world," he tells the television audience, "and I will fight anybody in the world."

The post-Ali era has finally ended.

* * *

Boxing is our most controversial American sport, always, it seems, on the brink of being abolished. Its detractors speak of it in contempt as a "so-called 'sport,'" and surely their logic is correct: if "sport" means harmless play, boxing is not a sport; it is certainly not a game. But "sport" can signify a paradigm of life, a reduction of its complexities in terms of a single symbolic action—in this case its competitiveness, the cruelty of its Darwinian enterprise—defined and restrained by any number of rules, regulations, and customs: in which case boxing is probably, as the ex-heavyweight champion George Foreman has said, the sport to which all other sports aspire. It is the quintessential image of human struggle, masculine or otherwise, against not only other people but one's own divided self. Its kinship with Roman gladiatorial combat—in which defeated men usually died—is not historically accurate but poetically relevant. In his classic *Theory of the Leisure Class* (1899), Thorstein Veblen speaks of sport in general as "an expression of the barbarian temperament," and it is a commonplace assumption for many boxers, particularly for young boxers like Mike Tyson, that in the ring they are fighting for their lives. (As Tyson said excitedly, following the Berbick fight, "I refuse to get hurt, I refuse to get knocked down, I refuse to lose—I would have to be killed—carried out of the ring. I would not *be* hurt.")

It should be kept in mind, however, that for all its negative publicity, and the sinister glamour of certain of its excesses, boxing is not our most dangerous sport. It ranks in approximately seventh place, after football, Thoroughbred racing, sports car racing, mountain climbing, et al. (It is far less systematically violent than professional football, for instance, in which, in a single season, hundreds of players are likely to be fined for the willful infraction of rules.)

And in a time of sports mania unparalleled in our history, boxing remains the only major sport accessible to what is piously called "underprivileged" youth—the others are Establishment-controlled, sealed off from penetration by men with the backgrounds of Larry Holmes, Hector Camacho, Marvin Hagler, Mike Tyson.

It has always been, in any case, from the days of bare-knuckle prizefighting to the present, the sport that people love to hate. Its image of men pitted against each other in man-to-man warfare is too stark, too extreme, to be assimilated into "civilized" society. "You're fighting, you're not playing the piano, you know," welterweight champion Fritzie Zivic once said.

"Yes, I'm fighting for my life in the ring," Mike Tyson tells me. And, "I love boxing." And, a little later, "Am I a born boxer? No—if I was, I'd be perfect."

In person Mike Tyson exudes the air of an intensely physical being; he is guarded, cautious in his speech, wary of strangers, unfailingly courteous. His intelligence expresses itself elliptically, as if through a mask—though not the death's-head mask of the ring that so intimidates opponents. No doubt the referee's classic admonition, "Protect yourself at all times!" rings in his ears in situations like this—an interview, one of numberless interviews, thrust upon him in the ever-burgeoning phenomenon of Fame. (It is difficult to believe Tyson will ever be fully—narcissistically—comfortable in his celebrity as Muhammad Ali and Sugar Ray Leonard are in theirs.)

Tyson is a young man, a phenomenon, one might say, of paradoxical qualities: more complex, and more self-analytical, than he has seemed willing, in public, to acknowledge. With his boyish gap-toothed smile and his earnest voice he has disarmed speculation about his future as a precocious titleholder by telling reporters repeatedly that his life is simple: "You wouldn't believe how simple it is. I'm too young to worry about so many things. I let them worry." (Meaning that his professional affairs are handled—and handled, it would seem, with consummate skill—by managers Jim Jacobs and Bill Cayton of Big Fights Inc. and trainer Kevin Rooney.) He acquiesces to media descriptions of himself as a "boy champion"; he speaks, not, it seems, disingenuously, of being a "kid" whose career is a masterwork guided by others—primarily, of course, by the late Cus D'Amato. ("Cus laid the groundwork for Mike's career," Jim Jacobs tells me. "And when I say Cus laid the groundwork, I mean he laid the groundwork—for Mike's entire future career.") The young boxer's relationship to his handlers and to his "family"—an intimate though not blood-related constellation of men and women linked by way of D'Amato—allows him the freedom-within-discipline of the child prodigy in music whose teacher and parents zealously protect him from the outside world. And it is readily clear, speaking with Mike Tyson in the presence of Jim and Loraine Jacobs (my interview was conducted in the Jacobses' apartment in the East Forties, Manhattan, surrounded by boxing memorabilia that includes an entire wall of films and tapes), that he is fully aware of his good fortune; he understands that his emotional-professional situation is close to unique in the notoriously unsentimental world of professional boxing. He is loved by his family and he loves them—it is that simple, and that enviable. If in one sense, like other star athletes of our time, Mike Tyson *is* a child, he is also a fully, even uncannily mature man—a twenty-year-old like no other I have ever encountered.

"I'm happy when I'm fighting. The day of the fight—leading up to it—I'm happy," he says. In his black wool-and-leather sweater, black brushed corduroy trousers, a jewel-studded gold bracelet on his wrist, Mike Tyson looks very different from the man who "destroyed" Trevor Berbick seven days ago in Las Vegas; very different from the iconographic photographs of him that have appeared in various publications, here and abroad. (The Japanese are much taken with Tyson: his photograph has been on the cover not only of sports magazines but of movie and general-interest magazines. How to explain his popularity there, where he has never visited? Tyson smiles and shrugs. "Who knows?") Loraine Jacobs shows me a remarkable photograph of Tyson by Ken Regan of Camera 5 in which, in his boxing trunks, eerily shadowed and outlined by light, Tyson looks like a statue, or a robot—a high-tech fantasy of sheerly masculine threat and aggression. I ask Tyson what he thinks of his image—does it seem strange to him, to be so detached from a "Mike Tyson" who both is and is not himself—and Tyson murmurs something vaguely philosophical, like, "What can you do?" Yet it is clear that he too is fascinated by the phenomenon of Tyson; he remarks, a little later, that it would be interesting if he could in some way be in the audience at one of his own fights, where the excitement is. In the ring, in the cynosure of action, the fighter does not experience himself; what appears to the crowd as an emotionally charged performance is coolly calibrated. If Tyson feels fear—which, he acknowledges, he does—he projects his fear onto the opponent, as Cus D'Amato instructed: but little emotion is ever visible on Mike Tyson's own face.

If Tyson is happy in the ring, unlike many boxers who come to dislike and dread their own life's work, it is perhaps because he hasn't been hurt; hasn't been seriously hit; has never met an opponent who was in any sense a match for him. (Do any exist? Right now? Tyson and his circle don't think so.) At the age of twenty he believes himself invulnerable, and who, watching him in action, would deny it? One of the fascinations of this new young titleholder is the air he exudes of "immortality" in the flesh—it is the fascination of a certain kind of innocence.

Asked after the Berbick fight why he is so concerned with establishing a record "that will never, ever be broken," Tyson said, "I want to be immortal! I want to live forever!" He was being funny, of course—he often is, making such pronouncements to the press. But he was also, of course, deadly serious.

Baptized Catholic, he no longer practices the faith; but believes, he says, in God. As for life after death—"When you're dead, that's it." He is quick to acknowledge the extraordinary good fortune, amounting very nearly to the miraculous, that has characterized his life beyond the age of twelve, when, as a particularly unhappy inmate of the Tryon School for Boys in Johnstown, New York, a juvenile detention facility to which he was sent after committing burglaries and robberies in the Brownsville section of Brooklyn, he was brought to the attention of the elderly Cus D'Amato— a man who, judging by the testimony of numerous observers, seems to have had the mystical qualities of a Zen Master. But Cus D'Amato was a boxing trainer par excellence who had already cultivated another juvenile delinquent, Floyd Patterson, into a prodigy-champion heavyweight in the 1950s, and had discovered José Torres (world light-heavyweight champion 1965–66 and current head of the New York State Boxing Commission) as an amateur boxer in Puerto Rico. The story is that, having observed the untrained thirteen-year-old Tyson box a few rounds in the gym he ran above the police station in Catskill, New York, D'Amato said to a Tryon School boxing coach: "That's the heavyweight champion of the world. If he wants it, it's his."

This is the stuff of legend, of course. Yet it happens

to be true. The precocious criminal-to-be—Tyson's earliest arrests were at the age of ten—is taken up by one of boxing history's greatest trainers; is released into D'Amato's custody and, two years later, is officially adopted by him; lives, trains, most importantly is nourished, in Catskill, New York, in a fourteen-room house shared by D'Amato and his sister-in-law, Camille Ewald—far from the corrosive atmosphere of the black ghetto, in which, judging from his record, the young Mike Tyson would have been doomed. "Cus was my father but he was more than a father," Tyson says. "You can have a father and what does it mean?—it doesn't really mean anything. Cus was my backbone. . . . He did everything for my best interest. . . . We'd spend all our time together, talk about things that, later on, would come back to me. Like about character, and courage. Like the hero and the coward: that the hero and the coward both feel the same thing, but the hero uses his fear, projects it onto his opponent, while the coward runs. It's the same thing, fear, but it's what you do with it that matters." (Jim Jacobs tells me afterward that much of what Mike says is Cus D'Amato speaking; much of what *he* says is Cus D'Amato speaking.)

Quite apart from his genius as a boxing trainer, D'Amato appears to have been a genius of a spiritual sort, if "genius" is not an inappropriate term in this context. Like a devoted religious elder he instilled in Tyson, and no doubt in others of his young boxer acolytes, qualities of an abstract nature: self-denial, discipline, will, integrity, independence, "character." It was D'Amato's belief that a fighter's character is more important ultimately than his skill: a perception proven, in the ring, only in the most arduous of fights—one thinks of the virtually Shakespearean struggles of the first Ali/Frazier match, the 1941 Louis/Conn match, the Leonard/Hearns. Most importantly, D'Amato instilled in Tyson that most invaluable and mysterious of gifts, an unwavering faith in himself. "He said I would be the youngest heavyweight in history," marvels Tyson. "And what he said turned out to be true. Cus knew it all along."

Jim Jacobs, D'Amato's devoted friend, a boxing manager of enormous reputation and prestige and the archivist of twenty-six thousand boxing films, says that D'Amato's word regarding Tyson's promise was enough for him: there was no one in the world whose judgment he trusted more than Cus D'Amato's. "When Cus told me that Mike Tyson was going to be heavyweight champion of the world, that's all I had to hear." So internalized is D'Amato's voice, and his instructions regarding the nurturing of the young heavyweight, Jacobs says that when he thinks about what he is doing, he has only to "press a button in my head and I can hear Cus talking to me. What I am doing is precisely and exactly what Cus told me to do."

If Tyson looked upon D'Amato as a father—Tyson's "real" father seems never to have figured in his life—it is evident that D'Amato looked upon Tyson as a son. In an interview for *People* shortly before his death, D'Amato told William Plummer that the boy meant "everything" to him. "If it weren't for him, I probably wouldn't be living today. See, I believe nature's a lot smarter than anybody thinks. During the course of a man's life he develops a lot of pleasures and people he cares about. Then nature takes them away one by one. It's her way of preparing you for death. See, I didn't have the pleasures any longer. My friends were gone, I didn't hear things, I didn't see things clearly, except in memory. . . . So I said I must be getting ready to die. Then Mike came along. The fact that he is here and is doing what he is doing gives me the motivation to stay alive." Though D'Amato died of pneumonia in November 1985, aged seventy-seven, approximately a year before Tyson became the youngest titleholder in heavyweight history, he seems to be alive, still, in Tyson's soul. One man's faith in another can go no further.

Yet it would be imprecise to say that Mike Tyson is D'Amato's creature solely. His initial social shyness masks a quick, restless intelligence; he is not without humor regarding even the vicissitudes of his early life. Of his years as a child criminal—during which time, as the youngest member of a gang, he was frequently entrusted with holding a gun during robberies—he has said, "Please don't think I was really bad. I used to rob and steal but other guys did worse things—they murdered people." At times Tyson lived on the Bedford-Stuyvesant streets, slept in abandoned buildings like a feral child. When he was arrested, aged eleven, and sent to the Tryon School for Boys, no one could have guessed how his life, ironically, had been saved. He was violent, depressed, mute; one of the most intractable of the "incorrigible" boys. When he broke loose it required several adult men to overpower him. One official recalls having seen him dragged away in handcuffs, to be locked in solitary confinement.

Mike Tyson's story reminded me of those legendary tales of abandoned children so particularly cherished by the European imagination—Kasper Hauser of Nürnberg, the "wild boy" of the Aveyron. Such tales appeal to our sense of wonder, mystery, and dread; and to our collective guilt. These children, invariably boys, are "natural" and "wild"; not precisely mute but lacking a language; wholly innocent of the rudiments of human social relations. They are homeless, parentless, nameless, "redeemable" only by way of the devotion of a teacher father—not unlike Tyson's Cus D'Amato. But even love is not enough to save the mysteriously doomed Kasper Hauser, whose story ends as abruptly and as tragically as it begins. And the "wild boy" of the Aveyron loses the freshness of his soul even as he acquires the skills of language and social intercourse.

There is nothing nostalgic, however, about Tyson's feelings for his past. Many of his boyhood friends are in jail or dead; both his parents are deceased; he has a sister and a brother, both older, with whom he appears to be on friendly but not intimate terms. If he returns to his old neighborhood it is as a visitor of conspicuous dimensions: a hero, a "boy champion," a *Sports Illustrated* cover in the flesh. Like Joe Louis, Sugar Ray Robinson, Larry Holmes, et al., Mike Tyson has become a model of success for "ghetto youth," though his personal code of conduct, his remarkably assured sense of himself, owes nothing at all to the ghetto. He is trained, managed, and surrounded, to an unusual degree, by white men, and though he cannot be said to be a white man's black man he is surely not a black man's black man in the style of, for instance, Muhammad Ali (whose visit to Tyson's grammar school in Brooklyn made a powerful impression on him at the age of ten). Indeed, it might be said that Mike Tyson will be the first heavyweight boxer in America to transcend issues of race—a feat laudable or troubling, depending upon one's perspective. (In the light of which, a proposed match between Tyson and the zealously overpromoted "White Hope" candidate Gerry Cooney would have interesting consequences: allegiances are likely not to break down along cursory color lines.)

He will do what he can, Tyson says, to promote blacks, but he does not intend to become involved in politics. He will visit schools, make public appearances, do anti-drug commercials for the FBI and the State of New York. If his replies to questions about black consciousness—its literature, art, history—are rather vague, it should be said that his replies to most questions that deal with culture in a larger sense are vague. Tyson dropped out of Catskill High School in his senior year—"I hated it there"—to concentrate on his amateur boxing in clubs and Golden Gloves competitions under the tutelage of D'Amato; and at this point his formal education, such as it was, seems to have ended. He has virtually no interest in music—"I could live without music." He shrugs aside queries about art, dance, literature; his reading is limited to boxing books and magazines. With Jim Jacobs's library of twenty-six thousand fight films at his disposal he watches old fights with an almost scholarly passion—surely this is unusual, in a practitioner? (Jim Jacobs assures me it is.) For entertainment Tyson watches videos of karate movies, horror movies, occasionally even children's cartoons: no serious dramas, and no movies about the lives of fictionalized boxers. I am spared asking him the obligatory question about the preposterous *Rocky* movies.

It should not be assumed, on the evidence of the above, that Mike Tyson is not intelligent; or that he is intellectually limited. On the contrary, I sensed in him the prodigy's instinctive husbanding of the self: he dares not allow his imagination freedom in areas only peripheral to the cultivation of his talent. Because he is an unusually sensitive person—sensitive to others' feelings, not merely to his own—he does not want to be forced to expend himself in feeling, or in thinking; except of course on his own terms. The awareness of life's tragic ambiguity that serious art provides—the perception, as Henry James describes it in the preface to *What Maisie Knew,* that no themes are so human "as those that reflect for us, out of the confusion of life, the close connection of bliss and bale, of the things that help with the things that hurt, so dangling before us for ever that bright hard medal, of so strange an alloy, one face of which is somebody's right and ease and the other somebody's pain and wrong"—would be disastrous for the warrior boxer.

When, the story goes, Alexis Arguello (the great champion of the featherweight, junior lightweight, and lightweight divisions) met Roberto Durán (the great champion of the lightweight and welterweight divisions) and proffered his hand to shake, Durán backed away and screamed, "Get away! You're crazy! I'm not your friend!" To acknowledge friendship, let alone brotherhood, always makes it difficult to kill—or to provide for spectators the extraordinary mimicry of killing that boxing of the quality of Mike Tyson's involves. Life is real and painful, and steeped in ambiguity; in the boxing ring there is either/or. Either you win, or you lose.

The brilliant boxer is an artist, albeit in an art not readily comprehensible, or palatable, to most observers. The instruments of his art are his own and his opponent's bodies. That it is, in a sense, a contemplative art—contemplated, dreamt-of, for weeks, months, even years before it is executed—is a proposition important to understand if one is to understand the boxer. ("It's a lonely sport," Mike Tyson, who is surrounded by people who love him, says.) Obsession is not greatness but greatness *is* obsession, so it is no accident that, in his ambition to be not only the youngest titleholder in heavyweight history but (I would guess) the greatest titleholder of all time, Tyson is always, in a spiritual sense, in training. His admiration for past boxers—Stanley Ketchel, Jack Dempsey, Henry Armstrong, Kid Chocolate—and, not least, Roberto Durán, of whom he speaks with genuine awe—is the admiration of the shrewd apprentice for his elders, not necessarily his betters. When I ask Tyson to assess his heavyweight contemporaries, men he will be meeting in the ring in the next few years, he again becomes purposefully vague, saying he doesn't think too much about them: "That would drive me crazy." Pinklon Thomas, Gerry Cooney, Carl Williams, Tyrell Biggs, Bert Cooper—he'd rather change the subject. And this instinct too is correct:

the boxer must concentrate upon his opponents one by one, each in turn: in the collective, they cannot be granted existence. I am reminded of a diary entry of Virginia Woolf's to the effect that she does not dare read her serious rivals. "Do I instinctively keep my mind from analysing, which would impair its creativeness? . . . No creative writer can swallow another contemporary. The reception of living work is too coarse and partial if you're doing the same thing yourself" (20 April 1935).

Similarly, Tyson does not want to think overmuch about fatal accidents in the ring. He takes it for granted that *he* will not, indeed cannot, be hurt—"I'm too good for that to happen"; on the subject of an opponent's fate at his hands he is matter-of-fact and pragmatic. He is a boxer, he does his job—throwing punches until his opponent is defeated. If, as in the infamous Griffith-Paret match of 1962, in which Paret, trapped in the ropes, was struck eighteen unanswered blows by Griffith, death does occur, that is no one's fault: it can be said to be an accident. "Each of you takes the same chance, getting into the ring," Tyson says in his soft, considered, alternately slow and hurried voice—one of the voices, perhaps, of Cus D'Amato. "That you might die. It *might* happen."

I ask Tyson what he was thinking when the stricken Berbick tried to get to his feet and he says quickly, "I hoped he wasn't hurt," and adds, "It was a deliberate punch, to the head—a bad intention in a vital area." The anatomical areas Tyson has been taught to strike with his sledgehammer blows include the liver, the kidneys, the heart, and, as in Berbick's case, a certain spot on the temple which, if struck hard enough, will cause a man to drop immediately to the canvas. He will be fully conscious, as Berbick was, but paralyzed. Helpless. Down for the count.

And Tyson is confident that he himself cannot be hurt—in any serious, permanent way?

"That's right. I can't be. I'm too good."

Following the accidental death of one of the Flying Wallendas some years ago, a surviving member of the family of famous aerial-trapeze performers told the press that none of them had any intention of quitting. "All of life," he said, "is just getting through the time between acts."

So too with the fighter who loves to fight; the man whose identity is so closely bound up with the ring that it might be said he has none, publicly speaking, outside it. His creative work is done only in the ring and only at certain designated times. Taped, it becomes permanent; it *is* himself—or all that posterity will know of him.

The extraordinary upward trajectory of Mike Tyson's career—twenty-eight professional fights in eighteen months—has been the result of discipline and concentration so fierce as to resemble monastic devotion. Now that he is a titleholder, and a celebrity, and no longer a hungry young contender, Tyson's sense of himself has irrevocably altered; though he has yet to unify the heavyweight title—to do so, he will have to beat "Bonecrusher" Smith for the WBA title and the elusive Michael Spinks for the IBF title—he is already being called, and, in excited moments, calls himself, the heavyweight champion of the world. He has outdistanced his contemporaries—the new young generation of boxers that includes such Olympic Gold Medalists as Tyrell Biggs, Mark Breland, Paul Gonzales, Meldrick Taylor, and Pernell Whittaker; he is the first among them to win not only a title but enormous popular success. "When I was a kid I wanted to be famous—I wanted to be somebody," Mike Tyson says. And: "If someone right now is going to be famous, I'm glad it's me." But fame and the rewards of fame are, in a very real sense, the counterworld of the boxer's training: they represent all that must be repressed in the service of the boxer's real, as opposed to his merely public, career. When boxers retire it is primarily because of the terrible rigors of training, not the risks of defeat, injury, or even death in the ring. (The boxer who is generally credited with having trained hardest is Rocky Marciano, who commonly spent upward of two months preparing for a fight. And when Marciano decided to retire, undefeated, at the age of thirty-three, it was because the sacrifices of the training camp outweighed the rewards of celebrity: "No kind of money can make me fight again," Marciano said.) The existential experience of the fight itself—spectacular, amplified, recorded in its every minute detail—is not only the culmination of the formidable training period but, in its very flowering, or fruition, it presents the boxer-as-performer to the world. Very likely this physical expenditure of the self (Tyson typically refers to it as "matching my boxing skills against my opponent's"), this bedrock of what's real, casts the remainder of life into a light difficult to assess. Life outside the ring is real enough—yet is it *really* real? Not public display as such but the joy of the body in its straining to the very limits of ingenuity and endurance underlies the motive for such feats of physical prowess as championship boxing or aerial-trapeze work. The performer is rewarded by his performance as an end in itself; he becomes addicted, as who would not, to his very adrenaline. *All of life is just getting through the time between acts.*

Since Mike Tyson is a young man gifted with a highly refined sense of irony, if not a sense of the absurd, it cannot have escaped his attention that, much of the time, in public places like the expensive midtown restaurant in which our party has dinner following the interview, or the reception two weeks later in a private suite in Madison Square Garden before the Witherspoon-Smith elimination match, he is likely to be the only black in attendance. He is likely to be the youngest person in attendance, and the only man not dressed in a suit and tie. Above all he is likely to be the only person with a gold tooth and a homemade tattoo ("Mike" on his right bicep); and the only person who, not many years before, was so violent and uncontrollable ("I went berserk sometimes") he had to be forcibly restrained. But when I mention some of this to a fellow guest at the Garden reception the man looks at me as if I have said something not only bizarre but distasteful. "I doubt that Mike thinks in those terms," he says. Not even that Tyson *is* the only black in this gathering of well-to-do white people, an observation that would appear to be simple fact? But no, I am assured: "Mike Tyson doesn't think in those terms."

Following a brief speech by the gentleman who runs Madison Square Garden, Tyson is presented with a ceremonial gift: a glass paperweight apple symbolizing New York City. He is photographed, he smiles genially, expresses his thanks for the paperweight, stands looking at it, for a moment, with a bemused expression. When, afterward, I ask Tyson how he likes being a celebrity—since, after all, he wanted to be famous—he says, "It's okay." Then: "Most of the time these things drive me crazy." I observe that he has learned to smile very nicely for photographers, and he responds with a violent parody of a celebrity smile: a death's-head grimace that is fierce, funny, self-mocking, inspired.

Four weeks later, still being photographed—this time by photographers for two magazines simultaneously—Tyson is back in training in Catskill, New York, in a third-floor walk-up gym above Catskill Police Headquarters on Main Street. The gym is small, well-weathered, romantically shabby; owned and operated by the city of Catskill but leased for $1 a year to the Cus D'Amato Memorial Boxing Club, a nonprofit organization. In the spareness of the gym's equipment as in the sentiment that so clearly accrues to its homeliest features, it is the very antithesis of today's high-tech high-gloss athletic clubs. It contains only a single ring and a few punching bags; its ceiling is high and blistered, its lights antiquated. Its peeling walls are covered with newspaper clippings, announcements of the Catskill Boxing Club, photographs and posters of great champions (Louis, Walcott, Charles, Marciano, Patterson, et al.), reproductions of magazine covers. Mike Tyson's entire career is recorded here, in miniature, and, beneath the legend WE MOURN HIS PASSING, there are numerous clippings and photographs pertaining to the late Cus D'Amato, who once presided over the Boxing Club. Tyson prefers this gym to any other, naturally: it was here he began training, aged thirteen, and here that D'Amato's spirit still resounds. The gym is as indelibly imprinted in Tyson's imagination as any place on earth, and one must suppose that his prodigious youthful success has consecrated it in turn.

No athletes train more rigorously than boxers, and no present-day boxer is more serious about his training than Mike Tyson. Indeed, for the first eighteen months of his career he seems to have kept in condition more or less as the legendary Harry Greb did—by fighting virtually all the time. Today Tyson has done his morning roadwork—"three to five miles; I like it then 'cause I'm alone"—and is now going through the exercises that constitute "preliminary" training. (In Las Vegas he will work with at least five sparring partners. As Jim Jacobs explains, the sparring partners need time to recover.) Dressed in a black leotard and blowsy white trunks he moves from "work" station to station, closely attended by his trainer, Rooney, whom he clearly respects, and for whom he feels a good deal of affection, perhaps, at

least in part, because Rooney is himself a D'Amato protégé—a welterweight who once boxed on the U.S. Boxing
Team—and even shared one or two cards with Tyson, when
he was already Tyson's trainer.

The drills are fierce and demand more concentration,
strength, and sheer physical endurance than any fight Tyson
has yet fought. Rooney has set a timer made up of two bulbs,
red and green, to monitor each drill, the red telling Tyson
to pause, the latter to resume. First he jumps rope, as if in
a kind of trance, the rope moving too swiftly to be seen; the
spectacle of a man of Tyson's build, so light on his feet, so
seemingly *weightless,* has a preternatural quality. Next the
heavy bag: Rooney wraps his hands with white tape, Tyson
puts on gloves, pushes the bag with his left, then pummels
it with combinations as it swings back to him. Rooney stands
close and after each flurry the two confer, even as the heavy
bag still swings treacherously in and around them. As he
launches his hooks Tyson leaps from point to lateral point
with extraordinary agility—as if his upper body remains sta-
tionary while his lower body moves in sharp angles out of
which solidly anchored punches are shot. These are blows
of such daunting power it is difficult to comprehend how
they could be absorbed by any human being . . . any fellow
creature of flesh, bone, and blood.

Rooney is game to try, at least for a while, wearing
padded mitts over his hands and forearms; then they move
on to the "slip" bag, where Tyson bobs and weaves, eluding
his invisible opponent's best-aimed blows to the head. Last,
the speed bag. In the blurred and confusing action of a fight
it is not so readily clear, as it is in the gym, that Tyson's
relative shortness (he is considered a "little" heavyweight) is
really to his advantage. Most of his opponents are taller than
he, if not invariably heavier, so that they are obliged to punch
at a downward angle, utilizing only their shoulder and arm
muscles; while Tyson can punch upward, utilizing not only

his shoulder and arm muscles but his leg muscles as well—and these muscles are massive. By crouching, he can make himself shorter, and yet more elusive. (As Jim Jacobs has explained, "People speak of a 'height advantage' when what they're really referring to is a 'height disadvantage.' If a boxer is good, and shorter than his opponent, the advantage is his, and not his opponent's. The same thing holds true with the fallacy of the 'reach advantage'—a boxer has a 'reach advantage' only if he is superior to his opponent.") But the strangest, most dazzling thing about Tyson's boxing style is really his speed: his incredible speed. How, one wonders, can he do it? Weighing what he does, and built as he is? And will he be able to keep it up, in the years to come?

"Eat, sleep, and train," says Kevin Rooney. "Mike loves to train."

But: "I'm tired," Tyson says several times, in a soft, nearly inaudible voice. (He is still being photographed.) In his black leotard, towel in hand, he is literally drenched in sweat; exuding sweat like tears. One can see how much easier fighting has been for him than the regimen Rooney has devised—so many of Tyson's fights have lasted less than five minutes, against opponents lacking the skill to so much as raise a welt on his face, or cause him to breathe hard. And this training session is only the beginning—on February 3 he leaves for Las Vegas and four weeks of "intensive" training.

He showers, dresses, reappears in jeans, a white tuniclike jacket, stylish tweed cap, brilliantly white Gucci sports shoes—surely the only shoes of their kind in Catskill, New York? When we're photographed together in a corner of the ring he complains in my ear of the hours he has endured that day alone, facing cameras: "You can't believe it! On and on!" Fame's best-kept secret—its soul-numbing boredom—has begun to impress itself upon Mike Tyson.

Catskill, New York, is a small town of less than six thousand inhabitants. Its well-kept wood-frame houses have that prewar American look so immediately appealing to some of us—the very architecture of nostalgia. Like Main Street, with its Newberry's Five-and-Dime, Joe's Food Market, Purina Chows, the Town of Catskill town hall a storefront facing the police station, and the village offices—clerk, treasurer, tax collector—in the same building as the Catskill Boxing Club. Parking here is five cents an hour.

Mike Tyson lives two or three miles away, in one of the largest and most attractive houses in town, the home of Mrs. Camille Ewald, Cus D'Amato's sister-in-law. The house is at the end of an unpaved, seemingly private road, immaculately kept outside and in, yet comfortable— "I've lived here for seven years now," Tyson says proudly. He leads me through a kitchen and through a parlor room gleaming with trophies he doesn't acknowledge and we sit at one end of an immense living room while, from varying distances, a photographer (from Japan) continues to take candid shots of him he doesn't acknowledge either.

Life in Catskill is quiet and nourishingly routine: up at 6 A.M., to bed at 9 P.M. Daily workouts at the gym with Rooney; a diet of meat, vegetables, pasta, fruit juice—never any alcohol or caffeine; a modicum, in this semirural environment, of monastic calm. But there are numerous distractions: last week Tyson addressed a junior high school in New York City, under the auspices of the Drug Enforcement Agency, and tomorrow he is due to fly to Jamaica for a boxing banquet at which, however improbably, Don King is going to be given a humanitarian award—"But I'm not going; I'm too tired." He speaks soberly of the responsibility of celebrity; the fact that fame requires, of its conscientious recipients, a degree of civic servitude. The awareness weighs upon him almost visibly.

With equal sobriety, and a mysterious conviction, Tyson goes on to say that friends, certain friends—"some of them the ones you like best"—can't be relied upon. "They want to be your friend, or say they do, then the least thing that goes wrong—" He makes a dismissive gesture. "They're gone." I suggest that this can't be the case with people he has known a long time, before he became famous, like Jim and Loraine Jacobs, and Tyson's face brightens. The Jacobses will always be his friends, he agrees. "No matter if I lost every fight from now on, if I was knocked down, knocked out—they'd always be my friends. That's right." He seems momentarily cheered.

Tyson's prize possession in Catskill is a young female dog of an exquisite Chinese breed, Shar-Pei, with an appealingly ugly pug face, rippling creases of flesh on its back, a body wildly animated by affection. He'd always wanted one of these dogs, Tyson says, but hadn't been able to afford it until now. "In China they were bred to hunt wild boars—that's why they have those wrinkles on their backs," he explains. "So when the boar bit into them they could twist around to keep on attacking." As Tyson speaks fondly of this uniquely evolved creature I am reminded of Tyson's own ring strategy—his agility at slipping an opponent's blows, ducking or leaning far to one side, then returning with perfect leverage and timing to counterpunch, often with his devastating right uppercut. The "little" warrior dramatically overcoming the larger. . . . He loves this dog, he says. For the first time today he looks genuinely happy.

On our way out of the house, Tyson shows me the dining room in which he ate so many meals with Cus D'Amato. The room is handsomely furnished, flooded with sunshine on this clear winter day. "Cus sat here," Tyson says, indicating the head of the table, "—and I sat here. By his side."

When Santayana said that another world to live in is what we mean by religion, he could hardly have foreseen how his remark might apply to the sports mania of our time; to the extraordinary passion, amounting very nearly to religious fervor and ecstasy, millions of Americans commonly experience in regard to sport. For these people—the majority of them men—sports has become the "other world," preempting, at times, their interest in "this" world: their own lives, work, families, official religions.

Set beside the media-promoted athletes of our time and the iconography of their success, the average man knows himself merely average. In a fiercely competitive sport like boxing, whose pyramid may appear democratically broad at the base but is brutally minuscule at the top, to be even less than great is to fail. A champion boxer, hit by an opponent and hit hard, may realize the total collapse of his career in less time than it takes to read this sentence. Boxing is not to be seized as a metaphor for life, but its swift and sometimes irremediable reversals of fortune starkly parallel those of life, and the blow we never saw coming—invariably, in the ring, the knockout blow—is the one that decides our fate. Boxing's dark fascination is as much with failure, and the courage to forbear failure, as it is with triumph. Two men climb into a ring from which, in symbolic terms, only one climbs out.

After the Berbick fight Tyson told reporters he'd wanted to break Berbick's eardrum. "I try to catch my opponent on the tip of the nose," he was quoted after his February 1986 fight with the hapless Jesse Ferguson, whose nose was broken in the match, "because I want to punch the bone into the brain." Tyson's language is as direct and brutal as his ring style, yet, as more than one observer has noted, strangely disarming—there is no air of menace, or sadism, or boastfulness in what he says: only the truth. For these reasons Mike Tyson demonstrates more forcefully than most boxers the paradox at the heart of this controversial sport.

That he is "soft-spoken," "courteous," "sensitive," clearly thoughtful, intelligent, introspective; yet at the same time— or nearly the same time—he is a "killer" in the ring. That he is one of the most warmly affectionate of persons, yet at the same time—or nearly—a machine for hitting "sledge-hammer" blows. How is it possible? one asks. And why? Boxing makes graphically clear the somber fact that the same individual can be thoroughly "civilized" and "barbaric" depending upon the context of his performance. "I'm a boxer," Tyson says. "I'm a warrior. Doing my job." Murder, a legal offense, cannot occur in the ring. Any opponent who agrees to fight a man of Tyson's unique powers must know what he is doing—and, as Tyson believes, each boxer takes the same chance: matching his skills against those of his opponent.

The fictive text against which boxing is enacted has to do with the protection of human life; the sacramental vision of life. *Thou shalt not kill* (or maim, wound, cause to suffer injury) and *Do unto others as you would have them do unto you* are the implicit injunctions against which the spectacle unfolds and out of which its energies arise. The injunctions are, for the duration of the "game," denied, or repressed, or exploited. Far from being primitive, boxing is perhaps the most highly regulated and ritualistic of sports, so qualified by rules, customs, and unspoken traditions that it stands in a unique, albeit teasing, relationship to the extremes of human emotion: rage, despair, terror, cruelty, ecstasy. It is an art, as I've suggested, in which the human body itself is the instrument; its relationship to unmediated violence is that of a musical composition to mere noise. There may be a family kinship between Bach and aleatory "music," but the kinship is hardly the most significant thing about either.

But what, one wonders, is the purpose of so extreme

an art?—can it have a purpose? Why do some men give themselves to it so totally, while others, as spectators, stare in rapt fascination—and pay so much money for the privilege of doing so?

Wallace Stevens's insight that the death of Satan was a tragedy for the imagination has no validity in terms of the curious aesthetic phenomenon that is professional boxing. In the boxing ring, elevated, harshly spotlighted, men are pitted against each other in one-on-one mirrorlike combat in order to release energies in themselves and in their audience that are demonic by the standards of ordinary—or do I mean noncombative?—life. The triumphant boxer is Satan transmogrified as Christ, as one senses sitting amid a delirium-swept crowd like the one that cheered Mike Tyson on to victory. Yet, even before Tyson began to fight, even before he entered the ring, the crowd was fixed upon him emotionally. (As the crowd was fixed, more evenly, upon Marvin Hagler and Thomas Hearns in their April 1985 match, shrieking as soon as the men appeared and scarcely stopping until the fight itself was stopped after eight very long minutes. Ecstasy precedes stimulus and may, indeed, help bring it into being.) For many, Mike Tyson has become the latest in a lineage of athletic heroes—a bearer of inchoate, indescribable emotion—a savior, of sorts, covered in sweat and ready for war. But then most saviors, sacred or secular, are qualified by a thoughtful "of sorts." In any case, it's Tyson's turn. A terrible beauty is born.

Materials used in the preparation of this article: Elliot J. Gorn, "The Manassa Mauler and the Fighting Marine: An Interpretation of the Dempsey-Tunney Fights," *Journal of American Studies,* Vol. 19 (1985); Nigel Collins, "Mike Tyson: The Legacy of Cus D'Amato," *The Ring,* February 1986; Jack Newfield, "Dr. K.O.: Mike Tyson—Cus D'Amato's Unfinished Masterpiece," *Village Voice,* 10 December 1985; John McCallum, *The Heavyweight Boxing Championship: A History* (Radnor, Pa.: Chilton Book Co., 1974); and articles in *The New York Times* by Dave Anderson and Phil Berger.

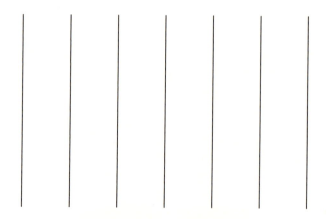

BLOOD, NEON, AND FAILURE IN THE DESERT

Other than boxing, everything is so boring.

—Mike Tyson

Las Vegas, Nevada. 7 March 1987. In a ring still stained with blood from the desperately fought heavyweight match that preceded it, Mike Tyson, World Boxing Council champion, at twenty the youngest heavyweight titleholder in boxing history, brings the fight for unification of the title to James "Bonecrusher" Smith, World Boxing Association champion, at thirty-three an aging athlete, and, yet more telling, the only heavyweight titleholder in boxing history to have graduated from college—but Smith will have none of it. He clinches, he backs away, he walks away, he clinches again, hugging his frustrated and increasingly infuriated opponent like a drowning man hugging something—anything—that floats. Referee Mills Lane calls "Break!" repeatedly during the twelve long rounds of this very long fight but Smith seems not to hear; or, hearing, will not obey. For the most part his expression is blank, with the blankness of fear, a stark unmitigated fear without shame, yet shameful to witness. "Fight!" the crowd shouts. "Do something!" In the ringside seats close by me Smith's fellow boxers Trevor Berbick (former WBC heavyweight champion) and Edwin Rosario (WBA lightweight champion) are particularly vocal, as if in an agony of professional discomfort. For it seems that the superbly conditioned Smith, who had performed so dramatically only three months ago in Madison Square Garden, knocking out Tim Witherspoon in the first round of his WBA title defense, is now, suddenly, not a boxer: though in that elevated and garishly spotlighted ring with another man, contracted for $1 million to fight him, performing in front of a crowd of some 13,600 people in the Hilton's newly erected outdoor stadium, and how many millions of television viewers, he cannot or will not fight. His instinct is merely to survive—to get through twelve rounds with no injuries more serious than a bleeding left eye and a bad swelling on the right side of his face; and to go back, professionally disgraced, to his wife, family, and plans for the future ("Being a champion opens lots of doors—I'd like to get a real estate license, maybe sell insurance") in Magnolia, North Carolina.

Berbick writhes in the folding chair beside me, muttering, laughing, derisive, very nearly as frustrated as Mike Tyson, and clearly resentful—after all, he is the man who fought Tyson here last November, and so spectacularly (and humiliatingly) lost to him, in the third minute of the second round of that fight. He too had tried to clinch with Tyson, had gripped the young man's arms and gloves in an effort to hold him back, slow him down, frustrate him, but Berbick had also fought him, or made a game attempt—"I wanted to prove my manhood," he said afterward, ruefully, "that was my mistake." In this match Smith's manhood is not evidently an issue. He has no "machismo" to display or defend; if he is a boxer it must be by default. Minute follows minute, round follows grinding round, as Tyson tries to get inside to throw the rapid-fire combinations for which he is famous, and Smith falls upon him and hugs him, clumsily, defiantly, desperately. Mills Lane, exasperated, penalizes Smith by deducting points from him after rounds two and eight. ("I could have deducted a point from him after each round," he said afterward, "but you don't like to do that in a title fight.") The 6-foot-4-inch 233-pound Smith is a zombie tonight, a parody of a boxer, so resistant to boxing's visible and invisible rules, that complex of mores that make boxing at once the most primitive and the most sophisticated of contact sports, it is fascinating to watch him—to a degree.

"I wasn't prepared for how strong Tyson is, how fast," Smith will say after the fight. "Tyson has a devastating left hook." And, defensively: "I did the best I could." Of current heavyweights Smith has invariably been the most erratic in performance, the most unpredictable—capable, under pressure, of boxing well, yet strangely and unprofessionally susceptible to vagaries of mood. Perhaps because he has no real vocation as a boxer—and no more instinct for fighting than one might expect from a man with a B.A. in business administration (from Shaw College, North Carolina)—he is easily demoralized in the ring, allowing childlike expressions of triumph, hurt, bewilderment, and acute unhappiness to show on his face, as boxers so rarely do; he boxes as an intelligent man might box whose intelligence is his only weapon in an action in which "intelligence" must be subordinated to something more fundamental. He draws upon no deeper reserves of self—no energy, imagination, emotion—beyond those of consciousness.

As for Tyson: unlike Dempsey, Marciano, and Frazier, those famously aggressive fighters to whom he is often compared, Tyson is not a reckless boxer; he is not willing, as so many boxer-fighters are, to take four or five punches in order to throw a punch of his own. His training is defensive and cautious—hence the peek-a-boo stance, a Cus D'Amato signature: for is not boxing primarily the art of self-defense? of hitting your man, and scoring points, without being hit in return? For two years, which must have been very long years, D'Amato trained Tyson to bob, weave, slip punches from sparring partners without throwing a single punch in response—a conditioning that has made Tyson an anomaly in the ring. His reputation is for power, speed, and aggression, but his defensive skills are as remarkable, if less dramatic. Confronted with an opponent like "Bonecrusher" Smith, who violates the decorum of the ring by not fighting, Tyson is at a loss; he hits his man after the bell, in an adolescent display of frustration; he exchanges insults with him during the fight, makes jeering faces; pushes, shoves, laces the cut over Smith's eye during a clinch; betrays those remnants of his Brooklyn street-fighting days (Tyson, as a child of ten, was one of the youngest members of a notorious gang called the Jolly Stompers) his training as a boxer should have overcome. In short, his inexperience shows.

So the pattern of the fight is immediately established: in the entire twelve rounds virtually nothing will happen that does not happen in the first thirty seconds of the first round. The spectator is gripped by stasis itself, by the perversity of the expectation that, against all expectation, something will happen. If this is theater, and boxing is always

theater, we are in the slyly teasing anti-worlds of Jarry, Io-
nesco, Beckett; the aesthetics is that of fanatic tedium, as in
John Cage and Andy Warhol. While my press colleagues to
a man will report the match boring—"Two interior decora-
tors could have done each other more damage" *(Los Angeles
Times)*—I find it uniquely tense, and exhausting; not unlike
the first Spinks/Holmes fight in which the frustrated Holmes
carried his right glove for round after round, a talismanic
club waiting to be swung. Poor Holmes! Poor Lear! This is
the very poetry of masculine frustration—the failure of
psychic closure. Such fights end, and are funny, in retrospect; but are never resolved.

    Tyson's predicament vis-à-vis "Bonecrusher" Smith
brings to mind Jack Dempsey, similarly frustrated in his
matches with Tunney, shouting at his retreating opponent,
"Come on and fight!" But, for all his renown, Dempsey was
not a strategic boxer of the sort Tyson has been meticulously trained to be; his ring style was virtually nonstop offense with very little defense, which means that he was willing to take punches in the hope of throwing his own.
Outboxed by the more cautious and more intelligent Tunney, he eventually lost both fights. In the Tyson/Smith match
there is no question that Tyson is the superior boxer; he
will win every round unanimously in what is in fact one of
the easiest fights of his two-year career as a professional.
But this is hardly the dramatic public performance he'd hoped
to give, and the fight's promoters had hoped to present. No
knockout—none of the dazzling combinations of blows for
which he is known; very little of what D'Amato taught his
protégés was the boxer's primary responsibility to his audience: to entertain. Winning too can be a kind of failure.

The fight recalls several previous fights of Tyson's with opponents who, out of fear or cunning, or both, refused to

fight him; yet more worrisomely it recalls Joe Louis's predicament as heavyweight champion in those years when, after
having cleared the heavyweight division of all serious con-
tenders, he was reduced to fighting mere opponents—"Bums-
of-the-Month" as the press derisively called them. Worse,
Louis's reputation as a puncher, a machine for hitting, so
intimidated opponents that they were frightened to enter
the ring with him. ("Enter the ring? My man had to be helped
down the aisle," one manager is said to have said.) For a
sport routinely attacked for its brutality boxing has had its
share of historically shameful episodes: Louis's title defense
against a long-forgotten challenger named Pastor, whom he
chased for ten dreary rounds of running and clutching, running and clutching, is invariably cited. While Rocky Marci-
ano/Jersey Joe Walcott I (September 1952) was notable for
both fighters' courage—this was the fight that gave Marciano
the heavyweight title—the rematch eight months later ended
with the first punch thrown by Marciano: Walcott sat on the
canvas and made no effort to get up as he was counted out.
("After twenty-three years as a professional fighter, the former champion went out in a total disgrace that no excuses
can relieve"—Red Smith, a former admirer of Walcott.) Both
Muhammad Ali/Sonny Liston title matches were memorable
for Liston's surprising behavior: in the first, in which Liston
was defending his title, he refused to continue fighting after
the sixth round, claiming a shoulder injury; in the second,
he went down with mysterious alacrity at one minute forty-
eight seconds of the first round, struck by a devastating, if
invisible, blow to the head. (This defeat disgraced Liston
and effectively ended his career: he was never to be offered
another championship fight. Even the circumstances of his
death some years later at the age of thirty-eight were suspicious.) There was Dempsey's notorious fight with Tommy
Gibbons in Shelby, Montana, in 1923, which made money

for Dempsey and his promoter, Kearns, while nearly bankrupting the town; there was the bizarre "Slapsie" Maxey Rosenbloom, world light-heavyweight champion of the early 1930s, a sort of pacifist of boxing, whose strategy was to hit (or slap, gloves open) and run—a boxing style as exciting to watch, it is said, as the growth of tree rings. While no one has ever questioned Marvelous Marvin Hagler's integrity, his defense of his middleweight title against Roberto Durán some years ago left many observers skeptical—the usually aggressive Hagler seemed oddly solicitous of his opponent. But the most scandalous boxing incident of modern times still remains Durán's decision, two minutes and forty-four seconds into the eighth round of his welterweight title defense with Sugar Ray Leonard in 1980, to simply quit the fight—*"No mas!"* No more! Leonard had been outboxing him, making a fool of him, and Durán had had enough. Machismo punctures easily.

Though most of Mike Tyson's twenty-eight fights have ended with knockouts, often in early rounds, and once (with Joe Frazier's hapless son Marvis) within thirty seconds of the first round, several opponents have slowed him down as "Bonecrusher" Smith has done, and made him appear baffled, thwarted, intermittently clumsy. "Quick" Tillis and Mitch Green come most readily to mind; and, though Tyson eventually knocked him out, in the final round of a ten-round fight, José Ribalta. Perhaps the ugliest fight of Tyson's career was with Jesse Ferguson, who, in a performance anticipating Smith's, held onto him with such desperation after Tyson had broken his nose that even the referee could not free the men. (Ferguson was disqualified and the fight was ruled a TKO for Tyson.) Such performances do not constitute boxing at its finest moments, nor do they presage well for Tyson's future: to be a great champion one must have great opponents.

* * *

Incongruity, like vulgarity, is not a concept in Las Vegas. This fantasyland for adults, with its winking neon skyline, its twenty-four-hour clockless casinos, its slots, craps, Keno, roulette, baccarat, blackjack et al., created by fiat when the Nevada legislature passed a law legalizing gambling in 1931, exists as a counterworld to our own. There is no day here—the enormous casinos are pure interiority, like the inside of a skull. Gambling, as François Mauriac once said, is continuous suicide: if suicide, yet continuous. There is no past, no significant future, only an eternal and always optimistic present tense. Vegas is our exemplary American city, a congeries of hotels in the desert, shrines of chance in which, presumably, we are all equal as we are not equal before the law, or God, or one another. One sees in the casinos, especially at the slot machines, those acres and acres of slot machines, men and women of all ages, races, types, degrees of probable or improbable intelligence, as hopefully attentive to their machines as writers and academicians are to their word processors. If one keeps on, faithfully, obsessively, one will surely hit The Jackpot. (You know it's The Jackpot when your machine lights up, a goofy melody ensues, and a flood of coins like a lascivious Greek god comes tumbling into your lap.) The reedy dialects of irony—the habitual tone of the cultural critic in twentieth-century America—are as foreign here as snow, or naturally green grass.

So it is hardly incongruous that boxing matches are held in the Las Vegas Hilton and Caesar's Palace, VIP tickets at $1,000 or more (and the cheapest tickets, at $75, so remote from the ring that attendance at a fight is merely nominal, or symbolic); it is not incongruous that this most physical of sports, like the flipping of cards or the throw of dice, is most brilliantly realized as a gambling opportunity.

In the elaborately equipped sports rooms of the big casinos, where television screens monitor various sporting events, sans sound, and betting statistics are constantly being posted, like stock market reports, one can bet on virtually any sport provided it is "professional" and not "amateur." The favorites are naturally baseball, football, basketball, boxing, and, of course, horseracing, the sport that seems to have been invented purely for gambling purposes. In these semidarkened rooms gamblers sit entranced, or comatose, drinks in hand, staring up at the television monitors and the hundreds, or is it thousands, of postings. Red numerals against a black background. A dozen or more television screens in an electronic collage. The upcoming "fight of the century"—Marvelous Marvin Hagler/Sugar Ray Leonard for Hagler's undisputed middleweight title, 6 April 1987 at Caesar's Palace—is the casinos' dream: as of 7 March odds are posted −3.25 Hagler, +2.25 Leonard, with these propositions: (1) the fight does not go twelve rounds; (2) Hagler by KO; (3) Hagler by decision; (4) Leonard by KO; (5) Leonard by decision. The Mike Tyson/"Bonecrusher" Smith odds are Tyson −7.00, Smith +5.00, which means that you would make a good deal of money betting on Smith, if Smith would only win. Since Tyson's victory is a foregone conclusion the bookmakers offer only one proposition: that the fight does, or does not, go four rounds. (Which accounts for the outburst of ecstatic cheering, the only cheering of the fight, when the bell rings sounding the end of round four and Smith, bleeding down the left side of his face, freshly admonished by Mills Lane for holding and refusing to break, nonetheless walks to his corner.)

While in the antebellum American South white slaveowners frequently pitted their Negro slaves against each other in fights of spectacular savagery, and made bets on the results, in Las Vegas the descendants of these slaves, and their black kinsmen from the West Indies, Africa, and else-where, freely fight one another for purses of gratifying gen-erosity: the highest paid athletes in the world are American boxers, and the highest paying fights are always in Vegas. Marvin Hagler, for instance, earned a minimum of $7.5 mil-lion for his April 1985 title defense against Thomas Hearns, who earned $7 million; in April 1987 he is guaranteed a minimum of $11 million against Leonard's $10 million in a fight that boxing promoters anticipate will make more money than any boxing match in history. ("I'm sure there will be $100,000 bets on both fighters," says a casino proprietor, "and we'll be right here to take them.") Mike Tyson will earn a minimum of $1.5 million for his fight with Smith (to Smith's $1 million) and if his spectacular career continues as everyone predicts, he will soon be earning as much as Hag-ler and Leonard, if not more. Though Tyson lacks Muham-mad Ali's inspired narcissism, he is not handicapped by Ali's brash black politics and Ali's penchant for antagonizing whites: for all his reserve, his odd, even eerie combination of shy-ness and aggression, his is a wonderfully *marketable* image. (See the iconic "Mike Tyson" of billboard and newspaper ads, a metallic man, no twenty-year-old but a robot of planes, angles, inhuman composure: "Iron Mike" Tyson.)

Yet how subdued the real Tyson appeared, following the inglorious fight, and the noisy press conference in a candy-striped tent in a corner of the Hilton's parking lot: one caught glimpses of him that night at the jammed victory party on the thirtieth floor of the hotel, being interviewed, photo-graphed, televised, and, later, being led through the hotel's crowded lobby, surrounded by publicity people, still being televised, wearing his preposterously ornate WBC champi-on's belt around his waist and his newly acquired WBA belt slung over his shoulder, his expression vague, dim, hooded, very possibly embarrassed ("It was a long, boring fight—

twelve rounds"), like one of those captive demigods or doomed kings recorded in Frazer's *Golden Bough*.

What is "taboo" except that aspect of us that lies undefined, and inaccessible to consciousness: the core of impersonality within the carefully nurtured and jealously prized "personality" with which we are identified, by ourselves and others. In his speculative essay *Totem and Taboo* Freud meditated upon the ambivalent nature of taboo: its association with the sacred and consecrated, and with the dangerous, uncanny, forbidden, and unclean. All that one can say with certitude about taboo is that it stands in perennial opposition to the ordinary—to the quotidian. Taboo has to do with the numinous, with the ineffable, with utter indefinable mystery: with something not us. Or so we tell ourselves.

To the boxing aficionado the sport's powerful appeal is rarely exponible. It seems to be rooted in its paradoxical nature—the savagery that so clearly underlies, yet is contained by, its myriad rules, regulations, traditions, and superstitions. It seems to make the quotidian that which is uncanny, dangerous, forbidden, and unclean: it ritualizes violence, primarily male violence, to the degree to which violence becomes an aesthetic principle. In this, men's bodies (or, rather, their highly trained employment of their bodies) are instruments and not mere flesh like our own. That a man is a boxer is an action, and no longer a man, or not significantly a "man," puzzles those of us who feel ourselves fully defined in any of our actions. The romantic principles of Existentialism in its broadest, most vernacular sense have much to do with one's volition and one's will in creating oneself as an ethical being by way of a freely chosen action. Boxing, more than most contemporary American sports, clearly inhabits a dimension of human behavior one might call meta-ethical or meta-existential. There is no evident relationship between the man outside the ring and the man inside the ring—the boxer who is, like Mike Tyson (or Joe Louis, or Rocky Marciano, or any number of other boxers of distinction), "courteous," "soft-spoken," "gentle," in private life, and, in the ring, once the bell has sounded, "brutal," "awesome," "murderous," "devastating," "a young bull"— and the rest. The aim is not to kill one's opponent, for one's opponent is after all one's brother: the aim is to render him temporarily incapacitated, in a simulation of death. "It's unbelievable," Mike Tyson has said of boxing. "It's like a drug; I thrive on it. It's the excitement of the event, and now I need that excitement all the time."

When the boxer enters the ring, ceremonially disrobes, and answers the summons to fight, he ceases being an individual with all that implies of a socially regulated ethical bond with other individuals; he becomes a boxer, which is to say an action. It might be argued that America's fascination with sports—if "fascination" is not too weak a word for such frenzied devotion, weekend after weekend, season after season, in the lives of a majority of men—has to do not only with the power of taboo to violate, or transcend, or render obsolete conventional categories of morality, but with the dark, denied, muted, eclipsed, and wholly unarticulated underside of America's religion of success. Sports is only partly about winning; it is also about losing. Failure, hurt, ignominy, disgrace, physical injury, sometimes even death—these are facts of life, perhaps the very bedrock of lives, which the sports-actor, or athlete, must dramatize in the flesh; and always against his will. Boxing as dream-image, or nightmare, pits self against self, identical twin against twin, as in the womb itself where "dominancy," that most mysterious of human hungers, is first expressed. Its most characteristic moments of ecstasy—the approach to the knockout, the knockout, the aftermath of the knockout, and, by way of television replays, the entire episode retraced in slow motion *as in the privacy of a dream*—are indistinguishable from obscenity, horror. In the words of middleweight Sugar Ray Seales, 1972 Olympic Gold Medalist, a veteran of more than four hundred amateur and professional fights who went blind as a consequence of ring injuries: "I went into the wilderness, and fought the animals there, and when I came back I was blind."

In Clifford Geertz's classic anthropological essay of 1972, "Deep Play: Notes on the Balinese Cockfight," the point is made that, in Bali, the now-illegal cockfighting obsession is wholly male, and masculine: the "cock" is the male organ, as the Balinese freely acknowledge, but it is more than merely that—it is the man, the maleness, codified, individualized, in a context of other individuals: which is to say, society. The cockfight is utterly mindless, bloody, savage, *animal*—and ephemeral: though a Balinese loves his fighting cock, and treats him tenderly, once the cock is dead it is dead, and quickly forgotten. (Sometimes, in a paroxysm of disappointment and rage, Geertz notes, cock-owners dismember their own cocks after the cocks are killed.) Boxing in the United States is far more complex a cultural phenomenon than the Balinese cockfight—it has much to do, for example, with immigrant succession, and with the ever-shifting tensions of race—but some of the principles Geertz isolates in the cockfight are surely operant: men are fascinated by boxing because it suggests that masculinity is measured solely in terms of other men, and not in terms of women; and because, in its very real dangers, it is a species of "deep play" (an action in which stakes are so high that it is, from a utilitarian standpoint, irrational for men to engage in it at all) that seems to demonstrate the way the world really is and not the way it is said, or wished, or promised to be. The boxer is consumed in action, and has no significant identity beyond action; the fight is a convulsion of a kind, strictly delimited in space (a meticulously squared circle bounded, like an animal pen, by ropes) and time. (Jack Dempsey, in whose honor the term "killer instinct" was coined, once remarked that he wasn't the fighter he might have been, with so many rules and regulations governing the sport: "You're in there for three-minute rounds with gloves on and a referee. That's not real fighting.") The passions it arouses are always in excess of its "utilitarian" worth since in fact it has none. As the bloody, repetitious, and ephemeral cockfight is a Balinese reading of Balinese experience, a story Balinese men tell themselves about themselves, so too is the American boxing match a reading of American experience, unsentimentalized and graphic. Yes, one thinks, you have told us about civilized values; you have schooled us in the virtues, presumably Christian, of turning the other cheek; of meekness as a prerequisite for inheriting the earth—the stratagems (manipulative? *feminine?*) of indirection. But the boxing match suggests otherwise, and it is that reading of life that we prefer. The boxers make visible what is invisible in us, thereby defining us, and themselves, in a single consecrated action. As Rocky Graziano once said, "The fight for survival is the fight."

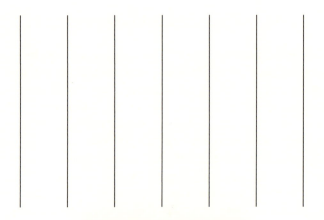

TYSON/BIGGS: POSTSCRIPT

It's like being in love with a woman.
She can be unfaithful, she can be mean,
she can be cruel, but it doesn't matter.
If you love her, you want her, even
though she can do you all kinds of harm.
It's the same with me and boxing. It can
do me all kinds of harm, but I love it.
—Floyd Patterson, former world
heavyweight champion

It is the boxing match with the distinct premise as its theoretical axis that is likely to be the most profound, and in our time the boxer whose matches are most consistently fueled by such interior—if rarely articulated—logic is Mike Tyson, the youngest undisputed world heavyweight champion in history.

The premise underlying Tyson's first title match, for instance, with World Boxing Council titleholder Trevor Berbick, which Tyson won in six brilliantly executed minutes, was that a boxer of such extreme youth (Tyson was twenty at the time, and fighting in a division in which boxers customarily mature late), who had never fought any opponent approaching Berbick's quality, could nonetheless impose his will upon the older boxer: thus Tyson was a "challenger" in more than the usual sense of the word, as, for instance, the luckless Marvis Frazier, son of Joe, had been in challenging Larry Holmes for his heavyweight title some years before.

The premise underlying Tyson's second title defense in Atlantic City, on 16 October 1987, was something along these lines: the twenty-six-year-old challenger, Tyrell Biggs, an Olympic Gold Medalist in the superheavyweight division in 1984, deserved to be punished for having enjoyed a smoother and more triumphant career as an amateur than Mike Tyson; and deserved to be punished particularly badly because, in Tyson's words, "He didn't show me any respect." (Tyson said, post-fight, that he could have knocked out Biggs in the third round but chose to knock him out slowly "so that he would remember it for a long time. I wanted to hurt him real bad.") That emotions between the boxers' managers ran high before the match, very nearly to the point of hysteria, did not assuage the situation.

As with the young, pre-champion Dempsey, there is an unsettling air about Tyson, with his impassive death's-head face, his unwavering stare, and his refusal to glamorize himself in the ring—no robe, no socks, only the signature black trunks and shoes—that the violence he unleashes against his opponents is somehow just; that some hurt, some wound, some insult in his past, personal or ancestral, will be redressed in the ring; some mysterious imbalance righted. The single-mindedness of his ring style works to suggest that his grievance has the force of a natural catastrophe. That old trope, "the wrath of God," comes to mind.

Though there were boxing experts who persisted in

thinking that Tyrell Biggs, with his "superior" boxing skills, and his height and reach advantage, could manage an upset against Tyson, for most spectators in the Atlantic City Convention Center the fight was a foregone conclusion. (The odds were ten to one in Tyson's favor.) Not which boxer would win but when would Tyson win, and how decisively, was the issue; and how badly after all would Biggs be hurt. Thus, when Biggs entered the ring, dancing, bobbing and weaving, shadow boxing, a singularly graceful figure in a white satin robe to mid-thigh, with built-up shoulders and fancy trim, accompanied by a sinister sort of music with a jungle-sounding beat, amplified but muffled, the vision was both alarming and eerily beautiful: for here was, not the champion's opponent, but the evening's sacrifice to the champion.

It is difficult to suggest to those whose experience of boxing has been limited to television how very different, and dramatically different, the "live" event is. For one thing, the live match is not filtered through the scrim of announcers' voices; it is voiceless, unmediated. Since words do not encompass it or define it one is not distracted by concepts, nor is one likely to know, from second to second, precisely what is happening, because it happens so swiftly, and irrevocably: no slow-motion replays. Announcers, too, develop homey, formulaic ways of talking about boxing; domesticating it, in a sense—as mellow-voiced narrators of African veldt documentaries domesticate the savage "natural" events of the animated food cycle. By naming, by conceptualizing, we reduce the horror of certain intransigent facts of life; by making the unspeakable speakable we bring it into a comfortable apotropaic relationship with us. Or delude ourselves that we have done so.

The live boxing match, however, suggests that such strategies are of no avail, and the more ferocious the fight, the more relentless the stalking of one man by the other, the wearing-down, the out-psyching, the approach to the knockout and the knockout itself, the more spellbinding the event. If refusing to look at the gouging out of Gloucester's eyes in *King Lear* could prevent that action, there would be some logic in refusing to look, but the event does occur, must occur, and by the terms of the contract we must watch. It is our obligation to the victim to witness, not his defeat, but the integrity with which he bears his defeat.

Real courage is required when you lose, Floyd Patterson once said. Winning is easy.

Matches of such spectacular action as Tyson/Berbick and Tyson/Biggs (arguably Tyson's most intelligently fought fight thus far) suggest boxing's kinship with ancient, or not-so-ancient, rites of sacrifice. The trappings of sport, let alone entertainment, simply dissolve away. One is witnessing the oldest story of our species, the battering of one man into submission by another, the triumph of one which is the loss (the mock death) of the other; but the significant issue, in boxing at least, is not this battering so much as the victim's accommodation of it, second after second, round after terrible round.

Like his predecessor Pinklon Thomas, whom Tyson handily knocked out to retain his World Boxing Association title last May, Tyrell Biggs was remarkably courageous in absorbing Tyson's hammerlike blows, those left hooks in particular, so that the theme of the fight as a drama became Biggs's quixotic, doomed determination in the face of Tyson's single-minded assault. The fascination lay in how long Biggs could endure it, or how long his cornermen would allow him to endure it. (What a surprise to afterward see the fight as Home Box Office televised it, and to hear Sugar Ray Leonard wonder aloud repeatedly why Biggs had "abandoned" his game plan—as if the helpless boxer had had any choice in the matter.) Biggs's strategy of lateral movement, quick jabs, constant motion was thwarted almost immediately, confronted by Tyson's superior will and strength; his much-publicized jab was a flicking sort of jab, a stay-away-from-me jab, while Tyson's newly honed jab was the real thing, a blow (with which, in the second round, Tyson split open Biggs's lip). In retrospect the match seemed a mismatch, like so many of Tyson's thirty-odd matches, but only in retrospect, since at the start—at the very start, at least—Biggs seemed to have had a chance. It was Tyson's unremitting pressure, the intensity of his concentration, his will to do hurt, that must have broken Biggs's spirit even before his blows began to take their toll, for never in Tyson's career had he seemed so grimly resolute, so fixed upon destruction, and so exhausting to watch. The tiredness that must have seeped into the very marrow of Biggs's bones, not to drain away, perhaps, for months, or years, was felt throughout the arena, a counterpoint to the nerved-up exhilaration of Tyson's attack. (Surely he is the oldest twenty-one-year-old on record?) Tyson has said that he doesn't think in the ring but acts intuitively; like his great predecessor Joe Louis, but unlike, for instance, Muhammad Ali, he gives the chilling impression of being a machine for hitting, and in this most rococo of his fights a machine for rapid and repeated extra-legal maneuvers—low blows, using his elbows, hitting after the bell. Never has a fight, in my limited experience at least, been so oppressively *communal* . . . as if we were all trapped inside the ring's foursquare geometry, with no way out except to be knocked through the ropes, as Biggs would be, at last, in the seventh round. And no way to be saved from annihilation except to succumb to it.

The tension generated by a typical Tyson fight—meaning one controlled and dominated by him—must be experienced to be understood. Tyson/Biggs struck its tone of high expectancy even before Tyson entered the arena (robeless, but wearing the three oversized and absurdly ornamental belts that are the warrior-symbols of his three titles) and built steadily, in some quarters very nearly unbearably, to its climax in the seventh round, when the blood-bespattered referee, Tony Orlando, stopped the fight after the second knockdown without counting over Biggs. Tyson's ring style, pitiless, forward-moving, seemingly invincible, evokes odd behavior in presumably normal people. Do most men identify with Tyson-as-potential-killer? Do most women identify with Tyson's victims? Or is "identification" in terms of the fight, the spectacle, the playing-out-of-action itself? When a great fight occurs—and Tyson has not yet had a great fight, for the reason that he has not yet had a worthy opponent—the spectator experiences something like the mysterious catharsis of which Aristotle wrote, the purging of pity and terror by the exercise of these emotions; the subliminal aftermath of classical tragedy.

These fights do linger in the mind, sometimes obsessively, like nightmare images one can't quite expel, but the actual experience of the fight, in the arena, is a confused, jolting, and sometimes semihysterical one. The reason is primary, or you might say primitive: either Tyson is hitting his man, or he is preparing to hit his man, and if nothing nasty happens within the next few seconds it will not be for Tyson's not trying. (For a man of Tyson's physical build he is extraordinarily fast with his hands, and he hits in combinations.) In the average boxing match, contrary to critics' charges of "barbarism," "brutality," et al., nothing much happens, as boxing aficionados affably accept, but in Tyson fights (with one obvious exception—last March's title fight with "Bonecrusher" Smith) everything can happen, and sometimes does.

Thus individuals in the audience behave oddly, and involuntarily—there was even a scuffle or an actual fight at the rear of the Convention Hall during the third or fourth round of the fight in the ring, not suggested by the television coverage, and a matter of some confused alarm until security guards broke it up. Some women hid their faces, some men emitted not the stylized cries of "Hit him!" or even "Kill him!" but parrotlike shrieks that seemed to be torn from them—perhaps the "womanlike" shrieks Tyson amusingly described coming from Biggs when he was hit. The boxing commissioner for New York State, ex-world light-heavyweight champion José Torres, seemed to forget himself as he shouted out commands to Tyson (who was oblivious to him as to everyone and everything outside the ring) and to Tyson's cornermen (who were too far away to have heard, should they have wished to hear). Torres's violent hand signals and shouted commands—"Six-five!" was one—would have seemed quite mysterious, if not deranged, had one not known that Torres, like Tyson, is a former D'Amato protégé, and had one not guessed that the ex-champion simply could not resist participating in the mesmerizing action. Strangest of all—and discreetly ignored by HBO television cameras—a fight threatened to ensue between Biggs's chief cornerman, the redoubtable Lou Duva, and the fight's promoter, Don King himself, at the immediate conclusion of the match; each man had to be forcibly restrained from rushing at the other. While television audiences watched the triumphant Tyson striding about the ring, and the dazed Biggs sitting on the canvas, attended by a physician, most of us were watching fascinated as the portly, not-young Lou Duva tried to climb through the ropes to get at Don King at ringside, the two gentlemen shouting at each other, for reasons only a few insiders would know: King had wanted the fight stopped immediately after the first knockdown, fearing "slaughter," but Duva had insisted that the fight continue, no matter the risk to Biggs. Duva had his way, and the fight continued a few more seconds, as if to fulfill its premise—Biggs deserved to be hurt, and to be hurt "real bad" by Tyson.

Boxing's spectacle is degrading, no doubt—in the most primary sense of the word: a de-grading of the self; a breaking-down, as if one's sensitive nerve-endings were being worn away. That the losing, failing, staggering boxer will not quit is very much a part of the degradation process, for boxing is as much about losing as winning, about being hurt as doing hurt, and even the most macho of spectators is roused to sympathy with the boxer who, though losing, has displayed that "grace" and "courage" of which, in another context, Hemingway spoke.

When the fight was over people remained for some minutes in their seats as if spellbound or dazed, like Biggs; or exhausted—the twenty minutes of action had seemed rather more like twenty hours. The prospect of surrendering Mike Tyson's display of *control* to the quotidian *controllessness* of the world seemed daunting, but we made our way, a crowd of thousands, milling and surging, headless, directionless—the yellow-clad ushers, so much in evidence earlier, seemed now to have entirely vanished—through dour dirty passageways with no EXIT signs and into cul-de-sacs of some terror, for what if, we were all thinking, what if there is a fire? a sudden panic? and we stampede one another to death? a fate some might consider only just, since we had all been witnesses to an action of indefensible savagery?—but, by sheer blind groping instinct, a sort of Brownian movement of human molecules, we made our way out to the street, or into underground passageways that led to the swanked-up tackiness of the Trump Plaza, where figured carpets in primary colors jolted the optic nerve and functionless silly mirrored columns blocked pedestrian movement, showing us what we could not have wanted much to see, our own faces. The fight being over, the "real" world floods back, and the powerful appeal of Mike Tyson, as of his great predecessors, is that, in however artificial and delimited a context, a human being, *one of us,* reduced to the essence of physical strength, skill, and ingenuity, has control of his fate—if this control can manifest itself merely in the battering of another human being into absolute submission. This is not all that boxing is, but it is boxing's secret premise: life is hard in the ring, but, there, you only get what you deserve.

4

A MISCELLANY

ANNIE JOHNSON: A "LOST" NEW ENGLAND ARTIST

The posthumous career of the New Haven artist Annie Johnson—she had no other—began by chance in 1971 when a Connecticut businessman collector with an avid interest in nineteenth-century American art, Bruce Blanchard, bought a portfolio of her watercolors at an estate sale. The paintings, unframed, dating from the 1880s, were primarily portraits of Victorian men and women of the middle or upper-middle class in the style of American "objective" realism; and though the finest of them struck Blanchard's eye as extremely skillful, far superior to the sort of sentimental genre art usually sold at such auctions, the artist "Annie Johnson" was evidently unknown: no one had heard of her or her work. (Eventually, years later, Blanchard was to locate a perfunctory notice of Johnson's death, aged eighty-four, in the *New Haven Evening Register* in 1937, but there was no mention of the fact that Johnson had been a prolific artist— or even that she had been one of the first woman students to attend the prestigious Yale University School of Fine Arts.) Nonetheless Blanchard pursued the phantom of Annie Johnson over the next sixteen years, visiting estate sales, flea markets, antique and even "junk" dealers, until by way of sheer persistence and devotion he acquired some two hundred works of hers—watercolors, charcoal sketches, a few pen-and-ink drawings. In 1984 he helped arrange for Johnson's first exhibit, in New Haven, a full century after most of her strongest work was done. Is Annie Johnson's story a tragic one or is it, perhaps, belatedly triumphant? It is in any case poignant and haunting—like this forgotten artist's work.

It was on the afternoon of an oppressively hot July day— temperature in the 90's, air heavy with humidity—that I visited Bruce Blanchard in his Federal-style red-brick house in Seymour, Connecticut, to be shown his Annie Johnson collection. To step inside Blanchard's house, however, was immediately to slip into another dimension, or era: the atmosphere was cool, rather dim; the dining room and the living room were given over completely to Blanchard's eclectic collection. Outsized vases; paintings by little-known nineteenth-century American artists (as many as twelve or fifteen crowded on a wall of modest proportions); antique rugs and antique furniture in various styles; audacious folk items (like four-foot-tall ceramic roosters, gaudily painted)—we might have been in an antique shop and not in a private home, surrounded by the artifacts of a collector who clearly collects out of love and not out of professional design.

Annie Johnson's work is uneven in quality, cast in a determinedly minor mode—no oils, no large or ambitious compositions, nothing even obliquely experimental—the sort of art appropriate for women artists, however gifted, in her time. This is a classically "feminine" art yet very gracefully executed—portraits of men, women, and children that show a precise, unsentimental eye and a subtlety in the revelation of character; landscapes of rural Vermont and other outdoor scenes painted with fresh, clear colors; a sick child in bed, cradling a kitten in the crook of one arm; a bridge, a waterwheel, a finely realized interior of a barn. There are no group scenes here, no crowds or public paintings—the portraits in particular communicate a sense of individual isolation, reverie, absolute stillness. The most haunting of the watercolors, dated 1880, is the portrait of a beautifully realized young woman with pale red hair, blue eyes, an aqua dress, delicate features, and an inscrutable expression—the very likeness of Henry James's Milly Theale, the doomed heroine of *The Wings of the Dove.* Here the artist reveals character "objectively" yet by no means harshly; nor is the portrait even remotely sentimental. There are striking, assured masculine portraits as well—an undergraduate member of the Yale Bicycle Club, 1885, posing beside his bicycle; a white-haired and -bearded patriarchal gentleman, seated, with a cane; a tennis player seated with racquet in hand and rakish red cap on his head. Academic painters of Johnson's time were inclined to idealize both men and women—in different ways, of course—but Johnson's portraits are direct, forceful, individualized. Even among the more conventional paintings of women and young children we have the unusual, poetic painting of the sick child and her kitten (and, balancing the kitten, a doll on the far side of the bed)—near-Impressionist in its swift brush strokes and composition—a subject that, in lesser hands, would surely have been softened and sentimentalized.

So it is that in paintings not otherwise distinguished, Annie Johnson's precise eye and her intelligent use of color—subdued for the most part, earthen or neutral—reward close scrutiny. Her simplest studies are often charged with emotion. And there are frequently quirky angles of vision, men and women grasped in profile or aslant, or head on but curiously flattened (as in a double portrait of two wan, staring children), suggestive of experimental impulses in the artist not fully explored, or not explored, at least, in the work of hers that has been uncovered to this date. (One of the mysteries of the Annie Johnson story, as it might be called, is the fact that no art of hers has been located dated beyond 1906, though she was known to have been painting well into the 1920s.) Of the numerous finely executed charcoal sketches, the most striking is that of a young black boy in profile—a powerful likeness executed with photographic clarity, worthy, perhaps, of Johnson's great contemporaries Thomas Eakins and Winslow Homer. And there are two small paintings among Blanchard's collection—a burning house at night, a river skyline above a dense marsh—very nearly abstract in design, enigmatic, dreamlike, reminiscent of the image-centered "mystical" canvases of Albert Pinkham Ryder, another contemporary of Johnson's whose work she probably did not know. It is tempting to speculate what directions Annie Johnson might have taken had she lived in a less provincial society and been in contact with a wider range of artists.

Because the watercolors are likely to fade in daylight, Bruce Blanchard keeps them carefully stored in an enormous wooden chest in his living room and in a cubicle off his kitchen. Out of these unromantic spaces his prized Annie Johnson collection was taken that afternoon, to be shown by lamplight; and back into the spaces the collection went. "It's a problem—storing art—even museums have," Blanchard said apologetically.

In her provocative and frankly polemical study of "lost" women artists, *The Obstacle Race: The Fortunes of Women Painters and Their Work* (1979), the feminist critic Germaine Greer argues convincingly that though some women artists are granted a modicum of success during their lifetimes—almost always as a consequence of their intimate relations with male artists of power and renown—they are invariably, and justly, forgotten after their deaths, and their work contemptuously dismissed. To be "feminine" is life's ideal but to be "feminine" in one's art is to be irrevocably second-rate.

Surely it is more often the case, however, that women artists of talent and integrity have failed to receive even this short-lived, condescending attention, while male artists no less limited in scope, and "minor," are preserved in museums, art histories, and studies of their great contemporaries. Why, for instance, did Annie Johnson never sell a single work of hers?—why no exhibit during her long career? Despite her serious commitment to her art—she intermittently attended the Yale School, for instance, over a prodigious thirty-two-year period—she would seem to have been a casualty of her sex and her era. She was unable, or unwilling, to cultivate a career independent of her family life: she rarely left New Haven except to vacation, evidently, in Vermont; she made no effort to see great art firsthand, by traveling to Europe (as, for instance, Thomas Eakins did, though Eakins's ties to Philadelphia were as strong as Johnson's to New Haven); she seems to have been content to learn from and to have been influenced by her Yale teacher, the popular realist artist John Ferguson Weir, a minor painter. She was a professional woman: she taught not art but mathematics, history, civics, and even astronomy in high school, but when she retired, after becoming financially independent, she made no effort to move out of her family home or to pursue her career in a more ambitious or aggressive fashion. Though she never married she was wed, it would seem, to the comforts of her provincial life. A photograph of Annie Johnson taken when she was in her thirties shows a woman of character—hardly a "feminine" woman in stereotypical Victorian terms—yet she so subordinated her art to her social role that there were relatives of hers who, after her death in 1937, professed surprise to hear that she had been an artist at all! What might have been Annie Johnson's fate, and the fate of her art, had she been a man; or had her era been more sympathetic to women artists?

It is tempting, as one art critic has done, to suggest a parallel between Emily Dickinson and Annie Johnson. Both women cultivated their art for many years without formal recognition of their effort; both were discovered—or uncovered—after their deaths. Dickinson, living more or less as a recluse in Amherst, Massachusetts, was more valued in her household for her bread and puddings than for her poetry; Johnson, hardly a recluse, taught for twenty-three years in the very high school from which she had graduated and became a popular chaperone at student gatherings. In each case we may assume that the inner woman was well hidden behind a pragmatic female façade. But the parallel is finally misleading: Emily Dickinson is after all one of the unquestionably great poets in the English language, while Annie Johnson is a minor, even a provincial artist; Dickinson pursued a stubborn, idiosyncratic, inimitable course, leaving not a few, or even a dozen, but literally hundreds of poems of astonishing genius, while Johnson, so far as we know, seems to have worked carefully within the clearly defined aesthetic boundaries of her time and place.

Yet to have accomplished the considerable body of work that Johnson did accomplish, and to have been belatedly honored as she has been, is surely triumph of a kind. And since there may well be any number of works of hers scattered, unsigned, "lost" in Connecticut at the present time, who can say that the Annie Johnson story is concluded—or even properly begun?

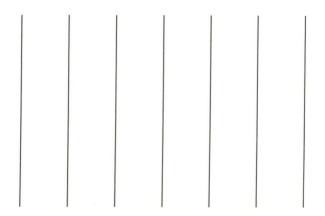

"LIFE, VIGOR, FIRE": THE WATERCOLORS OF WINSLOW HOMER

The life that I have chosen gives me my
full hours of enjoyment for the balance
of my life. The Sun will not rise, or set,
without my notice, and thanks.
                    —Winslow Homer, 1903

Winslow Homer's brilliant and innovative career as a water-colorist—he was to paint approximately 685 watercolors in thirty years—began in the summer of 1873 when, discouraged by unreliable sales and mixed reviews of his ambitious oil paintings, he vacationed in Gloucester, Massachusetts, and worked on a series of paintings that focused primarily on children against a seacoast background. The artist was thirty-seven years old at this turning point in his life and made his living as a free-lance illustrator for such magazines as *Harper's Weekly* ("a treadmill existence," as he called it, "a form of bondage"); he had had an early but misleading success at the age of thirty with his famous oil "Prisoners from the Front" (1866) but found, to his immense discouragement, that critics and collectors expected him to produce similar work: the chronic predicament of the artist of genius who almost at once leaves established taste behind, even as he has helped establish it. Homer's success at watercolors, however, not only allowed him to give up commercial art but freed him, for summers at least, from the concentrated labor of oil painting, which he assumed would be the primary focus of his career. It also freed him to experiment—to conceive of his art in terms of light, color, and composition, not merely in terms of subject. The artist could not have anticipated that, in a "lesser" medium to which relative failure had driven him, he would not only create an astonishing volume of exceptional work but would, in the words of the art historian Virgil Barker, remake the craft: "He invented the handling where everything depends upon a trained spontaneity. . . . No one since has added to its technical sources, and it is even unlikely that anyone can."

Just as Winslow Homer's watercolors span many years, so too do they focus upon greatly differing subjects and take up, sometimes obsessively, greatly varying themes. They are also closely identified with specific geographical settings: Gloucester, Massachusetts; Prouts Neck, Maine; the English fishing village of Cullercoats, Northumberland; the Adirondacks and the Canadian North woods; Florida and the Caribbean. "If a man wants to be an artist," Homer said as a very young man, "he should never look at pictures." This was in fact not Homer's practice—he was too intelligent to imagine himself truly superior to the historical development of his craft—but his art even at its most visionary is always in response to the physical world. The grim North Sea of England is very different from the benign and sunlit beach at Gloucester, Maine, and draws forth a radically different art; images of nostalgia evoked by upstate New York seem hardly to belong to the same sensibility—the same *eye*—as those so brilliantly and seemingly effortlessly evoked by the Caribbean. Except for his experimentation with light, color, and composition and the mastery of his brushwork, the Winslow Homer of Prouts Neck is not the Winslow Homer of the Adirondacks. "You must not paint everything you see," Homer advised a fellow artist, "you must wait, and wait patiently, until the exceptional, the wonderful effect or aspect comes." Homer's genius was to paint the exceptional as if it were somehow ordinary; to so convincingly capture the fluidity of motion of the present moment—its "life, vigor, fire," in the words of a contemporary critic—that other paintings, by other highly regarded artists, appear static by contrast. To observe the evolution of Homer's art from its earliest beginnings to its maturity is to be witness to the development of a major artist: an American painter of world stature and significance.

Winslow Homer was born in Boston in 1836, to educated and well-to-do parents; he would die in Prouts Neck, Maine, in September 1910, having lived in relative isolation for decades. At approximately the midpoint of his career he began to withdraw from society, though he was never, strictly speaking, a recluse; he went on frequent hunting and fishing expeditions, insisted upon first-rate accommodations in his frequent travels, was even something of a dandy. He never married, though he was said by a friend to have had "the usual number of love affairs." (In the 1870s Homer repeatedly painted studies of an attractive young redheaded woman whom he seems to have loved and, according to family legend, wanted to marry. But she disappeared from his work near the end of the decade and has never been identified.

See "Winslow Homer's Mystery Woman," by Henry Adams, in the November 1984 issue of *Art & Antiques*.) By adroitly resisting the advances of would-be acquaintances he acquired a reputation, only partly justified, for being rude and antisocial; he was in fact friendly enough, when he chose to be, and always remained on intimate terms with his family. Like most artists he lived more and more intensely in his art as he aged, and though he suffered periods of discouragement over poor or erratic sales there is no evidence that he ever suffered a moment's self-doubt. His extraordinary painterly genius remained with him to the very end: his last painting, an oil titled "Driftwood," 1909, painted after he had had a stroke, is a masterly Impressionist seascape.

As a boy Homer exhibited a precocious talent for drawing and painting, but he seems to have had no formal instruction apart from that given him by his mother, the gifted amateur watercolorist Henrietta Benson Homer. His work as a free-lance illustrator provided him with an apprenticeship in his craft: such early watercolors as "Fresh Eggs" and "Rural Courtship" have the look of magazine illustrations executed by a first-rate professional. There is a delight here in closely observed detail; colors are bright and fresh; the overall impression is affable, anecdotal, warmly nostalgic. Homer began his watercolor career at a time when post-Civil War America was rapidly changing, hence the avid interest in sentimental genre art depicting "typical" Americans in "typical" activities—the most popular being mass-produced, of course, by the printmakers Currier and Ives. He found that he could execute and sell these watercolors easily (he got about $75 apiece for them), yet his professional facility was not to interfere with his instinct for experimentation.

Homer's watercolors differed significantly from those painted by the majority of his American contemporaries, who

289

worked diligently, and often prettily, in the prevailing English style. Indeed, the medium of watercolor itself was not taken very seriously at this time, being largely the province of amateurs, for whom the rigor of oils was too demanding. Homer's first exhibits drew praise from critics, who thought him original and striking; but he was also faulted for what was perceived to be his crudeness and sketchiness—his conspicuous "lack of finish." The thirty-two-year-old Henry James, reviewing an exhibit of 1875, could not have been more ambivalent in his response to Homer's work:

> He is almost barbarously simple, and, to our eye, he is horribly ugly; but there is nevertheless something one likes about him. What is it? For ourselves, it is not his subjects. We frankly confess that we detest his subjects—his barren plank fences . . . his flat-breasted maidens, suggestive of a dish of rural doughnuts and pie. . . . He has chosen the least pictorial features of the least pictorial range of scenery and civilization; he has resolutely treated them as if they *were* pictorial, as if they were every inch as good as Capri or Tangiers; and, to reward his audacity, he has incontestably succeeded.

It may well have been that Homer himself was impatient with his American subjects or, in any case, with his mode of depicting them. In 1881 he went to live for twenty months in the fishing village of Cullercoats, Northumberland; he was in his mid-forties, no longer young, and ready for a complete break with his past. The paintings that derive from that period of isolation and intense work are like nothing he had ever done before, and represent a break too with the genteel tradition of American nature art. This is not the "English" England but the more primitive England of Shakespeare's Lear, Brontë's Heathcliff, Hardy's Tess. Homer's realistic rendering of the hardworking fisherfolk of Culler-coats—the women in particular—gives these paintings a dramatic urgency totally alien to his earlier work. His women are closely observed individuals, yet they are also monumental, heroic, mythic: they bear virtually no resemblance to women of the sort commonly depicted by Homer's American contemporaries. In "Fisherwoman, Tynemouth," a young woman strides along the beach wind-whipped and unflinching, a study in blues and browns, seemingly one with her element; the painting is a small masterpiece of design and execution. "Watching the Tempest" and "The Wreck of the Iron Crown" are yet more ambitious compositions, remarkable for the artist's success in capturing the wildness of a storm-tossed sea and the helplessness of human beings in confronting it. This is not the Romantic vision of a nature sublime and unknowable but bound up in some mystical way with man's own emotions; it is dramatically different from the pantheism suggested by the work of Homer's contemporaries George Inness, Frederick Church, Albert Bierstadt, and the Hudson Valley painters generally. The man who would one day stun and offend critics no less than potential customers by his unjudging depiction of acts of human violence—a hunter slashing a deer's throat, for instance—had found his subject and theme by way of the impersonal violence of the North Sea; in his later work even human figures were to be eliminated in the artist's obsessive contemplation of the forms and forces of nature.

After the Cullercoats series Winslow Homer's reputation was established, though sales of his work were, as always, erratic and unpredictable. He returned to Prouts Neck, Maine, where he was to live from 1884 onward, concentrating on marine paintings—watercolors and oils; he visited the Caribbean and Florida, where the dazzling sunshine had the effect of liberating his palette and inspiring him to open-air painting of a particularly lyric sort. If the watercolor bears a relationship to any literary form it is surely to the lyric poem: a work which, in Robert Frost's words, rides on its own melting, like a piece of ice on a hot stove. The transparent luminosities and compositional brilliance of such works as "Shark Fishing" (1884–85), "The Gulf Stream" (1889), and "After the Tornado" (1898) are extraordinary. Out of wholly realistic material, charged with intense but thoroughly muted emotion, the artist renders an art that suggests abstraction—the very reverse of "genre" or narrative painting. In this sun-flooded space we contemplate a fractured world of planes, angles, gradations of light, in which the human figure is but an element in design. Homer had long been conscious of the phenomenon of light and had experimented with its possibilities for years, like his Impressionist contemporaries Monet, Pissarro, and Sisley: "You have the sky overhead giving one light; then the reflected light from whatever reflects; then the direct light of the sun; so that, in the blending and suffusing of these several illuminations, there is no such thing as a line to be seen anywhere." The elegaic "Rowing Home" (1890) might be said to be a study in the withdrawal of light—a muted evening sun presides over the subdued and seemingly melancholy action of rowers on a lake or an inlet in the North Woods; faint grays and blues wash transparently together; the human figures bleed into the stillness of impending night. In this beautiful tone poem there are no lines or outlines, only shadowy, smudged silhouettes, on the verge of dissolution.

Along with his marine studies, it is Homer's Adirondacks and North Woods paintings that most admirers know, and upon which his popular reputation rests. Certainly these are dazzling works—bold, eye-stopping, executed with the bravura of a master. So exquisite is Homer's brushwork in the large Adirondack series, so absolute his confidence in his art, the "impression" one forms in contemplating such works of the early 1890s as "Adirondack Guide," "An Adirondack Lake," "Old Friends," and "The End of the Hunt" is that they are, despite their incalculable complexity, simple compositions. So too with the remarkable "Shooting the Rapids," where a sense of vertiginous motion is conveyed by the most economic means, as two canoers plunge through tumultuous white water, gripping their oars tightly. White paper breaks through transparent washes to suggest the dim reflections of the sky; all colors are muted—browns, blues, greens, black. Here as elsewhere Homer succeeds wonderfully in communicating the fluidity of the present moment, the experience of physical action, as few other painters have done. Set beside his seemingly effortless watercolors, the experimental work of certain avant-garde artists who similarly attempted "movement"—the Italian Futurists, for instance—seems studied and artificial. It is only Homer's occasional predilection for frank sentiment, or sentimentality, and for the emotional tug of narrative, in such paintings as "Old Friends" and "The End of the Hunt," that suggests his background in magazine illustration and his kinship with American genre artists of the nineteenth century.

But Winslow Homer was—and is—an artist to transcend all categories, as the 1986 exhibit of one hundred of his watercolors in the National Gallery attested. It might even be argued that, had Homer worked only in watercolor, he would still be considered one of America's most original artists. "Only think of my being *alive* with a reputation," he wrote to his brother a few years before his death. And living, still, today.

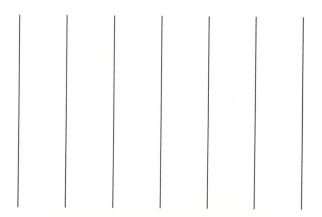

GEORGE BELLOWS: THE BOXING PAINTINGS

Though George Bellows (1882–1925) painted in a variety of styles, very often with great lyric power and an intensity that can only be called magical—see such unheralded paintings as "Cornfield and Harvest" and "The White Horse"—it is his "realistic" canvases for which he is known today, and, in particular, his boxing paintings that have established his reputation. Like his distinguished predecessor Thomas Eakins, the creator of numerous superb paintings and drawings of athletes, Bellows was clearly drawn to the spectacle of men in "sporting" combat and, to a lesser degree, by the very settings—theatrical, ceremonial, oddly formal—in which such combat is staged. Boxing is not, in theory, a blood sport: it descends from British bare-knuckle prizefighting, the "noble art of self-defense" as it was, not ironically, called; and is governed, one might say constrained, by rules devised by the Marquis of Queensberry in 1867. But, de facto, boxing has always been a bloody and dangerous sport, exciting both revulsion and fascination in onlookers. "I don't know anything about boxing," George Bellows once said. "I'm just painting two men trying to kill each other."

Bellows's boxing paintings are "Stag at Sharkey's" (1907), "Both Members of This Club" (1909), "Ringside Seats" (1924), and that most famous of 1920s paintings, the one with which the name George Bellows is perennially linked, "Dempsey and Firpo" (1924).[1] The early paintings are powerful evocations of emotion by way of stylized, heraldic images; the later paintings are formal compositions in a curious stilted mode—as if the artist had become, by this time, an artist historian or journalist, his focus more exterior, "objective." (In fact, Bellows was commissioned to cover important boxing matches for New York newspapers, including, for the *New York Evening-Journal,* the Dempsey-Firpo heavyweight title defense of 14 September 1923.) So different are the paintings of each period that they might well have been painted by two quite different artists. Even the subject matter—"prizefighting"—undergoes a radical change between 1909 and 1924.

Bellows can be linked temperamentally with such

---

[1] Bellows also did a number of boxing lithographs between the years 1916 and 1924, of varying degrees of quality, including "Training Quarters," "Preliminaries," "Between Rounds," "Introducing the Champion," "Introducing John L. Sullivan," "A Knock-Out," "The Last Count," "Counted Out," "The White Hope," "Introductions," "Introducing Georges Carpentier," and versions of "Dempsey and Firpo."

American realists as Stephen Crane, whose *Maggie: A Girl of the Streets* appeared in 1896, and Theodore Dreiser, whose *Sister Carrie* appeared, expurgated, in 1900; the images of his struggling, faceless boxers, animal-like in their desperation, suggest the tragic victims of Upton Sinclair's *The Jungle,* published in 1906. Like these writers, however, Bellows is best understood as a mythmaker or allegorist who uses the outward techniques of realism—an uncompromising fidelity to truth and to the textures, often disturbing, of its surface—in the service of a stern moral vision. His subjects are frequently crude, harsh, even sensational, as in the early boxing paintings, but his painterly control gives the canvases an eerie friezelike quality. A mysterious if brutal rite is being enacted, in an elevated, brightly lit ring, the natural focus of an audience's (and our) attention. However the eye moves outward it always circles back inward, irresistibly, to the center of frozen, contorted struggle, the blood-splattered core of life.

"Stag at Sharkey's" and "Both Members of This Club" are nightmare transcriptions of boxing scenes in private clubs in New York City at a time when public boxing was illegal—at a time, it is believed, when more boxing matches took place weekly than ever before or since. In these saloon clubs men of varying ages, weights, and experience were pitted together for the entertainment of a less than genteel sporting crowd that made bets on the outcomes of fights or on the number of rounds required to "put away" a man. If, as sometimes happened, a boxer died—usually by brain injury or bleeding to death—his body was dumped in an alley or in the river, without identification. No doctor was on hand; referees rarely stopped fights. As in Sinclair's *The Jungle,* there was never any scarcity of fresh talent.

In each painting the sport of boxing has been reduced to its barest, most brutal essence: hardly boxing in the traditional sense of the term; indeed, hardly "sport" at all, but mere fighting: man-to-man war. Here Bellows is clearly painting two men trying to kill each other, surrounded by caricatured—though perhaps not excessively caricatured—witnesses. Like George Luks's "The Wrestlers" (1905), presumably an influence at this time, the power of the paintings resides in their depiction of men as wholly physical beings in extremis, killer brothers, or twins, trapped in the madness of mutual destruction. "Both Members of This Club" is the more forceful for its image of a white man and a black man in mortal combat. (An exceptional image since, at this time in boxing's variegated history, white men were rarely pitted against black men: it was feared that such contests might cause race riots.) Is this murder, or suicide? Is there any distinction? The paintings are haunting, almost too painful to be contemplated. Unlike the Luks painting, which isolates the grimly struggling wrestlers in an inviolate darkness, Bellows's paintings make of us unwilling voyeurs: we are forced to take our place with the Goyaesque spectators—as if we too were members of the club.

"Stag at Sharkey's" and "Both Members of This Club," realistic in conception, are dreamlike in execution; poetic rather than naturalistic. In this lies their success. The ring—elevated, hellishly spotlighted, roped like a pen—provides a natural cynosure of action and attention: what more terrible images of mankind's demented instinct for war and self-destruction? Like the boxers, most of the spectators are effaced, their dubious humanity shading out into darkness. Colors are appropriately subdued—browns, beiges, shades of black, smudged white; the only brightness is, ironically, the boxers' blood, a fight's traditional badge of authenticity. For all its ugliness the subject is an inspired one, a metaphor of powerful moral significance that is also—and not least—the thing-in-itself.

Less successful as works of art, but memorable on their own terms, are the paintings of 1924, "Ringside Seats" and "Dempsey and Firpo." By this time boxing was legalized in New York State; the atmosphere of each—"Ringside Seats" in the old Madison Square Garden, "Dempsey and Firpo" at the Polo Grounds—differs radically from that of the squalid private clubs. Here, boxing has pretensions of being a sport; even, in the formally composed "Ringside Seats," with its youthful, handsome boxers and its suggestion of a better class of viewers, men and women both—note the man in black tie at the far right—a gentlemanly sport. In the 1920s boxing was at its zenith, revitalized by the young and seemingly invincible heavyweight champion Jack Dempsey, who won his title in 1919 in one of the great upsets—and one of the most savage of fights—in boxing history. In what is known as the Dempsey Era as many as 100,000 spectators would pay to see a title match involving Dempsey—the champion whom everyone loved, or loved to hate. Indeed, if "Dempsey and Firpo" is the most commonly reproduced of Bellows's paintings, it is probably because of Dempsey's charisma—though Bellows has captured the heavyweight titleholder in the most inglorious, and controversial, incident in his career.

"Dempsey and Firpo," inspired by a newspaper editor's assignment, records that moment—on canvas it looks absolutely timeless—when the Argentinian giant Luis Firpo knocked or, it's generally believed, pushed the champion Jack Dempsey through the ropes and onto the ring apron in the tumultuous first round of their five-minute title fight. By this time Dempsey had already been knocked down twice while Firpo, the much-publicized "Wild Bull of the Pampas," had been knocked down an extraordinary seven times; at which point, unexpectedly, acting out of sheer desperation, the dazed Firpo managed to stagger to his feet, avoiding Dempsey's assault, and, by trapping him in the ropes, knocked (or pushed) him out onto the ring apron. The fight remains controversial because it is not clear that Dempsey could have climbed back into the ring unaided before the count of ten; he *did* climb back (assisted, as legend has it, by the *Tribune* reporter upon whose typewriter he had fallen) and, in the second round, knocked Firpo down for a count of ten, to retain his heavyweight title. Seen on film, decades later, this infamous fight appears so violent it verges upon the surreal: its rhythms, exaggerated by the film medium, are comically percussive. Dempsey's characteristic ring style was nonstop offense with very little defense; so aroused was he by the act of fighting, he seems to have had no consciousness of fouling his opponents, nor did he much mind, or perhaps even notice, being fouled in return. Not a "boxer" in the style of his distinguished predecessor Gentleman Jim Corbett, Dempsey galvanized crowds by the sheer aggressiveness of his fighting: many of his pre-Tunney matches, like this one, would have been stopped early in the first round if they took place today.

By choosing to paint "Dempsey and Firpo" in a smoothly stylized manner suggestive of magazine illustration, Bellows makes no attempt to communicate what might be called the poetic essence of this barbaric fight, as he did, with such remarkable power, in the paintings of 1907 and 1909; he does not suggest the injured Firpo's manic desperation, nor is he probably accurate in showing Firpo having swung what appears to be a roundhouse left—wasn't it an overhand right? Seen from the back, Bellows's Dempsey might be any boxer; he is atypically pale for Dempsey, who trained out-of-doors and tanned darkly. Though the 88,000 people jammed into the Polo Grounds were said to have been hysterical by the time Dempsey fell through the ropes, Bellows's ringside spectators seem to register little more than gentlemanly if extreme surprise; they are so slickly executed as to resemble fashion mannequins.

Of course, "Dempsey and Firpo" is a painting, not journalism. It is under no obligation to be faithful to the historic event from which it derives. And there is something haunting in these stiff, frozen figures—the statuesque Firpo with his unbloodied, even composed face; the helplessly plunging Dempsey; the referee, however improbably, already in mid-count; the flat postage-stamp tonalities of the colors; the compulsive painterly detail in, for instance, the newspapermen's clothing and the ring ropes. No figure in the painting strikes the eye as truly alive, let alone involved in a frenzied dramatic action—but perhaps that was Bellows's point? That the Dempsey-Firpo match *was* unreal? Or did the painter's early intuitive genius, his sympathy for and identification with the dark fascination of man-to-man struggle, simply fail him in this instance? The risk for the artist in commemorating so historic and therefore impersonal an event is that the imagination, which feeds upon the subjective, is likely to be overcome. History and invention contend.[2]

In any case, such speculation is irrelevant. George Bellows's place in American art has long been assured; and "Dempsey and Firpo" will always be reproduced as his exemplary work. Perhaps in its way it is sui generis, like Jack Dempsey himself.

[2] Two stories are still extant concerning Bellows and "Dempsey and Firpo." The first, that Bellows thought the fight "the most exciting he'd ever seen"; the second, that he had not seen it at all—but had based his painting on secondary sources.

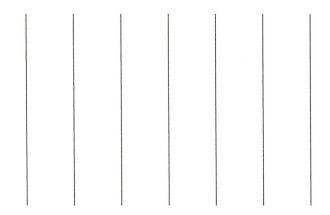

THE HEMINGWAY MYSTIQUE

All you have to do is write one true sentence.
—Hemingway, *A Moveable Feast*

Over a quarter century after his violent self-inflicted death in 1961, Ernest Hemingway remains the most controversial and very likely the most influential of American writers. His influence has been literary and personal, one might say idiosyncratic, not political—like that of Harriet Beecher Stowe and Upton Sinclair, for instance—and therefore incalculable. The ear, if not the eye, can detect Hemingwayesque cadences in the elliptical dialogue of Harold Pinter, the swift direct declarative sentences of the young (i.e., pre-Faulknerian) Gabriel García Marquez, the laconic first-person narratives of Albert Camus, the carefully honed, ironic prose of Joan Didion. Norman Mailer, strongly influenced by Hemingway's work in his early career, remains under the not altogether beneficent influence of the man: the Hemingway who believed that *afición* (passion) justified the expenditure of the self in public.

Like all major artists Hemingway arouses a diversity of critical responses, ranging from adulation to loathing. But in Hemingway's case the situation is confused by the highly visible presence—one might almost say the embarrassing intrusion—of the writer-as-celebrity, the flamboyant "Papa" Hemingway of the popular media whose advertisements for himself (as big-game hunter, deep-sea fisherman, grizzled sage, man among men) approached self-parody in the 1950s. (It is interesting to note that the expatriated Hemingway, long a derisory critic of American culture, succumbed to a distinctly American pathology, like Mark Twain and Jack London before him, and more recently Truman Capote: the surrender of the self to the public image, to the inevitable debasement of the self.) Perhaps because media celebrity came early and unbidden to Hemingway—at the age of eighteen, a driver for the Red Cross Ambulance Corps, he was wounded in Italy, cited for his extraordinary bravery under fire, and taken up for a time by American wire services and newsreels as a hero—he accepted fame as his due and believed that, though writing was a true end in itself, a pure activity, it might also be the means to an end: the enshrinement and immortalization of Ernest Hemingway.

As a consequence, attitudes toward Hemingway's considerable achievement now come sharply conditioned by attitudes toward Hemingway the man. How one feels, for instance, about his highly stylized religion of machismo (the glorification of the bullfight as a ritual of beauty; the camaraderie of men who are bonded by their "superiority" not only to women but to most other men as well); his rites of personal risk and exotic adventure ("It is certainly valuable to a trained writer to crash in an airplane that burns"); the equation of masculinity with greatness in literature. More than one acquaintance of Hemingway's made the observation that, despite his several wives and liaisons, he seemed to dislike women, at least women who did not know their place vis-à-vis men; and since he rarely wrote of women with sympathy, and virtually never with subtlety and understanding, feminist charges of misogyny are surely justified. (Yet in the context of American literature this is simply to accuse Hemingway of being a male writer. William Faulkner's equally insidious misogyny passes largely unnoted, perhaps because Faulkner's prose is less accessible and his manner more self-consciously "visionary.")

It cannot be surprising that Jewish readers have been disconcerted by the casual and unexamined anti-Semitism that pervades Hemingway's work; or that the sensitive are offended by his fascination with blood sports, like bullfighting (the inescapable "death" in the afternoon—for animals) and boxing, and that general air of indifference to the suffering of others that seems the more pitiless for being expressed in short, blunt, declarative sentences. (See the italicized passages in *In Our Time*, for instance: "They whack-whacked the white horse on the legs and he kneed himself up. The picador twisted the stirrups straight and pulled and hauled up into the saddle. The horse's entrails hung down in a blue bunch and swung backward and forward as he began to canter, the monos whacking him on the back of his legs with the rods. . . . Blood pumped regularly from between the horse's front legs. He was nervously unsteady. The bull could not make up his mind to charge." In *The Sun Also Rises*, Jake Barnes and his companions are contemptuous of the "kike" Robert Cohn because he is sickened by the bullfight and lacks the "healthy" stomachs of the others; they chide him at great length for looking green.)

Writers have always admired and learned from Hemingway, as Hemingway in his time admired and learned from any number of other, older writers, including Sherwood Anderson, but critics have been doubtful of his overall worth. Indeed, critical reassessment of Hemingway in the past two or three decades has been so harsh that Malcolm Cowley, in a sympathetic essay titled "Mr. Papa and the Parricides," analyzed the phenomenon in terms of Freud's highly speculative *Totem and Taboo*—the notion, never substantiated by anthropologists, that there might exist a primitive rite of murder, dismemberment, and devouring of the "primal" father by his own sons. Yet even the most severe critics have granted Hemingway a few classic books—*In Our Time* (1924), *The Sun Also Rises* (1926), *A Farewell to Arms* (1929), *Green Hills of Africa* (1935), the posthumously published *A Moveable Feast* (1964), and a number of masterly short stories including "The Snows of Kilimanjaro," "Hills Like White Elephants," "The Short Happy Life of Francis Macomber."

The Sun Also Rises, written in Paris and published when Hemingway was twenty-seven years old, immediately established his reputation as one of the most brilliant and original writers of his generation; he was lauded as an unsentimental, if not pitiless, interpreter of post–World War I society. The novel's idle, self-absorbed characters are American and English expatriates in Paris in the early 1920s, veterans in one way or another of the war: the newspaperman narrator Jake Barnes was wounded on the Italian front and is sexually impotent ("No," Jake says self-mockingly, "I just had an accident"); the woman he loves, Lady Brett Ashley, is estranged from an English baronet who became mentally deranged during his service in the Royal Navy, and is something of a nymphomaniac alcoholic ("I've always done just what I wanted," Brett says helplessly to Jake; "I do feel such a bitch"). The novel's title, perfectly chosen, taken from the first chapter of Ecclesiastes ("One generation passeth away, and another generation cometh; but the earth abideth for ever. The sun also ariseth, and the sun goeth down, and hasteth to his place where he arose"), strikes exactly the right chord of ennui and resignation and succeeds in lifting Hemingway's story of drifting, alienated, rather superficial men and women to a mythopoetic level. And the novel's other epigraph, long since famous, is Gertrude Stein's: "You are all a lost generation." (In fact, as Hemingway discloses in *A Moveable Feast,* Stein herself appropriated the remark from the manager of a Parisian gas station.)

Reading Hemingway's first novel today, one is likely to be struck by its "modern" sound: the affectless, meiotic prose, the confrontations that purposefully eschew emotion, the circular and even desultory movement of its narrative. The generation of the 1920s was perhaps no more lost than many another postwar generation, but the self-consciousness of being lost, being special, "damned," casually committed to self-destruction (Jake and his friends are virtually all alcoholics or on their way to becoming so) sounds a new note in prose fiction. Jake's impotence is of course not accidental. Being estranged from conventional society (that is, one's family back home) and religion (for Jake, Catholicism: a "grand" religion) establishes the primary bond between the novel's characters. Brett says defensively at the novel's end, after she has made a surely minimal gesture of doing good, "It makes one feel rather good deciding not to be a bitch . . . it's sort of what we have instead of God."

As for morality—Jake wonders if it isn't simply what goads a man to feel self-disgust after he has done something shameful.

It seems not to be generally recognized that Hemingway's classic novel owes a good deal to F. Scott Fitzgerald's *The Great Gatsby,* which Hemingway read in 1925, after having made Fitzgerald's acquaintance, and admired greatly. Each novel is narrated by a disaffected young man who observes but does not participate centrally in the action; each novel traces the quixotic love of an outsider for a beautiful if infantile woman; each is an excoriation from within of the "lost generation" and the "fiesta concept of life" (Hemingway's phrase)—the aristocratic rich "who give each day the quality of a festival and who, when they have passed and taken the nourishment they need, leave everything dead." Fitzgerald's Daisy is unhappily married to the wealthy Tom Buchanan, whom Gatsby bravely challenges for her love; Hemingway's Brett intends to marry the drunkard wealthy-bankrupt Mike Campbell, whom the hapless Robert Cohn fights with his fists. (Cohn knocks the inebriated Campbell down but loses Brett, at least temporarily, to a nineteen-year-old bullfighter.) In each novel men and women set themselves the task of being entertained, absorbed, diverted, not by work (though Jake Barnes is a newspaperman of a literary sort) but primarily by drinking and talking. Hemingway's people in particular are obsessed with various forms of sport—golfing, tennis, swimming, hiking, trout fishing, attending boxing matches and bullfights. And drinking. Only in Malcolm Lowry's *Under the Volcano* are drinks so rigorously catalogued, described: whiskey, brandy, champagne, wines of various kinds, absinthe, liqueurs. Long passages are devoted to the correct use of the wine bag in the Spanish Basque region: the drinker should hold the bag at arm's length, then squeeze it so that a long stream of wine "hisses" into the back of the mouth. After a long drunken sequence Jake thinks, "Under the wine I lost the disgusted feeling and was happy. It seemed they were all such nice people."

As a story, *The Sun Also Rises* depends primarily upon the reader's acceptance of Jake Barnes as an intelligent and reliable observer; and of Brett in the role of a thirty-four-year-old Circe awash in alcohol and cheery despair. Though based, like many of Hemingway's characters, on a real person (Lady Duff Twysden, a "legend" in Montparnasse during the time Hemingway and his first wife, Hadley, lived there), Brett is sketchily portrayed: she is "nice," "damned nice," "lovely," "of a very good family," "built with curves like the hull of a racing yacht," but the reader has difficulty envisioning her; Hemingway gives her so little to say that we cannot come to know her as a person. (Whereas Duff Twysden was evidently an artist of some talent and seems to have been an unusually vivacious and intelligent woman.) Another problematic character is the Jew Robert Cohn, who evokes everyone's scorn by "behaving badly"—he follows Brett around and intrudes where he isn't wanted. Cohn is so much the scapegoat for the others' cruelty ("That kike!" "Isn't he awful!" "Was I rude enough to him?" "He doesn't add much to the gaiety," "He has a wonderful quality of bringing out the worst in anybody") that most readers will end up feeling sympathy for him. The fact that Cohn cannot drink as heavily as the others, that the bullfight sickens him (especially the disemboweling of the picador's horse), that in this noisy macho milieu he finally breaks down and cries—these things seem altogether to this credit; he emerges as the novel's most distinctly drawn character. One waits in vain, however, for Jake Barnes to rise to Nick Carraway's judgment of Jay Gatsby: "You're worth the whole damn bunch put together."

The Sun Also Rises is a novel of manners and a homoerotic (though not homosexual) romance, merely in outline a "love story" of unconsummated passion. Like most of Hemingway's books, fiction and nonfiction, it celebrates the mysterious bonds of masculine friendship, sometimes ritualized and sometimes spontaneous; women are viewed with suspicion and an exaggerated awe that turns with mythic ease to contempt. Jake is happiest when he and his friend Bill are away from the company of women altogether and fishing alone in the Rio de la Fabrica valley in Spain. There they achieve a degree of intimacy impossible elsewhere. ("Listen," says Bill. "You're a hell of a good guy, and I'm fonder of you than anybody on earth. I couldn't tell you that in New York. It'd mean I was a faggot.") Of equal importance with male friendship is the worship of the matador, the master of the bull, the only person (in Hemingway's judgment) to really live his life to the full. *Afición* means passion, and an aficionado is one who feels intense passion for the bullfight. Says Jake, "Somehow it was taken for granted than an American could not have *afición.* He might simulate it or confuse it with excitement, but he could not really have it. When they saw that I had *afición,* and there was no password, no set of questions that could bring it out, rather it was a sort of oral spiritual examination . . . there was this same embarrassed putting the hand on the shoulder, or a 'Buen hombre.' But nearly always there was the actual touching." Only at certain rigorously defined moments are men allowed to touch one another, just as, in the ritual of the bullfight (bloody and barbarous to those of us who are not aficionados) the tormented bull and the matador "become one" (in Hemingway's repeated phrase) at the moment of the kill. These are quite clearly sacred rites in Hemingway's private cosmology.

If many men are disturbed by Hemingway's code of ethics—as, surely, many women are disturbed by it—it is because Hemingway's exaggerated sense of maleness really excludes most men. The less than exemplary bullfighter is jeered in the ring, even if he has been gored; poor Robert Cohn, whose flaw seems to have been to have felt too deeply and too openly, is ridiculed, broken, and finally banished from the clique.

If it seems to us highly unjust that Hemingway's men and women derive their sense of themselves by excluding others and by establishing codes of behavior that enforce these exclusions, it should be recalled that Hemingway prided himself on his ability to write of things as they are, not as they might, or should, be. One can object that he does not rise above his prejudices; he celebrates *afición* where he finds it, in the postwar malaise of the 1920s and in his own enigmatic heart.

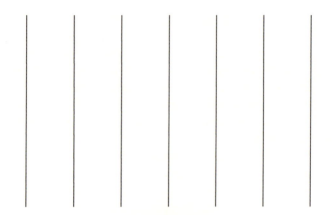

"FOOD" AS POETRY

Food, it might be said, is a kind of poetry. In even moderately affluent societies it seems scarcely to exist in itself but rather as an expression of metaphor. And just as, in poetry, the motive for metaphor remains an insoluble mystery, so too the peculiar symbolic value that food acquires strikes us as mysterious. No one eats merely to—eat.

For some of us food must be symbolic or it is nothing—it must be encapsulated in an "occasion" or it is nothing. Eating in the wrong circumstances, or with the wrong people, or under duress, or pressure, or in haste, is deeply repugnant if not impossible. (This is not to suppose that genuine hunger would not change our attitude, and change it fairly swiftly.) There are those for whom the prospect of a solitary meal seems very nearly a contradiction in terms; a melancholy proposition indeed. What is wonderfully enhanced by the presence of the Other, or of Others—of one's choice—is radically diminished by their absence. In such unhappy circumstances food doesn't *taste*. Eating is merely—eating.

That our deepest instincts are bound up inextricably with food as more-than-nourishment is so simple a truth it can be overlooked. "This is my body, this is my blood: take ye and eat," commands Christ. The savior as—perversely, yet ingeniously—both *male* and *maternal*.

In affluent societies, thinking about food in abstract and codified terms can come virtually to replace eating itself as a symbolic activity. Not *what* one eats but *how* it is prepared; not what food *is* but what it *means; who* has prepared it for you, or for *whom* you have prepared it. Human beings are symbolic animals, and their symbols are as sacred to them as life—perhaps more sacred since they will surrender their lives for these symbols.

In such societies the willful resistance to food—fasting to the point of anorexia nervosa, for instance—is a way of defining the self; the "will" as superior to "appetite." When the anorexic instinct is contained within a culturally coherent symbol system—religious fasting and self-mortification, for instance—it has the value of a transcendent act; to fast forty days and nights in the desert is a gesture of self-abnegation, not self-enhancement. When the anorexic instinct is unmoored, so to speak, from a social context, it seems merely stubborn, self-destructive, suicidal. But one can become as addicted to the systematic denial of food as to its more celebratory consumption. Anorexics speak ecstatically of a heightened consciousness, a world made more vivid and seemingly purposeful; their wasting bodies are vehicles of rebellion and transcendence, living (even as dying) symbols of pure asceticism. But how without meaning the anorexic's project, in a society of generalized hunger.

It might be theorized that both Simone Weil and Diamond Jim Brady died of an obsession with food, the one an anorexic saint—at least in the eyes of her admirers—and the other a bon vivant of the Gilded Age whose eating habits were prodigious. (Diamond Jim could devour dozens of oysters, washed down with champagne, as mere appetizers to Gargantuan meals.) Weil starved herself to death during World War II for religious and political reasons, but we know from her autobiographical writings that the will to die preceded theory: "I never think of the Crucifixion without feeling a pang of envy," she once said. Diamond Jim Brady would have required no theoretical framework to justify his eating binges except perhaps that of *carpe diem* and Why not?—you only live once. The pleasures of eating are perhaps so elementary as to need no articulation, but the pleasures of starving to death, and of achieving what Weil calls "decreation" or "disincarnation," are less obvious (if more sinister): "God grant that I become nothing," was Weil's secret prayer. "We must become nothing, we must go down to the vegetative level. It is then that God becomes bread." In which extreme case "bread" symbolizes biological death.

When Wittgenstein made the remark that he didn't care what he ate as long as it was the same thing every day, he was articulating the wish of many an "imaginative" person—we want to reserve our thinking, such as it is, for things other than food.

In literature, eating and not-eating are always symbolic. Food always "means" something other than mere food. Eating scenes, particularly scenes of overconsumption, seem to shade inevitably into comedy, satire—the famous eating episode in Fielding's *Tom Jones,* for instance (food as sheer sensuality, gluttony, sex-to-be); banquets in Flaubert's *Madame Bovary* and in the more sumptuous *Salammbô;* the holiday dinner in Joyce's "The Dead"; the "artificial sensation" of Huysmans's *À Rebours*—involving as it does, in one passage of inspired silliness, the Decadent hero "playing internal symphonies to himself [by] providing his palate with sensations analogous to those which music dispenses to the ear." (Des Esseintes imagines his liqueur casks as a "mouth organ": "Dry curaçao . . . was like the clarinet with its piercing, velvety note, kümmel like the oboe with its sonorous, nasal timbre; crème de menthe and anisette like the flute, at once sweet and tart, soft and shrill. Then to complete the orchestra there was kirsch, blowing a wild trumpet blast; gin and whisky raising the roof of the mouth with the blare of their cornets and trombones; marc-brandy matching the tubas with its deafening din; while peals of thunder came from the cymbal and the bass drum, which arak and mastic were banging and beating with all their might. . . . String quartets might play under the palatal arch, with the violin represented by an old brandy, choice and heady, biting and delicate; with the viola simulated by rum, which was stronger, heavier, and quieter; with vespetro as poignant, drawn-out, sad, and tender as a violoncello; with the double-bass a fine old bitter, full-bodied, solid, and dark. One might even form a quintet . . . by adding a fifth instrument, the harp, imitated to near perfection by the vibrant savour, the clear, sharp, silvery note of dry cumin.") Like any infant the Decadent wants to put the very world in his mouth—or *is* the world a mouth?

Many-coursed Victorian dinners of stupefying excess are described in Dickens's *Our Mutual Friend* and Mann's *Buddenbrooks* by way of poetically commenting on a self-indulgent bourgeoisie. (The Buddenbrooks' Sunday dinner is so heavy as to be fatal to one of the gentlemen.) One of the most powerful interludes in *Jane Eyre* is that of Jane's near-starvation as, in flight from her beloved Rochester, she is forced to beg food from strangers: a crust of bread becomes the symbol of her humbled pride. Christina Rossetti's "Goblin Market" is a virtual fruitcake of a poem, studded with delicacies of startling suggestiveness (the goblins offer their wares to innocent young women in "sugar-baited" voices: "Plump unpecked cherries," "Bloom-down-cheeked peaches," "wild free-born cranberries," "Currents and gooseberries,/ Bright-fire-like barberries,/ Figs to fill your mouth,/ Citrons from the South")—a feminist cautionary tale of subversive ingenuity.

By contrast, Hemingway's fiction abounds in scenes, often quite protracted, involving the convivial consumption of food and drink. Lovers, friends, comrades—all bond themselves, so to speak, by ritualistic excess; machismo demands a hearty indulgence in the pleasures of the flesh. (Indeed, if one were to delete all references to these activities—particularly to drinking—the size of Hemingway's books would shrink considerably.)

When Emily Dickinson writes, "It would have starved a Gnat/ To live so small as I –/ And yet I was a living Child –/ With Food's necessity/ Upon me – like a Claw –" (612) and "I had been hungry, all the Years –/ My Noon had Come – to dine –" (579), she is speaking of spiritual and emotional deprivation, and giving poetic voice to the variegated hunger of women of her place and time. But when most poets—among them Horace and D. H. Lawrence, Wallace Stevens and William Carlos Williams, Anne Sexton, Denise Levertov, Theodore Weiss, Maxine Kumin, Diane Wakoski, Robert Haas, Daniel Halpern, Erica Jong, Sandra Gilbert, Margaret Atwood, and numerous others—write about food, it is usually celebratory. Food as the thing-in-itself but also the thoughtful preparation of meals, the serving of meals, meals communally shared: a sense of the sacred in the profane. For if food is poetry, is not poetry also food?

THIS IS JUST TO SAY

I have eaten
the plums
that were in
the icebox

and which
you were probably
saving
for breakfast

Forgive me
they were delicious
so sweet
and so cold

—William Carlos Williams

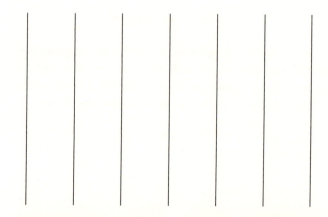

"WHERE ARE YOU GOING, WHERE HAVE YOU BEEN?" AND *SMOOTH TALK:* SHORT STORY INTO FILM

Some years ago in the American Southwest there surfaced a tabloid psychopath known as "The Pied Piper of Tucson." I have forgotten his name, but his specialty was the seduction and occasional murder of teen-aged girls. He may or may not have had actual accomplices, but his bizarre activities were known among a circle of teenagers in the Tucson area; for some reason they kept his secret, deliberately did not inform parents or police. It was this fact, not the fact of the mass murderer himself, that struck me at the time. And this was a pre-Manson time, early or mid-1960s.

The Pied Piper mimicked teenagers in their talk, dress, and behavior, but he was not a teenager—he was a man in his early thirties. Rather short, he stuffed rags in his leather boots to give himself height. (And sometimes walked unsteadily as a consequence: did none among his admiring constituency notice?) He charmed his victims as charismatic psychopaths have always charmed their victims, to the bewilderment of others who fancy themselves free of all lunatic attractions. The Pied Piper of Tucson: a trashy dream, a tabloid archetype, sheer artifice, comedy, cartoon—surrounded, however improbably, and finally tragically, by real people. You think that, if you look twice, he won't be there. But there he is.

I don't remember any longer where I first read about this Pied Piper—very likely in *Life* Magazine. I do recall deliberately not reading the full article because I didn't want to be distracted by too much detail. It was not after all the mass murderer himself who intrigued me, but the disturbing fact that a number of teenagers—from "good" families—aided and abetted his crimes. This is the sort of thing authorities and responsible citizens invariably call "inexplicable" because they can't find explanations for it. *They* would not have fallen under this maniac's spell, after all.

An early draft of my short story "Where Are You Going, Where Have You Been?"—from which the film *Smooth Talk* was adapted by Joyce Chopra and Tom Cole—had the rather too explicit title "Death and the Maiden." It was cast in a mode of fiction to which I am still partial—indeed, every third or fourth story of mine is probably in this mode—"realistic allegory," it might be called. It is Hawthornean, romantic, shading into parable. Like the medieval German engraving from which my title was taken, the story was minutely detailed yet clearly an allegory of the fatal attractions of death (or the devil). An innocent young girl is seduced by way of her own vanity; she mistakes death for erotic romance of a particularly American/trashy sort.

In subsequent drafts the story changed its tone, its focus, its language, its title. It became "Where Are You Going, Where Have You Been?" Written at a time when the author was intrigued by the music of Bob Dylan, particularly the hauntingly elegiac song "It's All Over Now, Baby Blue," it was dedicated to Bob Dylan. The charismatic mass murderer drops into the background and his innocent victim, a fifteen-year-old, moves into the foreground. She becomes the true protagonist of the tale, courting and being courted by her fate, a self-styled 1950s pop figure, alternately absurd and winning. There is no suggestion in the published story that "Arnold Friend" has seduced and murdered other young girls, or even that he necessarily intends to murder Connie. Is his interest "merely" sexual? (Nor is there anything about the complicity of other teenagers. I saved that yet more provocative note for a current story, "Testimony.") Connie is shallow, vain, silly, hopeful, doomed—but capable nonetheless of an unexpected gesture of heroism at the story's end. Her smooth-talking seducer, who cannot lie, promises her that her family will be unharmed if she gives herself to him; and so she does. The story ends abruptly at the point of her "crossing over." We don't know the nature of her sacrifice, only that she is generous enough to make it.

In adapting a narrative so spare and thematically foreshortened as "Where Are You Going, Where Have You Been?" film director Joyce Chopra and screenwriter Tom Cole were required to do a good deal of filling in, expanding, inventing. Connie's story becomes lavishly, and lovingly, textured; she is not an allegorical figure so much as a "typical" teenaged girl (if Laura Dern, spectacularly good-looking, can be so defined). Joyce Chopra, who has done documentary films on contemporary teenage culture and, yet more authoritatively, has an adolescent daughter of her own, creates in *Smooth Talk* a vivid and absolutely believable world for Connie to inhabit. Or worlds: as in the original story there is Connie-at-home, and there is Connie-with-her-friends. Two fifteen-year-old girls, two finely honed styles, two voices, sometimes but not often overlapping. It is one of the marvelous visual features of the film that we *see* Connie and her friends transform themselves, once they are safely free of parental observation. The girls claim their true identities in the neighborhood shopping mall. What freedom, what joy!

Smooth Talk is, in a way, as much Connie's mother's story as it is Connie's; its center of gravity, its emotional nexus, is frequently with the mother—warmly and convincingly played by Mary Kay Place. (Though the mother's sexual jealousy of her daughter is slighted in the film.) Connie's ambiguous relationship with her affable, somewhat mysterious father (well played by Levon Helm) is an excellent touch: I had thought, subsequent to the story's publication, that I should have built up the father, suggesting, as subtly as I could, an attraction there paralleling the attraction Connie feels for her seducer, Arnold Friend. And Arnold Friend himself—"A. Friend" as he says—is played with appropriately overdone sexual swagger by Treat Williams, who is perfect for the part; and just the right age. We see that Arnold Friend isn't a teenager even as Connie, mesmerized by his presumed charm, does not seem to *see* him at all. What is so difficult to accomplish in prose—nudging the reader to look over the protagonist's shoulder, so to speak—is accomplished with enviable ease in film.

Treat Williams as Arnold Friend is supreme in his very awfulness, as, surely, the original Pied Piper of Tucson must have been. (Though no one involved in the film knew about the original source.) Mr. Williams flawlessly impersonates Arnold Friend as Arnold Friend impersonates—is it James Dean? James Dean regarding himself in mirrors, doing James Dean impersonations? That Connie's fate is so trashy is in fact her fate.

What is outstanding in Joyce Chopra's *Smooth Talk* is its visual freshness, its sense of motion and life; the attentive intelligence the director has brought to the semi-secret world of the American adolescent—shopping mall flirtations, drive-in restaurant romances, highway hitchhiking, the fascination of rock music played very, very loud. (James Taylor's music for the film is wonderfully appropriate. We hear it as Connie hears it; it is the music of her spiritual being.) Also outstanding, as I have indicated, and numerous critics have noted, are the acting performances. Laura Dern is so dazzlingly right as "my" Connie that I may come to think I modeled the fictitious girl on her, in the way that writers frequently delude themselves about motions of causality.

My difficulties with *Smooth Talk* have primarily to do with my chronic hesitation—about seeing/hearing work of mine abstracted from its contexture of language. All writers know that language is their subject; quirky word choices, patterns of rhythm, enigmatic pauses, punctuation marks. Where the quick scanner sees "quick" writing, the writer conceals nine tenths of the iceberg. Of course we all have "real" subjects, and we will fight to the death to defend those subjects, but beneath the tale-telling it is the tale-telling that grips us so very fiercely. The writer works in a single dimension, the director works in three. I assume they are professionals to their fingertips; authorities in their medium as I am an authority (if I am) in mine. I would fiercely defend the placement of a semicolon in one of my novels but I would probably have deferred in the end to Joyce Chopra's decision to reverse the story's conclusion, turn it upside down, in a sense, so that the film ends not with death, not with a sleepwalker's crossing over to her fate, but upon a scene of reconciliation, rejuvenation.

A girl's loss of virginity, bittersweet but not necessarily tragic. Not today. A girl's coming-of-age that involves her succumbing to, but then rejecting, the "trashy dreams" of her pop teenage culture. "Where Are You Going, Where Have You Been?" defines itself as allegorical in its conclusion: Death and Death's chariot (a funky souped-up convertible) have come for the Maiden. Awakening is, in the story's final lines, moving out into the sunlight where Arnold Friend waits:

> "My sweet little blue-eyed girl," he said in a half-sung sigh that had nothing to do with [Connie's] brown eyes but was taken up just the same by the vast sunlit reaches of the land behind him and on all sides of him—so much land that Connie had never seen before and did not recognize except to know that she was going to it.

—a conclusion impossible to transfigure into film.

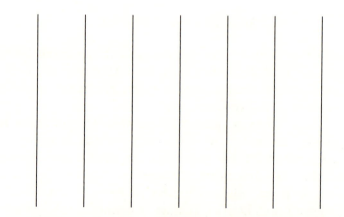

"STATE-OF-THE-ART CAR": THE FERRARI TESTAROSSA

Speak of the Ferrari Testarossa to men who know cars and observe their immediate visceral response: the virtual dilation of their eyes in sudden focused *interest*. The Testarossa!—that domestic rocket of a sports car, sleek, low-slung, aggressively wide; startlingly beautiful even in the eyes of non–car aficionados; so spectacular a presence on the road that—as I can personally testify—heads turn, faces break into childlike smiles in its wake. As one observer has noted, the Testarossa drives "civilians" crazy.

Like a very few special cars, the Ferrari Testarossa is

in fact a meta-car, a poetic metaphor or trope: an *object* raised to the level of a near-spiritual *value*. Of course it has a use—as a Steinway concert grand or a Thoroughbred racing horse has a use—but its significance hovers above and around mere use. What can one say about a street car (as opposed to a racing car) capable of traveling 177 effortless miles per hour?—accelerating, as it does, again without effort, from 0 mph to 60 mph in 5 seconds, 107 mph in 13.3 seconds? A car that sells for approximately $104,000—if you can get one? (The current waiting period is twelve months and will probably get longer.) There are said to be no more than 450 Testarossas in private ownership in the United States; only about three hundred models are made by Ferrari yearly. So popular has the model become, due in part to its much-publicized presence in the television series *Miami Vice* (in which, indeed, fast cars provide a sort of subtextual commentary on the men who drive them), that a line of child-sized motorized "Testarossas" is now being marketed—which extravagant toys range in price from $3,500 to $13,000. (Toys bought by parents who don't want to feel guilty, as one Ferrari dealer remarked.)

For all its high-tech styling, its racing-car image, the Ferrari Testarossa is a remarkably easy car to drive: its accelerative powers are first unnerving, then dangerously seductive. You think you are traveling at about 60 miles per hour when in fact you are moving toward 100 miles per hour (with your radar detector—"standard issue for this model"—in operation). In the luxury-leather seats, low, of course, and accommodatingly wide, you have the vertiginous impression of being somehow below the surface of the very pavement, skimming, flying, *rocketing* past vehicles moving at ordinary speeds; as if in a dream, or an "action" film. (Indeed, viewed through the discreetly tinted windshield of a Testarossa, the world, so swiftly passing, looks subtly altered: less assertive in its dimensions, rather more like "background.") Such speeds are heady, intoxicating, clearly addictive: if you are moving at 120 mph so smoothly, why not 130 mph? why not 160 mph? why not the limit—if, indeed, there *is* a limit? "Gusty/ Emotions on wet roads on autumn nights" acquire a new significance in a car of such unabashed romance. What godly maniacal power: you have only to depress the accelerator of the Ferrari Testarossa and you're at the horizon. Or beyond.

The mystique of high-performance cars has always intrigued me with its very opacity. Is it lodged sheerly in speed?—mechanical ingenuity?—the "art" of a finely tuned beautifully styled vehicle (as the mere physical fact of a Steinway piano constitutes "art")?—the adrenal thrill of courting death? Has it primarily to do with display (that of male game fowl, for instance)? Or with masculine prowess of a fairly obvious sort? (Power being, as the cultural critic Henry Kissinger once observed, the ultimate aphrodisiac.)

Or is it bound up with the phenomenon of what the American economist Thorstein Veblen so wittily analyzed as "conspicious consumption" in his classic *Theory of the Leisure Class* (1899)—Veblen's theory being that the consumption of material goods is determined not by the inherent value of goods but by the social standing derived from their consumption. (Veblen noted how in our capitalistic-democratic society there is an endless "dynamics" of style as the wealthiest class ceaselessly strives to distinguish itself from the rest of society and its habits of consumption trickle down to lower levels.)

Men who work with high-performance cars, however, are likely to value them as ends in themselves: they have no time for theory, being so caught up, so mesmerized, in practice. To say that certain cars at certain times determine the "state-of-the-art" is to say that such machinery, on its most refined levels, constitutes a serious and speculative and ever-changing (improving?) art. The Ferrari Testarossa is not a *car* in the generic sense in which, say, a Honda Accord—which my husband and I own—is a *car*. (For one thing, the Accord has about 90 horsepower; the Testarossa 380.) Each Ferrari is more or less unique, possessed of its own mysterious personality; its peculiar ghost-in-the-machine. "It's a good car," I am told, with typical understatement, by a Testarossa owner named Bill Kontes, "—a *good* car." He pauses, and adds, "But not an antique. This is a car you can actually drive."

(Though it's so precious—the lipstick-red model in particular such an attention-getter—that you dare not park it in any marginally public place. Meta-cars arouse emotions at all points of the spectrum.)

Bill Kontes, in partnership with John Melniczuk, owns and operates Checkered Flag Cars in Vineland, New Jersey—a dealership of such choice content (high-performance exotic cars, "vintage" classics, others) as to make it a veritable Phillips Collection amid its larger rivals in the prestige car market. It was by way of their hospitality that I was invited to test-drive the Ferrari Testarossa for *Quality,* though my only qualifications would seem to have been that I knew how to drive a car. (Not known to Mr. Kontes and Mr. Melniczuk was the ambiguous fact that I did once own, in racier days, a sports car of a fairly modest species—a Fiat Spider also in audacious lipstick-red. I recall that it was always stalling. That it gave up, so to speak, along a melancholy stretch of interstate highway in the approximate vicinity of Gary, Indiana, emitting actual flames from its exhaust. That the garage owner to whose garage it was ignominiously

towed stared at it and said contemptuously, "A pile of junk!"
That we sold it soon afterward and never bought another
"sports" car again.)

It was along a semideserted stretch of South Jersey
road that Mr. Kontes turned the Ferrari Testarossa over to
me, gallantly, and surely bravely: and conscious of the
enormity of the undertaking—a sense, very nearly, that the
honor of "woman writerhood" might be here at stake, a co-
lossal blunder or actual catastrophe reflecting not only upon
the luckless perpetrator but upon an entire generation and
gender—I courageously drove the car, and, encouraged by
Mr. Kontes, and by the mysterious powers of the radar detector to detect the presence of uniformed and sanctioned
enforcers of the law (which law, I fully understand, *is* for
our own good and in the best and necessary interests of the
commonwealth), I did in fact accelerate through all five gears
to a speed rather beyond one I'd anticipated: though not to
120 mph, which was Mr. Kontes's fairly casual speed a few
minutes previously. (This particular Testarossa, new to
Vineland, had been driven at 160 mph by Mr. Melniczuk
the other day, along a predawn stretch of highway presumably sanctioned by the radar detector. To drive behind the
Testarossa, as I also did, and watch it—suddenly—ease away
toward the horizon is an eerie sight: if you don't look closely
you're likely to be startled into asking, Where did it go?)

But the surprise of the Testarossa, *pace Miami Vice*
and the hyped-up media image, is that it is an easy, even
comfortable car to drive: user-friendly, as the newly coined
cliché would have it. It reminded me not at all of the tricky
little Spider I'd quite come to hate by the time of our parting but, oddly, of the unnerving but fiercely exhilarating experience of being behind the controls—so to speak—of a
two-seater open-cockpit plane. (My father flew sporty air-
planes years ago, and my childhood is punctuated with im-

ages of flight: the wind-ravaged open-cockpit belonged to a former navy bomber recycled for suburban airfield use.) As the Testarossa was accelerated I felt that visceral sense of an irresistibly gathering and somehow condensing power—"speed" being in fact a mere distillation or side effect of power—and, within it, contained by it, an oddly humble sense of human smallness, frailty. One of the perhaps unexamined impulses behind high-speed racing must be not the mere "courting" of death but, on a more primary level, its actual pre-experience; its taste.

But what have such thoughts to do with driving a splendid red Ferrari Testarossa in the environs of Vineland, New Jersey, one near-perfect autumn day, an afternoon shading romantically into dusk? Quite beyond, or apart from, the phenomenal machinery in which Bill Kontes and I were privileged to ride I was acutely conscious of the spectacle we and it presented to others' eyes. Never have I seen so many heads turn!—so much staring!—*smiling!* While the black Testarossa may very well resemble, as one commentator has noted, Darth Vader's personal warship, the lipstick-red model evokes smiles of pleasure, envy, awe—most pointedly in young men, of course, but also in older, even elderly women. Like royalty, the Testarossa seems to bestow a gratuitous benison upon its spectators. Merely to watch it pass is to feel singled out, if, perhaps, rather suddenly drab and anonymous. My thoughts drifted onto the pomp of kings and queens and maharajahs, the legendary excesses of the Gilded Age of Morgan, Carnegie, Rockefeller, Mellon, Armour, McCormick, et al.—Edith Rockefeller McCormick, just to give one small example, served her dinner guests on china consisting of over a thousand pieces containing 11,000 ounces of gold—the Hope Diamond, and Liz Taylor's diamonds, and the vision of Mark Twain, in impeccable dazzling white, strolling on Fifth Avenue while inwardly chafing at his increasing lack of privacy. If one is on public display one is of course obliged not to be conscious of it; driving a $104,000 car means being equal to the car in dignity and style. Otherwise the public aspect of the performance is contaminated: we are left with merely conspicuous consumption, an embarrassment in such times of economic trepidation and worldwide hunger.

Still, it's the one incontrovertible truth about the Ferrari Testarossa: no matter who is behind the wheel people stare, and they stare in admiration. Which might not otherwise be the case.

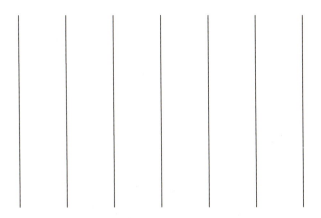

BUDAPEST JOURNAL: MAY 1980

In the spring of 1980, accompanied by my husband, Raymond Smith, I visited a number of European countries under the auspices of the United States Information Agency, including Poland and Hungary. Following is an edited version of a journal kept in Budapest.

21 May 1980. Deftly taken through Customs at the Warsaw airport by a Polish liaison official, hence avoiding—guiltily, shamefacedly—the long slow-moving lines other less fortunate travelers must endure. One gathers from remarks made frequently in Warsaw that private travel in this part of the world is not generally encouraged and is rather an ordeal. *You will be going next to Budapest? I envy you.* Our Polish acquaintances—writers, translators, professors—told us repeatedly during our week in Warsaw that we would like Budapest immensely: Budapest is the city Poles visit on holiday if they can afford it. *Budapest is a jewel of a city. I envy you.* On one of our last evenings in Warsaw a specialist in American literature at the University of Warsaw took us out to his favorite restaurant—a Hungarian restaurant.

On the Soviet plane, en route to Budapest: Russian flight attendants in chic blue suits, white turtleneck blouses; long hair braided and fixed at the back of the head and caught with a barrette. The international stamp of a certain kind of cosmetic prettiness: very red lips, eyes carefully enlarged by mascara and pencil, emphatically rouged cheeks. These young women seem to have stepped out of American advertisements. (They are serving us box lunches, minimal in both quantity and quality: cheese, cold cuts, slightly stale rye bread. And Pepsi-Cola—ubiquitous in East Europe—in small plastic cups.) Seated at the rear of the plane we are forced to endure dreadful American rock music for much of the flight, turned up to full volume. Our trash culture seems to follow us everywhere, even in anti-imperialist zones.

I have told no one that I am apprehensive about visiting Budapest because my family background is partly Hungarian on my mother's side. My grandparents emigrated to the States steerage class at the turn of the century, not yet married but acquainted, having been urged to come by relatives already settled in the Buffalo, New York, area. My grandfather's name was Büs—Americanized to Bush; my grandmother's, Torony. Their relatives had written that life in the States was far more prosperous and promising than in Budapest in the early 1900s, yet when they came to Buffalo things were very difficult for them, as one might expect. (I never read Upton Sinclair's *The Jungle* without a powerful reaction; surely Sinclair was describing my grandparents' lives as well as those of his hapless Lithuanian immigrants.) Most of what was Hungarian in my life was ignored, or denied, or repressed, very likely for reasons of necessity; too personal for me to describe. I will say that my grandfather's Hungarian temperament asserted itself in ways that sound flamboyant and colorful if seen through the retrospective of years and the prudent filter of language; and that my grandmother's refusal to learn to read English—she'd come to the States at the age of sixteen and reasoned that it was too late for her to learn, though she lived well into her eighties—is associated in my mind with a peculiar sort of Old World obstinacy and self-defeat. There has been no contact between members of my mother's family and their Hungarian kin in sixty years, and though my mother can speak Hungarian with one of her sisters, neither my brother nor I knows a word of it. That a number of my books have been translated into Hungarian and are said to sell fairly well there has always made me feel slightly guilty: the languages I've studied are French and German, and, apart from admiring the Hungarian surrealist Géza Csáth, the contemporary novelist and cultural critic Georg Konrad, and scattered translations of Hungarian poets in recent volumes edited by William Smith and Miklós Vajda, I know virtually nothing about Hungarian literature.

And Budapest turns out to be a jewel of a city indeed, like no other city I have ever visited.

□　□　□

22 May 1980. Traveling under the benign auspices of the United States Information Agency, as guests of the Hungarian government and Hungarian PEN, we are put up at the luxurious Budapest Hilton overlooking the Danube and Parliament House on the facing embankment. (At night the Parliament dome is illuminated, rather like a neo-Gothic version of the White House. It's an extraordinarily beautiful building, not old—built in the late nineteenth century—with pinnacles, allegorical statues, stone latticework, columns, and numberless smaller domes surrounding the central dome.) We know ourselves privileged, and we intend to be grateful. From our splendid hotel room window we look down not only at Parliament but immediately out onto stone steps, cobblestone walks, immaculately tended lawns; then the Danube. Our hotel room, indeed the entire Hilton, built with ingenious care and taste above and partly in the ruins of a thirteenth-century monastery, are in painful contrast to the run-down condition of the Europejski Hotel in which we stayed in Warsaw. The Hilton is a typical American hotel in every particular except for the fact—absurd in theory, rather wonderful in execution—that it has somehow managed to incorporate an actual ruin (towers, turrets, cloisters, walled pathways) into its structure. The Hungarians we meet appear to have no strong opinions about the Hilton or about the odd marriage of American imperialism and Communist shrewdness it represents; or, at any rate, no opinions they share with us. One of the striking features of the hotel is that, from the outside, its windows are bronze-tinted and mirror the Danube, the sky, the ruins, a nearby church: self-effacing yet majestic at the same time.

Budapest in late May is a city of lilacs. The sweet, languid, rather sleepy smell of lilacs wafts everywhere. And it is a city of lovers, many of them quite middle-aged. Walking with their arms around each other, embracing and kissing on park benches. A sensuousness very much bound up (it seems to me) with the heady ubiquitous smell of lilacs.

Cobblestone walks and streets, narrow passageways, friezes, iron grillwork, ornate façades of buildings, steep hills, many carefully restored old churches. . . . This is a haunting city, medieval, Gothic, neo-Gothic, yet modern in many respects; one's first impression is that it is rather Western (in East European terms, that is) despite its architecture. Certainly the Hungarians we see appear far happier and freer than their Polish compatriots. The economy is visibly healthier, the government less restrictive. A young writer who takes us sightseeing in his Soviet-built Fiat tells us proudly that he is able to visit England and Japan frequently in connection with his work. (Though another, older, Hungarian writer tells us that all Hungarians vividly remember the catastrophe of 1956, the short-lived rebellion, the terrible consequences. We know the tanks are close by, waiting, he says. But we must live.)

□ □ □

23 May 1980. Struck by the disquietingly familiar look of strangers glimpsed on the streets: the eyes, the cheekbones, skin coloring, the general bearing. Several of the Hungarians to whom I have been introduced (including the young writer, himself part Jewish) resemble me more closely than my brother does, and far closer than either of my parents. Uncanny sensation!—as if I had stepped into a dream. Yet I behave perfectly normally, impersonating the American writer "Joyce Carol Oates."

Prices are high in Hungary. Our camera, stolen this morning (with remarkable adroitness: my husband had set it down on a ledge close by, we'd turned our backs only a minute), would cost $1,000 to replace, though in the States it had probably cost less than $200. (Out of a desire not to upset our Hungarian hosts we are saying that our camera was "lost.")

A Hungarian cultural official alludes frankly to Hungarian dislike of Germans and Russians. ("Germans and Russians"—invariably linked, both here and in Poland.) Yet he's critical of his countrymen as well; the Hungarian people, he says, are constitutionally incapable of unifying their strengths. During the two months of the Revolution, for instance, in 1956 (called here the "Counterrevolution") there were no less than fifty factions opposing the Russians. . . . Which leads me to think of my stubborn Hungarian grandparents, and to speculate, as one really shouldn't, about national traits, "characteristics." Perhaps they are legendary. Or perhaps historical.

The hooded dwarf Telesphorus, the "bringer of the end"— on a red marble sarcophagus. An ancient gnomish gargoyle entrusted with the task of escorting the dead to the underworld.

The loneliness of travel in a country in which one's language is not spoken: underscoring the loneliness of travel anywhere: the loneliness of being.

□   □   □

24 May 1980. Walking for hours, miles. A sense of exhilaration bordering on intoxication. This is a city of steep hills, narrow winding streets, unexpected archways, traffic-clogged squares, culs-de-sac. Gellért Hill looking dramatically down upon the residential hills of Buda and the more urban, flatter Pest (these towns were united only recently, I learn to my surprise—1872); the "beautiful blue" Danube which is in fact an exquisite silver-blue in the sunshine, very placid, and indeed beautiful; in the distance Margitsziget (Margaret Island, where the famed health spa is located); a suspension bridge; the Sztálin-híd (Stalin Bridge); the cross of old Matthias Church; the bronze-glaring façade of the Hilton; a good deal of traffic, ceaseless streams over the bridges, an air that tastes of exhaust and lilacs. I keep seeing half-familiar faces, I keep feeling a tug of recognition, pleasurable yet disturbing; a melancholy predicament. I have been told that beneath their gaiety Hungarians are melancholy people and of course it's true: I know the temperament from within.

We visit Matthias Church, seven hundred years old, shamelessly tourist-ridden. A mass is in session and I am surprised to see girl altarboys. The priest is elderly, stiff, slow-moving, with a high nasal droning voice, a resolutely soporific manner. But the church interior is extraordinary: every square inch is decorated, like a body totally tattooed. There is a gorgeous rose window, there are vertiginous zigzag designs on the walls, a baroque nightmare or a baroque fantasy depending upon one's taste. Dimensions seem out of scale: the pulpit, for instance, richly carved, is enormous, with a canopy that must measure ten feet in height; the priest in his heavy ornamental vestments—white and red satin, gold brocade—looks dwarfed, doll-sized. Around us people are milling and shuffling constantly. Tourists and worshipers both, evidently. The atmosphere is almost psychedelic—noisy, crowded, eerie, mesmerizing. So very different from my memory of attending mass back home, years ago, that it seems another religion entirely; a truly foreign religion.

A large PEN meeting in a municipal building in downtown Pest. It occurs to me that virtually everything Americans write is perceived as allegorical and self-consciously "American" abroad: what is idiosyncratic becomes symbolic. Or is it that we write parables of American life without knowing what we do? During this lengthy program I am distracted a good deal by a woman seated to the left in the first row of the audience. She is in her thirties; with large eyes, striking features, a rather melancholy cast to her face; brown hair, an olive-pale skin, sloping shoulders. Of course she reminds me of myself. I watch her covertly, I'm frankly fascinated by her. We might be cousins. We might be sisters. . . . At the end of the program I am introduced to her: she is one of my Hungarian translators: she knows me, as she says shyly, very well—my writing, that is. And how wonderful that at last we should meet. We stare and stare at each other, not quite able to acknowledge how very much we resemble each other. We might be sisters, perhaps we *are* sisters, who is to say? Her name is Annamária Széky.

□ □ □

25 May 1980. Margitsziget Spa, Budapest. Ancient artesian wells, medicinal waters, and hot springs, known in the early fifteenth century and most fully realized in the nineteenth century; even today the magic waters are being investigated by the Budapest Institute of Balneology.

The thermal waters of Margitsziget Spa have played a prominent role in the curing of the sick. Rheumatic diseases of motorial organs, degenerative-inflammation diseases of muscles and joints, hypertension, myocardium, coronary artery disease, catarrhous diseases of the ureter, arthritis (polyarthritis and chronic), spondylarthritis ankylopoietica, discopathy, neuotis, myositis, tendovaginitis, bone-disease locomotive disorders, gout, old age, chronic inflammation of female sexual organs, defatigation, catarrhous respiratory ailments. . . . The miracle waters are 70° Centigrade. Consisting of sulphate which decomposes gradually (with no repellent odor). Also available are low- and high-frequency electric treatments: iontophoresis, galvanic current, supersonic wave, interference current, microwave. Also, mechanotherapy. Warning: If you suffer from leukemia, tuberculosis, malignant tumors, spinal sclerosis, thrombosis, tracheal asthma, or hyperthyreosis, Margitsziget Spa is not for you.

The diseases of a bygone era sound so quaint, their treatments so quixotic, one has the mistaken notion that perhaps suffering too was inconsequential.

□   □   □

26 May 1980. The busyness of the city, the welcome anonymity of the streets in Pest. When we are not in our official roles—accompanied by liaison officers or the embassy's
cultural attaché—we are treated fairly rudely by shopkee-
pers, waiters, waitresses; yet perhaps it isn't rudeness precisely, merely a sullen withheld charm. Where the Hungarian intellectuals whom we've met are uncommonly gracious,
the man-in-the-street, so to speak, isn't gracious at all: why
should he be?

An hour at Europa publishers; a luxurious view of the Danube and Parliament. The director of the publishing house
speaks of his astounding publishing empire through an interpreter, not pausing to remark that after all if one is *the*
publishing house of an entire language, responsible for
translating into Hungarian all of the world's literature from
Chaucer to "Joyce Carol Oates," it cannot be surprising that
one's list is formidable. Brandy is served; "Traubisoda"; cof-
fee in tiny cups (very bitter). Ritual courtesies. "Our mil-
lionaire uncle, the Hungarian state, supports us if we need
money," Mr. Domokus says with a pleasant smile. I am informed that an extraordinary number of copies—can it be
42,000?—in a *second* edition?—of a volume of my short stories has just been printed. And Europa is planning 35,000
copies for the first edition of the translated *A Garden of
Earthly Delights* (which surely sold little more than 10,000
copies in the States when it was first published in 1967).
And the population of Hungary is perhaps ten million people, of whom two million live in Budapest, of whom how
many might be readers of serious literature?

Visit to the village of Szentendre, sped along in a hired lim-
ousine, the young Hungarian chauffeur with hair styled like

Elvis Presley's, pomade, sideburns, slick oiled wings of hair meeting at the back of his head, *Texas* stitched on his denim jacket. Here in this famous little village—yes, it is genuinely picturesque, preserved, "quaint," very much worth the hour's trip—we visit a Byzantine church museum; an exhibit of presumably Matisse-inspired paintings; an unusually interesting exhibit of sculpture and ceramic works by an artist named Margit Kovács—famous in Hungary; unknown, unfortunately, elsewhere. (But one really can't be sentimental about the quality of life, as it might be called, in Hungary. The general atmosphere of bossiness, rudeness; a sort of Teutonic sternness; the futility of certain mechanical customs.) In the Margit Kovács museum, middle-aged women guards, uniformed, call out snappish orders to visitors again and again—and again—and *again*—simply because no signs are posted indicating which way one is to turn. Why not post a sign? thinks an American. But no: the women guards are jealously watching; this is their place, this is their role, to mechanically snap out orders to amiable if confused tourists, both foreign and Hungarian; never will the tradition be violated, it must be ingrained in the very soul. And in virtually every restaurant we have gone to, unfailingly slow service, distracted waiters and waitresses, an air of awkward improvisation, as if each customer, each meal, were somehow unexpected, an interruption of the quotidian. Yet they mean well, surely? They mean to be friendly though they so rarely smile? Even here in touristy Szentendre, which must have thousands of visitors each year, the best restaurant (serving traditional "peasant" food) is crowded and ill-managed, with soiled tablecloths, no napkins, greasy French fries (that ubiquitous libel against the French!), stale bread, no mineral water, not even any tea . . . not even any *tea?* One is thrown back upon the dismaying pettiness of travel, which must mimic, in its obsession with trivia, with elementary creature comforts and assurances, the humiliating circumscriptions of old age. Our Hungarian hosts apologize for the inadequacy of the restaurant. They are never prepared, we are told, for the many customers who arrive.

Hypnosis: the ritual of speaking (elaborately, slowly, with appropriate gestures) through an interpreter. One looks of course not at the interpreter (the fiction being that he or she does not exist) but at the party being addressed. It's uncanny, gradually mesmerizing, hearing one's words given significance by way of this ritual; hearing then the always-unintelligible response—an outburst of wonderful sounds that constitute a "language" to which one hasn't the code.

Fantasies slowly diminish of meeting remote cousins. Büs, Torony. Who might they be? And what connection between us? The writer purposefully mythologizes; is in danger (in life, not in art) of seeing what might not be present and failing to see what might very well be present, staring one in the face.

□ □ □

27 May 1980. A besieged country, a bloody history, not yet completed. The Hungarians await deliverance, but from what?—history itself? Ottó says that he was born during an air raid in 1944; Anna can vividly recall the seven-week siege of the Russians against the Germans; László speaks of the days and weeks of the "Counterrevolution" of 1956. We are told (by Americans, not Hungarians) of a mass graveyard in one of the city's suburbs—very likely in Rákoskeresztúr—a "prisoners' cemetery" which is under constant Soviet guard and surrounded by barbed wire. In it are an unknown number of men and women who were executed after the Soviets invaded Budapest in November of 1956; but none of the families of the executed is ever allowed to visit the cemetery. "In fact, the existence of the cemetery itself is a state secret."

Melancholia deeply ingrained in the spirit, hence the propensity toward laughter, gaiety, infectious high spirits. When we are part of a group here in Budapest—in a splendid restaurant near Castle Hill, for instance, and in a café near the Pest embankment—yet again in the American embassy, at a small reception arranged for us this afternoon—we feel extraordinarily happy; very much at home. And then the dilemma of the Hungarians strikes us anew. That they are not (politically, hence in any way) free; that they closely resemble us yet are not us; haven't our privileges, our good fortune. And yet they aren't bitter. Ottó speaks quietly of the "difficulties" of being a Jew in Hungary. He tells of his grandparents, "shipped to Germany" in March 1944. As we walk along a narrow path near the river, we are conscious of several Hungarian youths in black leather motorcycle jackets, eyeing us curiously; on the verge, it seems, of jeering. But nothing happens. They turn aside, they ignore us, we pretend not to be aware of them. But Ottó is nervous and falls silent.

"After a wait of twenty minutes they are seated at a table in the noisy restaurant. The table is covered with a coarse red tablecloth, soiled. There is only goulash soup on the menu—fatty meat of an indefinable species, potatoes, globules of salty grease. Stale crusts of bread to be dunked in the soup and chewed hungrily. For they *are* hungry. They will eat quickly, like everyone else in the restaurant, without needing to taste their food."

Everywhere lilacs, the lush confectionery smell of lilacs. Even small boys run through the streets with ragged bouquets.

Cobblestone lanes . . . stone steps . . . cannons displayed along a rampart . . . odd charming slapdash houses, very narrow, jammed together . . . postwar "modern" houses, rather square-built, grim, with grillwork over the windows . . . then again there are the "medieval" houses (rebuilt after the war, when the destruction of baroque buildings exposed the older structures): queer, wonderfully appealing, possessed of a storybook quirkiness: quite right, one thinks, for a city of such hills. Turkish-built bastions, some with the remains of dungeons; battlements; long curving stairs leading nowhere. Outside our hotel room is the locally famous Fisherman's Bastion, built in a fairly recent time (late nineteenth century) in a "romanesque" style. And behind the formidable Hilton are hills of "medieval," "baroque," and "classical" houses, many with striking façades. Statues high in niches, ornamental work around the windows and doors, great attention to detail. Perhaps the most interesting fact about Budapest architecture is that war damage and reconstruction exposed older structures, some medieval, some claimed to be four thousand years old (in the area of the Royal Palace). In one neighborhood an entire network of medieval defense walls was discovered. The Kafkaesque fantasy of a secret city beneath one's familiar city. A dream not one's own hovering close beneath the threshold of consciousness. These indefinable dimensions of the soul . . . where "I" is not "I" but "they."

In Budapest, the Poles are pitied; Warsaw was "formerly a beautiful city." Ah, but Prague, truly the jewel of Middle Europe!—it is too late for us to see Prague, we are told. Too late, too late, it is really not Prague any longer.

Our Hungarian hosts take us to hear gypsy music; we dine on Hungarian cuisine of the highest quality; and here, where most of the diners are foreigners, the service too is of the highest quality; the linen tablecloths are assuredly not soiled. Affluent Budapest, rather garish, old-fashioned, splendid and overblown, inaccessible to most Hungarians. (The Hungarian forint, for instance, is not accepted at the Hilton and at other first-class places. Hard currency only—the American dollar, the formidable deutsche mark.) Ottó told us of the bitter irony in the fact that busloads of well-to-do West Germans visit Budapest regularly; they dine in expensive restaurants that were formerly Nazi fortifications and headquarters, restaurants few Hungarians can afford. Thus, the whimsical cycles of history. But must one be bitter? One *must* live.

The tourist in East Europe quickly becomes aware of the servitude of an entire class of people; and that class of considerable size. For instance, the chambermaids in the hotels. Some are in their sixties, some are as young as fifteen or sixteen. They wear ill-fitting uniforms and canvas lace-up boots with open toes and heels. They appear to be working at odd hours, very late at night sometimes. Pushing carts, sorting laundry, dragging vacuum cleaners along the carpeted corridors; scrubbing sinks, showers, toilets; quite oblivious of the foreigners they serve; not ignoring but truly not hearing the English spoken behind their backs. Strong, muscled, attractive women, clearly women who feel no self-pity and no self-consciousness.

☐ ☐ ☐

28 May 1980. An autographing session at a bookstore in Pest; a long queue of "readers" of "Joyce Carol Oates"; even television cameras. Many handshakes, many kind comments, translated by way of Miss Annamária Széky, who is more or less in charge of me. I am a little light-headed with telling so many people of my Hungarian background, hearing the same words, saying the same words, buoyed along by that sense of euphoria that only certain very intense and very temporary occasions evoke. Though I don't feel quite myself, still less do I feel like the American author whose *A Földi Gyönyörök Kertje (A Garden of Earthly Delights)* so many people are buying. . . . Lovely Budapest: I don't know where I am, but I think I am at home.

There are no speed limits posted in the country, and there are no official speed limits in the city of Budapest; the reason why remains unclear. Thus everyone drives at his own speed, following his own whim: on treacherous steep hills, on narrow cobblestone streets, along wide congested avenues, across bridges, in the very heart of Pest. Our Hungarian chauffeur with his rakish d.a. haircut and his *Texas* denim scarcely notices how close he comes to striking pedestrians, bicyclists, other cars; he is simply driving his car, performing his function with admirable skill. And he hasn't had an accident yet.

☐ ☐ ☐

29 May 1980. Our last day in Budapest; tomorrow we fly out to Copenhagen. We are feeling beforehand a sense of regret and loss. The tourist may see and acquire all that he can afford, and feel gratified, ready to move on to the next spectacle, but the traveler inevitably feels a sense of incompletion and dissatisfaction . . . a knowledge that in some indefinable way he has failed. But at what he has failed, at what he imagines he might have succeeded, he doesn't know. The euphoric expectations of the first day of a visit give way with discomforting rapidity to the melancholy sense of loss of the last day: this too is a pattern, a ritual of travel.

It's a dazzling sunny Sunday. We are sitting in an outdoor café in Matthias Square; close about us large buoyant Hungarian families are treating themselves to exquisite pastries, tea, beer. So supremely rich and effortless does life seem at such times, one might very well doubt the invisible realms (of politics, for instance, and "history") and their power. . . . I recall with embarrassment the awkward comment made by a colleague of mine (a fellow writer, a New Yorker) in Warsaw a week ago, at a PEN program: he said speculatively that censorship might be "helpful" for a writer in that it forces him or her to invent strategies, select metaphors . . . or whatever . . . and his words trailed off into silence . . . and no one spoke, not even to challenge him . . . and what the Poles were thinking, or what they said later to one another, an American can only guess.

(The predilection for Americans to read themselves into others; seeing their faces mirrored in the faces of uncomprehending strangers.)

Eleven o'clock, and the bells of Matthias Church are ringing. Mourning doves circle overhead, the sky is a faint filmy blue, the sunlight very white. I am reading a highly poetic and rather mysterious short story by one of the young writers we met, György Odze, in the *New Hungarian Quarterly*. (Odze and I have promised to write to each other after I return to the States. I will write to him, in fact I will send him a package of a number of American paperback books, but I will never hear from him; and wonder—was the package lost? confiscated by the Hungarian authorities? Did Odze ever receive it? Or might his own reply have been confiscated?) These mysteries. East Europe in our time.

This brief visit to Budapest, from which my impoverished grandparents fled some eighty years ago, has been an extraordinary experience in ways I will never be able to define. Writers characteristically seek images to convey emotions too subtle and too elusive for words, but what is the image I seek?—not a stolen camera, surely?—an inexpensive Japanese-made camera, shrewdly lifted while its owners were looking in another direction? I envision our roll of film, partly used, taken out and unceremoniously tossed away. Perhaps, though, if the thief is economical, and not overly prudent, he will take his own pictures on the remainder of the roll and have all the snapshots developed together . . . a mysterious mix; but evidence, perhaps, of theft. Yet I hope he took that course. I love the cavalier air of the gesture: careless, pragmatic, daring, supremely Hungarian.

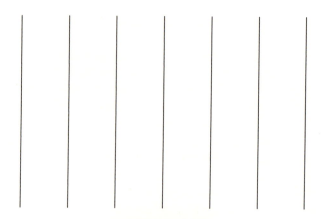

VISIONS
OF DETROIT

Hazy skylines. Chemical-red sunsets. A yeasty gritty taste to the air—how easy to become addicted! And elsewhere, whatever constitutes elsewhere, will never quite satisfy. Much motion—Brownian, ceaseless—mesmerizing—a landscape of grids interrupted by sharp-slanted drives, freeways snaking through neighborhoods, cutting streets in two. A city of streets. Freeways. Overpasses, railroad tracks, razed buildings and weedy vacant lots and billboards, and houses, houses, blocks and acres and galaxies of houses, stretching out forever. I shut my eyes and suddenly I am there again driving south along Livernois in the rain, meaning to get on the John Lodge just above Fenkell. Or I am driving on Six Mile Road east to Woodward. Or making the turn off Eight Mile and Litchfield, grateful to be home. (But which home? It must be the first house my husband and I owned when we were new to Detroit, young instructors at Wayne State University and the University of Detroit respectively—a conventionally attractive two-story four-bedroom "colonial" house with white aluminum siding, blue shutters, a large corner lot, many trees, at the corner of Woodstock Drive and Litchfield. The price, in 1963?—$17,900.)

Those streets. Those years. *Livernois. Gratiot. Grand River. John R. Outer Drive. Michigan. Cass. 2nd. 3rd. Woodward. Jefferson. Vernor. Fort. Jos. Campau. Dequindre. Warren. Hancock. Beaubien. Brush. Freud. Randolph.* Ceaseless motion, the pulse of the city. The beat. The beat. A place of romance, the quintessential American city.

We were so happy there, why did we leave?

We arrived in the early summer of 1962 and left in the early summer of 1968. A brief six years but a lifetime, in fact, a sentimental education never to be repeated for me. We lived for the first year on the second floor of a two-story apartment building on Manderson Road, just south of Palmer Park and north of Six Mile/McNichols Road: I was an instructor in English at the University of Detroit (four courses, two of them expository writing—and I loved it) and my husband, Raymond Smith, was an instructor in English at Wayne State University (though soon to be invited to join the faculty at the University of Windsor, across the border in Canada). Our second house, on Woodstock, was acquired perhaps a year later, or sometime in 1964 (I remember typing out the final draft of *Expensive People* there—a novel not to be published until 1968, when I too was teaching at the University of Windsor). Our third and largest house was on Sherbourne Road just above Seven Mile, on the corner of Berkeley, two or three blocks from Livernois. During the 1967 riots—not a singular "riot," and not truly a "race riot"—there was looting and burning on Livernois but our neighborhood was not seriously disturbed, and I doubt that we would have moved away, at least at that time, had we not both been teaching at the University of Windsor, a hardy commuting trip away.

So much of my writing from approximately 1963 to 1976 centers upon or has been emotionally inspired by Detroit and its suburbs (Birmingham, Bloomfield Hills, to a lesser degree Grosse Pointe) that it is impossible for me now to extract the historical from the fictional. Life is fecund, art is selective. Even the photographer, that most apparently forthright of artists, isolates the subject, enhances it, drops out the surrounding world. If we had never come to the city of Detroit I would have been a writer (indeed, I had already written my first two books before coming here, aged twenty-three) but Detroit, my "great" subject, made me the person I am, consequently the writer I am—for better or worse. I see now in retrospect that the extraordinary emotional impact Detroit had on me in those years must have been partly due to the awakening of submerged memories of childhood and adolescence in and around the equally "great" city of Buffalo, New York. But Detroit was—still is?—Motor City, U.S.A. For a while Murder City, U.S.A.

The quintessential American city. That fast-beating stubborn heart.

* * *

(What *is* the motive for metaphor? the writer wonders. Why do some events, some people, some landscapes urban or rural fall upon us with an almost inhuman authority, dictating the terms of our most private fantasies, forcing upon us what amounts very nearly to a second birth—while others, most others, make virtually no impression at all and quickly fade? Why the desire to transcribe the physical world into the metaphorical?—into language? Why the hope to make of the temporary and fluid an artifact as "permanent" as the print, paper, and binding of a book?)

There's never any answer, it seems. We live what is random and are pierced by it, accept it, as Fate.

Detroit. Those streets. Those skies. Years. Less a city—for who has *seen* this city whole, even from the sky?—than a brooding presence, a force, larger and more significant than the sum of its parts. It is a curiosity of the writer's life that his or her books are codified transcripts of the secret emotional life of the writer along with being generally "about" other things, public matters. The years pass, however, and the secret life is forgotten except in outline, even the key to the code is haphazardly recalled, for past secrets are never so valuable—so tantalizingly secret—as those of the present. But the books remain, as testimonies of a kind. To the modest extent to which any book, any work of art, can assert itself as a unique entity in the world.

Still, the code isn't invariably so difficult to break. Private memory fades, public event remains. Much of my novel *Expensive People* did occur, if not in Birmingham, Michigan, strictly speaking, then in one or another Detroit suburb. *them* (1969) is partly made up of "composite" characters and events, clearly influenced by the disturbances of the long hot sum-

mer of 1967. *Cybele* (1979, originally published by Black
Sparrow Press and now reissued by Obelisk) is entirely a
Detroit/Detroit-suburban creation, whose predominant image is the view as one drives beyond Northland on the John
Lodge Freeway headed into Southfield and points beyond.
My play *Miracle Play* was inspired by drug dealing–related
crimes in the city in 1971, as reported in the *Detroit News*
and the *Detroit Free Press;* oddly, it was written in London,
England, during the sabbatical year 1971–72, as was—with
even more passion—*Do With Me What You Will* (1973),
surely the only novel in our language whose key scene occurs close by the statue of the Spirit of Detroit in downtown
Detroit.

I could not list the many stories in the collections *The Wheel
of Love, Marriages & Infidelities,* and *The Goddess* that would
have been unimaginable apart from Detroit. "A Middle-Class
Education" and "The Tryst" of the relatively recent *A Sentimental Education* (1980) are equally bound to their geographical sources—the first, Highland Park and the area
around the Fisher Building, West Grand and Woodward;
the second a fictitious neighborhood in Birmingham. A more
recent story, "Last Days," originally published in *Michigan
Quarterly Review* and reprinted in a collection, *Last Days*
(1984) is a reimagining of the Detroit tragedy that informed
an early story, "In the Region of Ice"—written in 1964, two
decades previous, and surely a very long time for a short
story to gestate.

□ □ □

I have not returned to Detroit since 1978, when my husband and I moved from Windsor to Princeton, New Jersey,
where we continue to live. So the spell has been lifting
gradually. Perhaps in truth it *has* lifted—barring stray frag-

ments of memory, unsought visions, of the kind given shape in some recent poems and in the story "Double Solitaire," included in a special issue of *Michigan Quarterly Review*. But do we really want our demons exorcized? And, if they are exorcized, what will take their place?

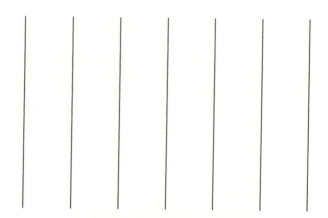

MEETING THE GORBACHEVS

A great man? All I see is the actor creating his own ideal image.
　　　　　　　　　　—Nietzsche

Listening to Mikhail Gorbachev's impassioned address in the rococo white-and-gold ballroom of the Soviet embassy on Sixteenth Street in Washington, D.C., on the late afternoon of 8 December 1987, in a heterogeneous gathering of some fifty fellow American "intellectuals" and "artists," I recalled these cryptic words of Nietzsche's, but wondered if my habitual skepticism, particularly regarding politics in its most public, theatrical mode, might be irrelevant here; unjustified. Simply because one of the world's most powerful men, indeed, the world's supreme Communist leader, the General Secretary of the Central Committee of the Communist Party of the Soviet Union, Mikhail Gorbachev, was speaking to us in warmly seductive tones, employing words reminiscent of the social mysticism of the sixties—*interrelatedness, integral, global peace, democratization*—and assuring us of matters that sounded almost literally too good to be true, as if our deepest, most desperate wishes were being uttered in an exotically foreign language and translated into our own, did it mean that these matters could not be true?—or even probable? Though the grim lessons of history suggest otherwise, and idealism's trajectory usually sinks rapidly downward, man is of all creatures the hopeful animal; and it is a hard task to resist believing in the very things (above all an end to the fanatic arms race of past decades: the suicidal stockpiling of nuclear weapons) that we have been talking about for so long. Shaking Mikhail Gorbachev's hand, looking the man in the eye—he is famed for making "eye contact" and is clearly happiest in such quasi-intimate public situations—one comes away with the visceral certitude that this is a person of surpassing integrity; a man of the utmost sincerity; somewhat larger than life, perhaps. And so brimming with energy! And a sense of his own historic worth! Yet one recalls too, more soberly, that the political enthusiasms of past eras (for "Uncle Joe" Stalin, for the bearded revolutionary Castro, for the ascetic Ayatollah Khomeni, among others) can look rather bleakly ironic in retrospect. History is the only true philosophy.

It was with the evident intention of circumnavigating, perhaps frustrating, conventional political and media channels, and speaking directly to a presumed intelligentsia, with a presumed power of its own to shape public opinion, that Gorbachev chose to arrange a special meeting at the Soviet embassy, on his own territory, so to speak, with American "intellectuals" and "artists" in the midst of his heroically crammed three-day schedule. Here, in an elegantly Old World sort of setting, with enormous crystal chandeliers hanging from the ceiling, and vases of white tulips on our tables, the already heated air given an added incandescence by ubiquitous television cameras, Gorbachev spoke with disarming candor of domestic Soviet problems, economic and moral; of the political necessities that brought *glasnost* into being; of his many-times-reiterated hope for world disarmament and peace; of his sense of the world's nations as "contradictory" yet "integral." Such words and noble concepts are hardly new but their utterance, by a Soviet leader of proven shrewdness and prescience, is certainly new; even rather astonishing. From where, within the repressive Soviet system, did such a man come? And how, and why? In Gorbachev, the personal anecdote has the weight of a political parable, conversationally, even confidentially, delivered: he told us of vacationing in Italy some years ago, with his wife, Raisa, and attending an evening entertainment in their hotel in which actors playing national types greeted one another and behaved in comically characteristic ways, and when the "American" and the "Russian" met each man looked stonily away without acknowledging the other. The Italian audience laughed at such idiotic behavior, Gorbachev said, and he was struck by the irony that two "such great nations" were at an impasse, and that the rest of the world should laugh. "I thought, why can't something be done to change our mutual attitudes? Why should the world find Americans and Russians so laughable?"

Though by this time Gorbachev had been speaking for perhaps a half hour without pause, only now and then glancing down, unobtrusively, at his notes, he is so practiced and charming a speaker that those of us who are usually stupefied by speeches remained attentive, even rapt, throughout. Yes, really, why can't something be done? The question hung in the air, eminently answerable. Though Paul Newman would afterward comment that Gorbachev is a gifted performer in whom you don't see the "machinery" of his technique, does it necessarily follow that histrionic gifts exclude sincerity? Must surface and substance be at odds?

I asked Henry Kissinger, seated beside me at our table, whether Mr. Gorbachev was radically different from other Soviet leaders he had known, and Kissinger paused, thought, and said, "This one is more skillful."

When, at about 10 P.M. on 30 November, the wholly unexpected telephone call came from the cultural attaché of the Soviet embassy in Washington, inviting me to meet Mr. Gorbachev and the U.S.S.R. ambassador to the United States, Yuri Dubinin, at a reception for artists, writers, and intellectuals the following week, I must confess that my first instinct was to decline: Thank you for the honor, I said, but I'm afraid I am too busy. (Such is the introvert's habitual response: did not William Faulkner laconically decline an invitation to dine at the White House, with the remark that it was too far to go for dinner?) But my husband was appalled and insisted I rethink my decision. It was a "historic" occasion, he said.

And so it was, and so I did, telephoning back the next morning to accept. And were spouses included in the invitation? I asked. Sorry, spouses were not.

(For two days following the call from the Soviet embassy our telephone line was disturbed by loud nervous clicks of a kind we had never heard before. Wiretapping? Could it be? A friend whose telephone conversations were monitored when he traveled in Korea told me yes, he recognized the sounds; another friend, a Princeton colleague who recently taught a seminar on American intelligence operations, assured me that it was nothing to be upset about.

Probably, no one was listening; conversations were just being taped. "These things are perhaps done routinely for security purposes," he said. Meaning Gorbachev's security.)

When we arrived in Washington for the 4:30 to 6:00 P.M. reception we discovered that the block containing the Soviet embassy at 1125 Sixteenth Street N.W. was officially cordoned off; the area was alarmingly aswarm with officers, both uniformed and plainclothes, and one could not help but imagine marksmen hidden in upstairs windows, regarding targets thoughtfully through telescopic lenses. It did not escape my attention that the large, prosperous-looking national headquarters for the National Rifle Association was a stone's throw, so to speak, from the heavily guarded Soviet embassy; nor that, of the streams of people entering the embassy building, not another woman was within sight. (In all, I would see perhaps four or five women at the reception, amid a crowd of as many as one hundred men.) Guests to the reception were required to proceed through three checkpoints, the first on the street, where an unidentified man (Soviet? American?) examined my gilt-embossed invitation, checked my name on his list, and allowed me through. My husband, who had accompanied me, stood behind watching the activity in the sealed-off zone—with virtually hundreds of police milling about, he thought, something was sure to happen—but simply by standing there, outside the barrier and gazing in, he aroused the suspicion of a Washington city policeman, who advanced upon him belligerently. "He's just watching his wife walk away," the man with the checklist explained. But by this time my husband had become discouraged at the prospect of participating in the historic event.

Guests went through a second, less formal checkpoint in front of the heavy wrought-iron gates of the embassy, and, inside, just beyond the mirrored foyer, we were asked to walk through a metal-detector frame. Handbags and attaché cases were carefully examined, with apologies—"We are very sorry to do this," an embassy official said. I said, "I understand." I didn't want any violence at the reception either.

At the crowded buzzing reception I gravitated toward Bill Styron, the only familiar face. Invitations to the meeting had gone out so mysteriously, with no American involvement, we were at a loss as to which of our friends and colleagues might be there. Norman Mailer had been mentioned, but we hadn't yet sighted him. And who else? Anyone else? "Look over there," I said, pointing to a far corner of the room, "that man in profile: isn't he Paul Newman?" Styron considered, but shook his head. "Too young," he said.

A few minutes later we were introduced to Paul Newman, whose left arm was in a sling, and who was a member of our very small "cultural" contingent. Most of the invitations to the reception had gone to American scientists, academicians, and men of the stature of Henry Kissinger, John Kenneth Galbraith, George Kennan, and Cyrus R. Vance; the "artists" consisted of William Styron, Norman Mailer, Paul Newman, Sidney Pollock, John Denver, Yoko Ono, Bel Kaufmann (whose *Up the Down Staircase* was enormously popular in the Soviet Union), one or two others, and me. Amid the crowd Paul Newman, slender, almost slight, with his eerily lapidary features, stood out dramatically: introduced, he had the guarded expression of a man who has been told too frequently that his eyes are blue. "Why are you here?" someone asked. "I was invited," he said.

And then there was a murmur of excitement, and the Gorbachevs were entering the room, and it was as if royalty had appeared in our midst; or media celebrities whose actual faces—youthful, high-colored, smiling, assured—were considerably more attractive than their reproductions. In newspaper photographs Gorbachev has looked jowly, heavy-set, and stolid; in person, he fairly radiates energy and vigor, the warmth of a naturally charismatic leader who knows his worth and delights in its reflection in others' eyes. The first thing one sees about him is the cranberry-red birthmark, descending on the right side of his head, with a look of a hieratic (or demonic) sign out of Dostoyevski. To shake hands with Gorbachev—that is, to have one's hand shaken vigor-ously by Gorbachev—is to feel the grand conviction, no less powerful because it is absurd, that the man has hurried to you for this purpose alone; that, for a blurred moment, *you* are indeed the center of *his* universe. By way of his inter-preter the General Secretary seemed to be telling me that he was an admirer of my work—or was it, yet more unex-pectedly, "I am a great admirer of your work, Mrs. Oates"? To this I could say only, "I am honored to meet you, Mr. Gorbachev," or some such banality, for to my shame I had not read the Gorbachev *Perestroika,* and at this great mo-ment the inappropriate thought had entered my mind that the real Mrs. Oates, my mother, was in upstate New York.

Then I was shaking hands with Raisa Gorbachev, yet more warmly, and through the interpreter we managed to talk, to a degree, for as it turned out Mrs. Gorbachev too declared herself a "great admirer" of my work, and had read two novels, *A Garden of Earthly Delights* and *Angel of Light,* the latter published in 1987 in Russia. Mrs. Gorbachev, pe-tite, stylish, a beautiful woman only slightly past the bloom of her beauty, held my hand in both of hers and told me that my books are "much read" and "much admired" in her homeland: "You write of women well? And of politics?" The Gorbachevs moved on, meeting my fellow Americans, art-ists, writers, intellectuals, scientists, shaking hands happily, not at all as if it were a duty, or even a gesture of *noblesse oblige;* there were television cameras and flashbulbs everywhere; and suddenly everyone was craning to see a photo opportunity of some significance—the several-times-posed handshake of Mikhail Gorbachev and Henry Kissinger. As Bill Styron observed, "It *is* a historic occasion; it's hard to stay away from things like this."

The reception ended punctually at 5 P.M. and the guests were ushered into another, even larger and grander ballroom, and seated at numbered tables; fifteen little round tables, six people at each, mainly Americans, with a scattering of Soviets. The color scheme was white and gold, or white and gilt; white tulips, an unexpected choice for December, but beautiful, and fragile, beginning to wilt in the over-warm atmosphere; bottles of mineral water, that Eastern European staple, on each of the tables. I saw to my mild alarm that I was seated beside Henry Kissinger, about whom I had written, briefly, though perhaps critically, in my Washington-set novel *Angel of Light;* but surely, I thought, he had not read those paragraphs? Surely he had never read a word I'd written? When we introduced ourselves Mr. Kissinger said, unsmiling, "Of course I know who you are."

Like an expert leading a university seminar Gorbachev addressed the gathering, telling us much, I suppose, that was familiar, yet speaking with surprising candor. On the subject of the new era in Soviet politics, *glasnost, perestroika,* "openness," "restructuring," he said: "Why are we moved to this? Because we have no choice. The people have lost their tolerance." If socialism seems to have failed it is because it has not been imaginatively utilized; its potential has been thwarted. "But this is our problem, not yours." As Gorbachev spoke he looked out at his audience steadily, and smiled almost steadily, like a popular and aggressive professor who needs to establish rapport with his charges as a way of suggesting not camaraderie but control; thus, sighting John Kenneth Galbraith, he made reference to Galbraith's books, which, he said, he had studied; sighting Henry Kissinger he made a humorous remark to him, as if inviting complicity. Kindred souls; Alpha males. He also recognized John Denver by sight—as few of the intellectuals and academicians would have.

Part of Gorbachev's now legendary charm for Americans is that he tells us things we desperately want to hear, as religious and political leaders have always told their listeners what is most desperately wanted. That Gorbachev comes from the far side of the world, as through a murky looking-glass, only intensifies the drama of the situation: recall the hugely popular quasi-mystical films of recent years, *2001, Close Encounters of the Third Kind, E. T.,* the latter two rather juvenile retellings of wisdom/savior myths; sitcom variants of the archetype in the human psyche that craves an other-worldly confirmation of our hopes for salvation, redemption, unique and individual worth. So it is not surprising that the leader of the most powerful Communist nation on earth, the United States's shadow-figure, or dreaded twin, should prove so charismatic to Americans. What is surprising is the historic phenomenon of Mikhail Gorbachev himself: that the man should have such ideas, such revolutionary courage, one might say such amazing faith in the possibility of a radical transformation of his long-repressed and calcified society, in a context of power politics. For after all Gorbachev is not royalty—Raisa is not "the little empress"—but both are subject to censure by the Politburo.

The question-and-answer part of the session was less rewarding than Gorbachev's presentation, perhaps because, in such contexts, the more thoughtful tend to remain silent while others plunge forward to speak. In fact there were few questions, but rather mini-speeches of varying degrees of coherence and plausibility. "Who the hell is that?" and "Who the hell is *that?*" Henry Kissinger several times murmured in my ear, as well-intentioned but possibly rather naïve ideas were aired. One unidentified man, speaking almost rhapsodically, suggested that instead of organizing exchange programs between our two countries involving small numbers of students and professionals, tens of thousands of citizens should be exchanged, not unlike hostages—"taxi drivers, farmers, factory workers"; a woman involved in a worldwide children's fund made an impassioned plea, throwing her arms wide to Gorbachev, while saying in a voice that seemed close to tears, "We throw our arms wide to you!" There were proposals for joint U.S.–U.S.S.R. research into AIDS, and travel to Mars; a suggestion that the arms manufacturers in the United States begin to produce automobiles, computers, and other domestic machines, to be donated to the U.S.S.R. One histrionic gentleman spoke of a multinational production of a Shakespearean play, in different languages. "Who is *that?*" Henry Kissinger asked several of us. But no one knew.

And so it went, until, near the end of the session, Gorbachev called upon a Russian Orthodox priest (incongruous in our midst, fiercely bearded, and wearing sacerdotal robes) to tell the gathering about Soviet freedom of worship, which, in rather vague rhetorical terms, the priest did. "And tell us, what are the statistics? How many marriages each year in the churches? How many baptisms?" Gorbachev smilingly inquired; but the priest backed down, faltering, or missing his cue entirely, saying only vaguely that religion in Russia was a "mass movement" and that "we don't keep records." There was an awkward pause. Had something gone wrong? Was Gorbachev disappointed in his countryman's performance? But the General Secretary's affable calm was not rippled, not once, in our presence.

Punctually at 6 P.M. the session ended, and Mr. and Mrs. Gorbachev were hurried away to their next appointment, at the White House. The protracted formality of a state dinner awaited; one could not envy them, much. I was thinking how anachronistic the tragic sense of life had come to seem, suddenly—at least in this cordoned-off ballroom in the Soviet embassy, with dozens of security men—KGB? Secret Service?—stationed obtrusively against the walls; and Gorbachev's measured, reasonable, persuasive words, everything electronically recorded for posterity. I was thinking, It is all too good to be true but does it logically follow, then, that it is not true; or that some of it, some day, might become true? We want so badly to believe.

In parting, Henry Kissinger shook my hand and said, with an unreadable expression, "I am a great admirer of your work." I was so taken by surprise I had not the wit to call after him, as of course I should have done, "And I'm a great admirer of your work too."

5

SELVES AND PSEUDONYMOUS SELVES

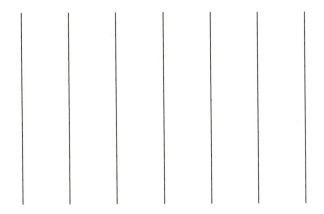

FIVE PREFACES

1. *them*

Alone among my novels *them* is prefaced by an Author's Note, terse, equivocal, and possibly helpful—at the very least by directing the reader's attention to the fact, not a negligible one, that the title *them* refers to certain people and is not a shorthand "poetic" way of alluding to all Americans. Who are these people?—Loretta and her children Jules and Maureen, and to a lesser extent their father, their stepfather, their uncle Brock, their lost sister Betty, their young brother Randolph? They are Americans of a certain class and era—infected, in part, by the glamour of America, the adventure of aggressive and futile dreams—but they are not Americans most of us know. Neither impoverished enough to be italicized against the prodigious wealth of their culture, nor affluent enough to be comfortably assimilated into it, the Wendalls exist—and they continue to exist—in a world for which, for the most part, despair itself is a luxury, incompletely understood, and failure unthinkable: because no American and no public models for failure are available with whom the disenfranchised might identify. If their lives are temporarily "unhappy," it never occurs to such people (not even the quick, intelligent, sweetly crafty Jules) that their dreams are at fault for having deluded them; they think instead, and indeed must continue to think, that success—that is, "happiness"—lies not far ahead in the future and can be grasped if only one knows how to play the game.

Of course, I lived in Detroit up to and including the days of the 1967 riots, and was shaken by the experience, and brooded upon it, like most Detroiters, and came to see that the genesis of these specific acts of violence lay far in the past and were certainly not limited to one troubled city (which, since 1967, has in fact become increasingly troubled). *Fire burns and does its duty* is a mystic utterance, characteristically misunderstood by Jules Wendall, and misunderstood, in effect, by his culture; but there is no mistaking the mad, demonic certainty with which its psychological message is comprehended by the disenfranchised, who must live out their lives in so publicly celebratory an affluent society. The instinct to destroy is inadequately understood by those of us who work to create, and who are governed by a sense, itself instinctive, of the need to preserve the past, which is always embodied in a healthy society; I have come to feel that it is not an instinct that can be, in any helpful way, *understood.* We look upon the murderer, or the rapist, or the vandal, and try to project our own selves, our ways of perceiving, into him; and we inevitably fail. There *are* others, and we are not among them. Though we all share emotions (and long before modern psychological theory it was recognized that the human psyche is universal, that we are all capable of one another's crimes and one another's virtues), very few of these emotions are allowed above the threshold of consciousness; we do not *know,* we do not *understand,* unless we experience. And it is only through art, an art seriously committed to the portrayal of a dense, complex, stubborn, and irreducible reality, one in which human beings are presented honestly, without sentimentality and without cynicism, that we can hope to approximate the experience of another's life. Tragedy, it is said, breaks down the barriers between human beings: but it should be argued that all serious works of art break down these barriers, affirming our kinship with one another.

From the very first, when *them* was published in 1969, I received letters from readers who inquire, at times with a desperation I find guiltily moving, what has become of the Wendalls—of Jules primarily, and of Maureen. Have I kept in contact with them? Is Jules really in California? Is Maureen married, and is she happy or unhappy? And what of the feckless Loretta—what is she doing *now?* The most extraordinary letter I received was written in longhand and covered many pages of scented stationery; it was a troubled appeal from a disturbed woman who believed that she was hopelessly in love with Jules . . . since she thought about him constantly, was unfaithful to her husband with him in her imagination, and would I please send her Jules's address so that she might go to him at once . . . ? Since I shared, to a limited extent, her deep regard for Jules, I sympathized with her predicament, but wrote to explain that Jules Wendall, while "real" enough in *them,* is a fictional character so far as the world itself goes. If he and Maureen and Loretta are to be located anywhere, it is in my imagination; just as the ghostly "Joyce Carol Oates" who appears, indirectly, obliquely, in the narrative, is a fictional character who, though driving the very car I drove in those years, is assuredly not me.

Yes, readers have said, but surely Maureen was "real"—surely you did have a student like her who told you her family history, as the Author's Note claims? True: and yet not true. Maureen Wendall, like her brother Jules, is a composite character. While she sets herself in opposition to me, to the person she imagines me to be (happily married, economically secure, fruitfully engaged in a profession that is, even at the worst of times, rewarding and stimulating and worthwhile), I see shadowy aspects of myself in her, and recognize my voice in her in ways I would not have understood when I wrote the novel. I was troubled in writing it, for indeed the Wendalls' lives became my own, and their souls entered mine; but it was, and remains, a work of love; and like all those who love, I cannot set myself up to judge. Are Jules and Maureen criminals . . . or are they tragically heroic (as survivors of any catastrophe might be considered "heroic") in their surprisingly similar ways? For nearly a decade now I've wondered, but I can't say; I can't judge.

2. *BELLEFLEUR*

The "key" to most works of fiction is a voice, a rhythm, a unique music; a precise way of *seeing* and *hearing* that will give the writer access to the world he is trying to create. (Yet this world is sometimes so real in the imagination that its construction, in terms of formal art, seems rather like a re-creation, a re-construction.) Sometimes one must wait a long time for this key to present itself—sometimes it comes rather quickly. In the case of *Bellefleur* I waited several years.

The entire novel grew out of a haunting image: there was a walled garden, luxurious but beginning to grow shabby; overgrown, "old," yet still possessing an extraordinary beauty. In this mysterious garden the baby Germaine was to be rocked in her regal cradle; and a less fortunate baby was to be carried off by an immense white bird of prey. My vision gave me the Bellefleur garden with an intimidating clarity, yet I could gain entry to it only by imagining all that surrounded it—the castle, the grounds, the waters of Lake Noir, the Chautauqua region, the State itself with its turbulent history, and the Nation with its still more turbulent history. In the foreground the Bellefleur family emerged as prismatic lenses by which the outer world is seen—an "outer" world abbreviated and in some cases mocked by the Bellefleurs' ambition for empire and wealth. It had always interested me that in the nineteenth and early twentieth centuries in America wealthy men were eager to establish themselves as "nobility" of a sort by reconstructing immense castles, and in many cases importing great sections of European castles for this purpose. (A castle, after all, is a castellated structure—that is, it is fortified for war.) The American castles were fascinating in themselves (the most notorious being of course Hearst's San Simeon) and in what they symbolize. Naturally the walled garden was a garden attached to a castle—though the Bellefleurs, with an air of unconvincing modesty, preferred to speak of their home as Bellefleur Manor.

It took several years for me to acquire the voice, the rhythm, the tone of *Bellefleur*. Before I finally began writing it I had acquired more than one thousand pages of notes—some of them mere scraps of paper, some fairly complete dramatic scenes that would emerge, in the novel's narrative, without many changes. It became the most demanding and the most mesmerizing novel I have written. Though I came to think of it as the months passed as my "vampire novel"—for it seemed that it was draining me of vitality in ways I could not control—I passed through a spell of what might be called acute homesickness after completing it, and feel rather melancholy now, at times, when I think of Bellefleur—the landscape, the castle, the people whom I came to love in odd surprising ways.

The imaginative construction of a "Gothic" novel involves the systematic transposition of realistic psychological and emotional experiences into "Gothic" elements. We all experience mirrors that distort, we all age at different speeds, we have known people who want to suck our life's blood from us, like vampires; we feel haunted by the dead—if not precisely by the dead then by thoughts of them. We are forced at certain alarming periods in our lives not only to discover that other people are mysterious—and will remain mysterious—but that we ourselves, our motives, our passions, even our logic, are profoundly mysterious. And we sense ourselves accursed at times; and then again blessed; singled out, in any case, for what feels like a special destiny. We are superstitious when events—usually coincidences— argue that "superstition" may be a way of grasping an essentially chaotic world. All these factors the novelist who wants to write an "experimental Gothic" will transpose into Gothic terms. If Gothicism has the power to move us (and it certainly has the power to fascinate the novelist) it is only because its roots are in psychological realism. Much of *Belle-fleur* is a diary of my own life, and the lives of people I have known. It must be significant that my father, Frederick Oates, as a young man, succumbed to the lure of flying, and took me up innumerable times in small planes; it must be significant that my mother, Caroline, was, like Leah, a very *young* mother whom I can remember as young—only a girl, really. But "Gideon" and "Leah" are by no means modeled on my parents.

Bellefleur is more than a Gothic, of course, and it would be disingenuous of me to suggest otherwise. It is also a critique of America; but it is in the service of a vision of America that stresses, for all its pessimism, the ultimate freedom of the individual. One by one the Bellefleur children free themselves of their family's curse (or blessing); one by one they disappear into America, to define themselves for themselves. The castle is destroyed, the Bellefleur children live. Theirs is the privilege of youth; and the "America" of my imagination, despite the incursions of recent decades, is a nation still characterized by youth. Our past may weigh heavily upon us but it cannot contain us, let alone shape our future. America is a tale still being told—in many voices— and nowhere near its conclusion.

3. *MYSTERIES OF WINTERTHURN*

Mysteries of Winterthurn is the third in a quartet of experimental novels that deal, in genre form, with nineteenth-century and early twentieth-century America. A family saga (*Bellefleur,* 1980), a romance (*A Bloodsmoor Romance,* 1982), a detective-mystery (*Mysteries of Winterthurn,* 1984), a Gothic horror set in turn-of-the-century Princeton (*The Crosswicks Horror,* forthcoming)—the novels, thematically linked, might be described as post-modernist in conception but thoroughly serious in execution. Primarily, each novel tells a story I consider uniquely American and of our time. The characters of the quartet are both our ancestors and ourselves.

But why "genre," one might ask. Does a serious writer dare concern herself with "genre"? Why, in imagining a quartet of novels to encompass some six decades of American history (beginning in the remarkable 1850s, in *Bloodsmoor*) and to require some two thousand pages of prose (the romance being, of necessity, the longest of the four)—why choose such severe restraints, such cruelly confining structures? But the formal discipline of *genre*—that it forces us inevitably to a radical re-visioning of the world and of the craft of fiction—was the reason I found the project so intriguing. To choose idiosyncratic but not distracting "narrators" to recite the histories; to organize the voluminous materials in patterns alien to my customary way of thinking and writing; to "see" the world in terms of heredity and family destiny and the vicissitudes of Time (for all four of the novels are secretly fables of the American family); to explore historically authentic crimes against women, children, and the poor, in the guise of entertainment; to create, and to identify with, heroes and heroines whose existence would be problematic in the clinical, unkind, and, one might almost say, fluorescent-lit atmosphere of present-day fiction—these factors proved irresistible. The opportunity might not be granted to me again, I thought, to create a highly complex structure in which individual novels (themselves complex in design, made up of "books") functioned as chapters or units in an immense design: America as viewed through the prismatic lens of its most popular genres. The sequence begins with a quotation attributed to Heraclitus ("Time is a child playing a game of draughts; the kingship is in the hands of a child"), at the start of *Bellefleur,* and ends with the concluding section, a sermon, in *The Crosswicks Horror.* But the novels, in any case, are independent of one another so far as the experience of reading is concerned.

The three cases that constitute *Mysteries of Winterthurn* are variations on the enigma of mystery itself. In "The Virgin in the Rose-Bower" the detective seeks to discover *who* has committed the murders, and *why;* in "Devil's Half-Acre" the identity of the probable murderer is less uncertain than whether, granted the prejudices of his society, he can be brought to justice. The special puzzle of "The Blood-Stained Bridal Gown" has to do with the detective's inability to solve the crime when various clues and motives will strike the attentive reader as self-evident. In the laconic words of Poe's Monsieur Dupin: "Perhaps it is the very simplicity of the thing that puts you at fault."

Xavier Kilgarvan as idealist and lover is the quintessence of the late-nineteenth-century sensibility. From boy-hood onward he is fascinated by the prospect of mystery and its "solution" or exorcism; his imagination is inflamed by the obdurate nature of certain puzzles—why? where? who? with what consequences? He is thoroughly American in his zeal to make a distinguished name for himself, and the buoyant optimism to which he confesses ("crime, if not the criminal heart itself, might someday be eradicated by *the in-tellectual, pragmatic, and systematic unification of the numerous forces for Good*") is in the spirit of mid- and late-nineteenth-century dreams of progress. Xavier comes of age and begins his rather glamorous professional career in those decades in which a passionate belief in evolution (in society and morals no less than in Nature) was widely shared by men and women of education, intelligence, and sensitivity. He withdraws from his career—for mysterious but privately logical reasons—not long before the collapse of these dreams with the outbreak of the Great War. So far as Xavier's personal story is con-cerned, it might be seen to end happily, or tragically, or ironically, or, indeed, wisely, depending upon one's point of view.

Aficionados of classic American murder cases will recognize here, in transmogrified and modulated forms, cer-tain old favorites about which I dare not be more specific, for fear of revealing too much. The fictional cases are meant to bear a sort of dreamlike (or nightmarelike) relationship to the originals, one or two of which have never been sat-isfactorily solved; but they have been chosen because they deal with ongoing themes of the quartet—the wrongs per-petrated against women, for instance, and the vicious class and race warfare that has constituted much of America's do-mestic history. Xavier Kilgarvan is a fictitious person but in many ways he follows the pattern of the nineteenth-century "amateur" detective, tireless in his research into the latest forensic discoveries, pioneering in a new and undefined and thoroughly exciting profession. (It is quite likely, for instance, that a promising young man with Xavier's ambition would visit the Paris Sûreté and speak with the famous Alphonse Bertillon, and that he would be treated kindly by Scotland Yard—men with a penchant for detective work, whether associated with police forces or not, constituted an informal brotherhood within a great sea of ignorance, incompetence, and corruption.)

Yet Xavier's temperament is also that of an artist. His cases are, perhaps, stories, parables, "mysteries" that yield their meaning only after much frustration and mental anguish . . . the meaning being the very pattern of the work of art, its voice, its tone, its spirit. Hence my feeling of intense identification with him, and my sense that, at this time at least, *Mysteries of Winterthurn* is my favorite among my own novels.

4. *MARYA: A LIFE*

Marya: A Life will very likely remain the most "personal" of my novels (along with the later novel *You Must Remember This),* though it is not, in the strictest sense, autobiographical. It contains some autobiographical material, particularly in its opening sections, and it is set, for the most part, in places identical with or closely resembling places I have lived—Innisfail and its surrounding countryside are akin to Lockport, New York, and its surrounding countryside, where I grew up; Port Oriskany shares some characteristics with Syracuse, New York, where I went to college—but I am not Marya Knauer (who stopped writing fiction because it disturbed her too deeply) and Marya is surely not I (who have been spared Marya's grimmer experiences with men). Though her author's feelings toward her are sisterly, if at times ambivalent, I don't believe that Marya represents me any more than do several other of my female characters of recent novels—Sheila Trask, for instance, of *Solstice,* or Deirdre of the Spirits of *A Bloodsmoor Romance;* or even the unregenerate murderess Perdita of *Mysteries of Winterthurn.*

Marya was an extremely difficult novel to write, perhaps because it is both "personal" and "fictional." Many of Marya's thoughts and impressions parallel my own at her approximate age but the circumstances that provoke them have been altered, as have most of the characters. To the author, *Marya*'s mixture of intimacy and strangeness suggests a dream in which the domestic features of one's life appear side by side with unrecognizable elements; yet, evidently, all constitute a pattern. What is most autobiographical about the novel is its inner kernel of emotion—Marya's half-conscious and often despairing quest for her own elusive self.

Of all my novels *Marya* is the only one I could not approach head-on. I had to write it in self-contained sections, each dealing with a specific phase of Marya's life, and after finishing each of these sections I was determined not to write another—the tension was too great. I worried that I might be trespassing—transgressing?—in some undefined way venturing onto forbidden ground. At least one family secret I had not known, or had not, in any case, known that I knew, was explored in fictional form before it was revealed to me in life, by a relative. But it was not until I wrote the sentence "Marya, this is going to cut your life in two" on the novel's final page that I fully understood Marya's story, and was then in a position to begin again and to recast it as a single work of prose fiction. As I recall now how obsessively certain pages of the novel were written and rewritten, it seems to me miraculous that the novel was ever completed at all.

The spirit of William James, our greatest American philosopher, pervades Marya's story. *My first act of freedom,* James says, *is to believe in freedom.* For James it is the fluidity of experience and not its Platonic "essence" that is significant, for truth is relative, ever-changing, indeterminate; and life is a process rather like a stream. Human beings forge their own souls by way of the choices they make, large and small, conscious and half-conscious. James's philosophy is ideally suited to the New World in which identity (social, historical, familial) is not permanent; it is a philosophy of the individual, stubborn, self-reliant, and ultimately mysterious. The democratic "pluralistic" universe of which James wrote in such startlingly contemporary terms is one in which old traditions and standards of morality are judged largely useless unless they can be regenerated in uniquely individual terms. This is of course Marya Knauer's universe, in which one forges one's own soul, for better or worse.

For the novelist, the act of writing even a short novel is an act of faith sustained through many months. It has been said by Aldous Huxley that all art is a quest for grace, and it has been said, by Flannery O'Connor among others, that merely to write fiction is an optimistic gesture: pessimists don't write novels. To write is to make a plea for some sort of human sympathy and communication. To write is to risk being rejected, ridiculed, misunderstood. To write is to attempt to make contact between the world *out there* and the world *in here,* both of them mysterious, perhaps ultimately unknowable.

Whether Marya Knauer's story is in any way my own "story," it became my story during the writing of the novel; and it is my hope that, however obliquely and indirectly, it will strike chords in readers who, like Marya, choose finally not to accept the terms of their own betrayal.

5. *YOU MUST REMEMBER THIS*

Its working title was *The Green Island*, and so, during the approximately fifteen months of its composition, I thought of this chronicle of the Stevick family from 1946 to 1956, suffused, in a sense, with greenness: green of romance, of nostalgia, of innocence; green of an epoch in our American history that, for all its hypocrisies, and its much-documented crimes against its own citizens, has come to represent an innocence of a peculiarly American kind. And this greenness is an island: insular, self-contained, self-referential; doomed. Passion plays itself out on both the collective and the personal scale, and is best contemplated at a distance, by way of memory.

You Must Remember This, like *Marya: A Life* (1986), is one of the most personal of my novels; though it is not, except in its setting, and certain of its specific incidents, autobiographical. It takes place in a fictitious city, Port Oriskany, an amalgam of two cities in upstate New York—Buffalo (the first large city of my experience) and Lockport (the city of my birth, my paternal grandmother's home, suffused forever for me with the extravagant dreams of early adolescence—I attended sixth grade in Lockport, and all of junior high school there; the city is probably more real to me, imaginatively, than any I have known since). While writing the novel I had a map of Port Oriskany taped to my wall so that, dreamy as all novelists are, when not in the throes of acute anxiety or the fabled and so often elusive heat of composition, I could simply stare at it; and, like Enid Stevick, in fact very much like Enid Stevick, the contours of whose soul so resemble my own, traverse its streets, ponder its buildings and houses and vacant lots, most of all the canal that runs through it, as it runs through Lockport, New York . . . that canal that, in Enid's heightened and often fevered imagination, as in my own, seemed an object of utter ineffable beauty. (It must be remembered that beauty does not mean mere prettiness but something more brutal, possessed of the power to rend one's heart.)

Where *Marya: A Life* grew slowly out of an accretion of memory, and did not take its final compositional shape until Marya's story was complete, *You Must Remember This* was immediately conceived as a family chronicle, of sorts; a memoir-as-narrative; its focus upon Enid Stevick and her uncle Felix, who loses his youth in the course of the novel, as Enid loses, by degrees, in a countermovement, her attraction for death. By way of passion Enid exorcises an instinct for suicide; by way of passion, and its somber consequences, Felix exorcises an instinct for self-destructive violence. The one suggestively "female," the other "male": poles of masochism and sadomasochism. Which is not, of course, to suggest that we are defined by such poles; only that they exert a gravitational pull, weak in some, powerful in others.

The novel's primary excitement for the author was its evocation of that now-remote decade 1946–1956; its focusing upon certain selected areas of American life, notably politics (the antipodes of the Red Scare and the early, pioneering, antinuclear arms movement), popular culture (primarily music and Hollywood films), and professional prizefighting (when vast numbers of Americans routinely watched weekly boxing matches on television, and the great champions Sugar Ray Robinson, Rocky Marciano, Archie Moore, Jersey Joe Walcott, Willie Pep, Carmen Basilio, and others were in their prime). The Stevicks live through the era and, to a degree, embody it; but should not be thought of as representative. They are too real, in my imagination at least, and surely too idiosyncratic, to bear the weight of allegory.

Boxing is an American sport—a "so-called sport" to many— in which images of incalculable beauty and violence, desperation and ingenuity, are routinely entwined; the sport that evokes the most extreme reactions—loathing, revulsion, righteous indignation; a fierce and often inexplicable loyalty. Freud spoke of taboo as evoking such ambivalent reactions, and it is probable that boxing, like few other legalized, or "civilized," activities, has the power to disturb because it violates taboo . . . or excites it. Like any ritualized action in which risk would seem to outweigh reward—that mysterious species of "play" to which the adjective "deep" has been assigned by anthropologists—its participants appear, to the neutral observer, to be, if not mad, touched with madness; yet boxing is, in another sense, the most fully conscious of sports since the *agon* at its very core is direct and acknowledged. To love life for some men is to love fighting, for fighting, and not love, is seen as man's deepest passion. *Why do you love fighting?* the boxer is asked, and his answer, in effect, is, *Why do you love life?*

Though one might claim any number of parallels, most of them theoretical, between the life of the fighter and that of the writer, it is probable that the writer conceives of himself, fundamentally, as a nurturer; a practical-minded dreamer; a creator who never creates out of nothing but out of a palpably living, immediate reality. By way of the imagination one world is transposed, and given a unique aesthetic significance, into another world: the permanence, or semiper-manence, of art. *You Must Remember This* is a novel, rather than a romance, but it might be said that all novelists, in love with their material, still more with the inimitable voices their material yields, are romantics. Imaginative literature is meant to be a form of sympathy, as D. H. Lawrence saw it, and of all my novels this one seems, to its author at least, the most "sympathetic"—its vision large enough to accom-modate seemingly disparate and even contentious impulses of love and war.

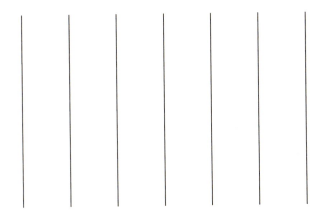

PSEUDONYMOUS SELVES

"It was a new birth. I was renewing myself. Everything was being given me one more time."

So Romain Gary said in his posthumously published *The Life and Death of Émile Ajar,* which appeared in France in 1981, the year after Gary's suicide. The book created a literary sensation in Paris since in it Gary acknowledged that he was the author of four popular novels published under the pseudonym "Émile Ajar." (The first "Ajar" novel, *Gros-Câlin,* had been a best-seller in 1974; the second, *La Vie devant soi,* was named winner of the Prix Goncourt for 1975, but, because one of the rules of the Goncourt is that a writer can win it only once, and Gary had already won, he was forced to decline the prize.) The publishing strategy for the "Ajar" books was artful: manuscripts were mailed to Paris from Rio de Janeiro, and a surrogate "Ajar," a cousin of Gary's, allowed himself to be interviewed and photographed. Explaining his motives in the posthumous memoir, Gary claimed he was tired of being "the famous Romain Gary"; he wanted to be someone else. By the age of fifty-nine he had written thirty-three books, had won numerous prizes, and was one of the most successful and admired of French writers. "I have always been someone else," he said. And: "I wanted to be a spectator at my own second life." And, quoting the Polish writer Witold Gombrowicz: "There comes a day when a writer is held prisoner by 'la gueule qu'on lui a fait' ('the mug which the critics have given him')— an appearance which has nothing to do with his work or himself."

In 1984 the American Academy and Institute of Arts and Letters awarded one of its distinguished fiction prizes to a new and presumably young Chicano writer named Danny Santiago, for his first novel, *Famous All Over Town*. Subsequent to the award it was revealed, with some embarrassment, that the newly discovered Chicano writer was not Chicano at all: "Danny Santiago" turned out to be the pseudonym of seventy-three-year-old Daniel James, author of several previously published books, and better known as a playwright and screenwriter; and a former Communist Party member who had been blacklisted by Hollywood in the 1950s. By his account, James wrote *Famous All Over Town* as a consequence of his experience doing volunteer social work in Mexican-American districts of Los Angeles in the 1950s and 1960s, and chose to publish it under a Hispanic pseudonym because he had lost confidence in his own writing ability. Yet it is plausible to assume that he chose "Santiago" over "James" because, while writing the novel—which is narrated by the fourteen-year-old Chicano boy—he felt closer to "Santiago" than to "James."

(Though *Famous All Over Town* alone should have been the issue, and not its author's identity, the awards committee confessed that they might have had second thoughts about giving the novel their prize, had they known its author was "Anglo" and not "Chicano.")

It may be that, after a certain age, our instinct for anonymity is as powerful as that for identity; or, more precisely, for an erasure of the primary self in that another (hitherto undiscovered?) self may be released. Romain Gary, writing as the unknown "Émile Ajar," is no longer writing as Gary, but as Gary-through-"Ajar"; the Danish noblewoman, Baroness Karen Blixen, choosing "Isak Dinesen" ("Isak": one who laughs) as a pseudonym, is writing as Blixen-through-"Isak Dinesen," thereby evoking an ancestral, magisterial, and certainly unfeminine self. Jonathan Swift, behind the mask of "Isaac Bickerstaff, Esq." in the deadpan satire of 1708–1709 known as the *Bickerstaff Papers,* is Swift-through-"Bickerstaff"—and should one doubt the existence of "Bickerstaff," his thought-tormented likeness is reproduced in *The Tatler* in 1710. For a woman to write under a male or a male-sounding pseudonym—"Currer Bell," for instance, instead of Charlotte Brontë; "George Sand" instead of Amandine Aurore-Lucie Dupin, Baroness Dudevant—may be a decision based upon practical expediency in a male-dominated culture; but it may also stimulate the imagination in unanticipated ways. Daniel Defoe's "true histories" of such adventurers as "Robinson Crusoe," "Moll Flanders," and "Captain Singleton," recounted in their own words, ingeniously blurred the line between fiction and what the credulous reading public might call outright hoax, as did the ancient Gaelic epic by a Scottish poet named "Ossian" which was allegedly discovered and translated by one James Macpherson, a contemporary of Samuel Johnson's whom Johnson publicly accused of imposture in 1775, and, in the 1760s, the "medieval" Rowley sequence by Thomas Chatterton. (Romain Gary compared his "doubling" with "Ajar" in terms of Macpherson's with "Ossian.") When the now-famous Karen Blixen/"Isak Dinesen" published a parablelike novel called *The Angelic Avengers* in 1944 under the pseudonym "Pierre Andrézel," she arranged for her longtime secretary-companion Clara Svendsen to be named on the title page as the translator. Here we have Blixen-through-"Isak Dinesen"-through-"Pierre Andrézel"-through-"Clara Svendsen, translator." Not even Vladimir Nabokov's catoptric imagination can take us further.

And there is the mysterious relationship between the Oxford clergyman and mathematics lecturer Charles Lutwidge Dodgson and the author of the *Alice* books, "Lewis Carroll." "Lewis Carroll" was created to accommodate Dodgson's extraordinary storytelling imagination and as a means by which a series of remarkable photographs was taken—photographs of theatrically posed little girls, sometimes nude, more often costumed and caught in moments of dramatic intensity, suggestively "erotic" yet more disturbing, perhaps, to contemporary eyes than they were to Victorian. Without the scrim of "Lewis Carroll" and the inspired brilliance of "Carroll's" art, to what end the genius of Dodgson?

Though the imagination delights in freedom and play, and it is arguable that, in its earliest manifestations, in childhood, art *is* play, the professionalism that overtakes writers like Romain Gary often has very little that is playful about it. The more successful the writer, the more secure his "international reputation," the greater the temptation to consider oneself in the third person; which is not so very different from the posthumous. Each work of fiction or poetry, unique to its creator, requiring, certainly, a unique expenditure of effort, is nonetheless judged as part of the *oeuvre*—"*oeuvre*": that soul-numbing word!—or, if not judged, assumed to possess a tactical position in it, an inevitable part of the design. Radical departures from what has come to seem one's métier may be met with disapproval, disappointment—to quote Nietzsche, "When we must change our minds about someone, we charge the inconvenience he causes us heavily to his account." (Isak Dinesen's most fervent admirers were angry with her, for instance, for her deviation as "Pierre Andrézel," though one might have thought the pseudonym-atop-the-pseudonym might have protected her.) Who, having created an identity in the world's eyes, an indestructible *persona,* has not subsequently wished to escape from it!—for such is the perversity, the instinct for freedom and newness, in the human psyche.

When not for such interior motives, or for political reasons, or for reasons of scandal, or as the brimming-over of sheer energy (Georges Simenon, for instance, author as Simenon of hundreds of mystery novels, also publishes under "Christian Brulls," "Jean Du Perry," and "Georges Sim"), pseudonymous works are often playful; experimental; "entertainments," as Graham Greene rather disarmingly called certain of his novels. Or, like Dinesen's elegantly artificial narratives, they may reflect a transpersonal, even transcendental consciousness, not to be linked with or explained by the merely personal. When Walter Whitman, aged thirty-five, renamed himself "Walt Whitman," the gesture had the effect of cutting his life in two. (The first edition of *Leaves of Grass,* issued on 4 July 1855, contained no author's name on the title page: "Walt Whitman, an American, one of the roughs, a kosmos,/ Disorderly fleshy and sensual" was not announced until page twenty-nine.) Young David Henry Thoreau became "Henry David Thoreau" as if to declare not only self-dependence but self-genesis. Marie Henri Beyle into "Stendhal"; Marian Evans into "George Eliot"; Sidonie Gabrielle Colette into "Colette Willy" and finally "Colette"; Józef Konrad Korzeniowski into "Joseph Conrad"; Andrei Codrescu into "Tristan Tzara"; Giorgos Stylianous Seferiades into "George Seferis"; Reyes Basoalto into "Pablo Neruda"; Hector Hugh Munro into "Saki"—each suggests an interior and not merely an outward transformation, a conspicuous redefining of the self. Though Eric Blair, prior to the publication of *Down and Out in Paris and London,* allowed his publisher to choose his pseudonym from several names Blair provided, "George Orwell" shortly became the name by which he was known, even by friends: thus, George Orwell the man, "Eric Blair" an early and outgrown identity. Samuel Langhorne Clemens, a young humorist and newspaperman, baptized his writing self with the riverboat leadsman's exuberant cry "Mark Twain": by that gesture assuring an irrevocable split in his life, if not in his conception of himself, suggested by the title of Justin Kaplan's excellent biography *Mr. Clemens and Mark Twain.* More practicably, Ford Madox Hueffer became "Ford Madox Ford" (and, upon occasion, "Daniel Chaucer" and "Fenil Haig") at a time when the Germanic ring of "Hueffer" sounded discordantly in English ears.

Like the experience of first authorship, writing under a pseudonym gives one the sense of discovering oneself by way of redefining oneself, even if it is only for the space of a single book. There is the possibility, however quixotic, of making a fresh start—in Romain Gary's words, "renewing" oneself—and not being held to severe account for it. Trollope, that indefatigable master craftsman of the English novel, chose to publish one book under a pseudonym; it aroused no particular attention, sales were poor, and Trollope quietly returned to "Trollope." Though Doris Lessing's publicly acknowledged motives for publishing two novels in the early 1980s, *The Diary of a Good Neighbor* and *If the Old Could . . .* as "Jane Somers" ("the pseudonym of a well-known British journalist," as the dust jacket noted), were to test the integrity of the publishing industries of England and the United States, which she believed would have honored the "Somers" novels with major reviews had they been issued under the name "Lessing," it is probable that, like Romain Gary, she too hoped to make a fresh start; to return to realism of a scaled-down, human dimension in the style of her short fiction and not that of her more vatic utterances; to be rediscovered, perhaps, as a writer of talent, and accorded the kind of excited attention "Émile Ajar" received in the French press. Had the "Somers" novels been as radically different from Lessing's realistic fiction as her science-fiction sequence has been, or as *The Golden Notebook* seemed in the context of British fiction of the 1960s, the venture would have taken an entirely different course. As it is, Doris Lessing's curious experiment, though idealistic in outline, failed to prove anything of significance for at least two reasons: each season, there are first novels that do receive a good deal of attention, presumably because they deserve it; and novels by many previously published writers are often reviewed with less interest and respect than the unknown "Jane Somers" received.

When, for instance, Gore Vidal published several mystery-thrillers in the 1950s under the name "Edgar Box," the novels were praised as successes of their genre by the very publications that were, at the time, ignoring Vidal's serious fiction. (By Vidal's account, the American literary establishment was so offended by his third novel, *The City and the Pillar,* for its "perverted"—i.e., homosexual—subject matter, that his next five books were boycotted by major reviewing publications. In order to support himself he wrote the "Box" novels, each in eight days. And though they were well received when issued under the name "Edgar Box" they were conspicuously less well received when reissued under "Gore Vidal" some years later.) Norman Mailer's *Barbary Shore* and *The Deer Park,* following the prodigious critical and commercial success of his first novel *The Naked and The Dead,* would surely have fared better under pseudonyms since, given the nature of the intemperate feelings the author seems to have aroused in reviewers at that time, they could scarcely have done worse.

John Updike has not, to my knowledge, published under a pseudonym—"Updike" is a name bankable in ways too sweet to relinquish—but he has created in the person of comically beleaguered Henry Bech an alter ego who clearly speaks for Updike, masking his hurt in ironic tones.

> It was his fault; he had wanted to be noticed, to be praised. He had wanted to be a man in the world, a "writer." For his punishment they had made from the sticks and mud of his words a coarse large doll to question and torment, which would not have mattered except that he was trapped inside the doll, shared a name and a bank account with it. He was, for all his brave talk . . . too alone.
>
> ("Bech Swings?" from *Bech: A Book*)

Why punish a writer for writing?—a reviewer recently asked, beginning a review of a book of mine. The tantalizing question hovered in the air, unanswered.

The advantages of publishing under a male or a male-sounding pseudonym, for a woman writer, have always been self-evident. As Robert Southey, then the Poet Laureate of England, explained to young Charlotte Brontë: "Literature cannot be the business of a woman's life, and it ought not to be." Consequently the Brontë sisters chose androgynous pseudonyms: "Currer Bell" (Charlotte Brontë), "Ellis Bell" (Emily Brontë), "Acton Bell" (Anne Brontë) for *Jane Eyre, Wuthering Heights,* and *Agnes Grey,* respectively. When *Jane Eyre* appeared in 1847 it was an immediate success—"Currer Bell" became famous overnight—and much speculation raged concerning the probable sex of the author. The intelligence, vigor, and passion of the work argued for its having been written by a man, commentators noted; at the same time, its sensitivity, and, of course, its point of view in the heroine Jane, argued for its having been written by a woman. Harriet Martineau shrewdly saw that the author *must* be a woman because of the way Grace Poole, mad Bertha's caretaker, is depicted sewing rings onto curtains. When it was revealed that "Currer Bell" was in fact a woman, the tone of criticism changed and became more pejorative. Now, the (female) author was charged with "coarseness" and an "unseemly knowledge of passion." As Elaine Showalter suggests in *A Literature of Their Own: British Women Writers from Brontë to Lessing,* the fantasy of male personae, as well as the depiction of male protagonists, was a part of the Brontë sisters' lives long before they considered sending their work out to publishers. In the Angrian chronicles the Brontës had a dozen male alter egos; Charlotte used several male aliases as a child, among them "Captain Thunder," "Charles Townsend," and "Captain Tree." Charlotte's "maleness" was very likely identified with the active, creative side of her personality, her "femaleness" with the more passive.

Alert to the dangers of publishing under a woman's name, Marian Evans, with the counsel and support of her common-law husband, George Henry Lewes, made the decision to use the pseudonym "George Eliot" for *Scenes of*

Clerical Life, her first book, which appeared in 1856. It was a considerable success, like the more ambitious *Adam Bede* two years later, and the author's secret was generally intact until the publication of *The Mill on the Floss,* in 1860, when exposure of "Eliot's" identity as Marian Evans adversely affected the novel's fortunes. George Eliot's feminist sympathies were strong yet ambivalent; she freely conceded the prejudices of the era, asking, in 1855, that a writer-friend not reveal the fact that she was the author of an essay in the *Westminster:* "The article appears to have produced a strong impression, and that impression would be a little counteracted if the author were known to be a *woman.*"

An impressive number of British women writers have used male pseudonyms, among them Harriet Parr ("Holme Lee"), Mary Molesworth ("Ennis Graham"), Mary Dunne ("George Egerton"), Violet Page ("Vernon Lee"), Margaret Barber ("Michael Fairless"), Olive Schreiner ("Ralph Iron"), Gillian Freeman ("Eliot George"). Others have used names of dubious gender: Storm Jameson, Radclyffe Hall, I. Compton-Burnett, V. Sackville-West, A. S. Byatt. The American Hilda Doolittle followed the advice of her friend Ezra Pound and published her poetry under the neuter, if rather diminutive, "H.D."; Janet Flanner became "Genêt"; Florence Margaret Smith became "Stevie Smith"; Lula Mae Smith became "Carson McCullers"; Janet Taylor Caldwell published as "Taylor Caldwell" (and as the yet more virile "Max Reiner").

Conversely, the mid-nineteenth-century American writer Sara Payson Willis Parton, novelist and first woman newspaper columnist in the United States, chose the pseudonym "Fanny Fern": a name that, for all its satirical intent, has had a detrimental effect upon this gifted, and largely unknown, writer's reputation.

Among the plethora of entries in the *Pseudonyms and*

Nicknames Dictionary—627 densely printed triple-columned pages that take us from "A. A." (Anthony Armstrong Willis, Canadian author, 1897–1976) to "Z. Y. X." (Arthur Alkin Sykes, British author, 1861–?)—are hundreds of women writers, most of them unknown today, who elected to write under male or androgynous pseudonyms. Some mix male and female names, as do a number of male writers, but William Butler Yeats's Scottish poet-friend William Sharp, who published as "Fiona Macleod," is a rare example of a man who disguised his writing self as a woman. (And underwent what seems to have been a schizoid breakdown of a kind, of which "Fiona Macleod" must have been more consequence than cause.) Yeats's celebrated use of his wife Georgie Hyde-Lees as a medium to whom spirit-"communicators" dictated answers to his questions for *A Vision* might be seen as an ingenious variation on the female-pseudonym/persona phenomenon. Without Mrs. Yeats, the poet insisted, no "vision" would have been possible.

Of course, motives for writing under a pseudonym are likely to be as varied and idiosyncratic as there are pseudonymous writers, though some decisions, in the contexts of their authors' lives, are clearly more explicable than others. When, in 1963, the year of her suicide, thirty-year-old Sylvia Plath published her first, transparently autobiographical, novel, *The Bell Jar,* it was under the pseudonym "Victoria Lucas": Plath feared, and with justification, that her harsh satirical portrait of her protagonist's mother would deeply wound her own mother. (Which of course it did.) It seems likely that W. S. Snodgrass, whose *Heart's Needle* was one of the early and conspicuously successful examples of "confessional" poetry, chose to write under the pseudonym S. S. Gardens, for some time in the late 1960s, for much the same reason.

Karen Blixen, forty-eight years old when her first

book, *Seven Gothic Tales,* was completed, chose to publish it under a pseudonym in the hope of avoiding the excessive attention, some of it malicious, she did in fact receive when the Danish press finally tracked her down. Ezra Pound, that most ambitious of poets and poet-theorists, published occasional music and art criticism under the names "William Atheling" and "Alfred Venison"; twenty-two-year-old James Joyce, later to consign to Leopold Bloom the banal *nom de plume* "Henry Flower," published early versions of three *Dubliners* stories in the *Irish Homestead* under the distinctly un-Irish pseudonym "Stephen Dedalus"—Joyce's reason for disguise being that he was ashamed of publishing "in the pigs' paper." While living in Berlin, as a Russian émigré, Vladimir Nabokov published several novels in his native Russian between 1925 and 1940 under the pseudonym "Vladimir Sirin" or "V. Sirin" (funnily misprinted in the *Pseudonyms and Nicknames Dictionary* as "V. Siren," a superb Nabokovian pun). "Sirin" is only the best-known of Nabokov's Russian pseudonyms; he had others, among them "Vaseli Shiskov" and "Vivian Calmbrood" (precursor of the author "Vivian Darkbloom" of *Lolita?*), and in Nabokov's fiction generally there is a virtuoso's delight in the willful shifting of identities: the masquerade of *Lolita*'s deadpan foreword, for instance, in which "Humbert Humbert" is revealed as the pseudonymous creation of one "John Ray, Jr., Ph.D." (John Ray was a seventeenth-century English naturalist and taxonomist); the mad but inspired commentary of "Charles Kinbote" on the long poem "Pale Fire" by "John Francis Shade"; the eerie monologue of "Hugh Person" ("You Person") of *Transparent Things.* Jonathan Swift commonly employed not pseudonyms precisely but personae, by way of which his satire acquired its particular dramatic resonance. The doggedly sincere narrator of "A Modest Proposal," like "Isaac Bickerstaff, Esq." of the *Bickerstaff Papers,* and "M.

B.," the Dublin linen drapier of *The Drapier's Letters,* is himself a brilliant literary creation. Swift illuminated religious and political polemics with the imagination of genius but his writing, with the exception of *Gulliver's Travels,* was usually for specific and limited purposes; the narrating self is an aspect of the satire, and not a mask or voice of the author himself. Charles Lamb's much-imitated "Elia" essays, published as the observations of an Italian clerk named Elia, whom Lamb had known slightly, allowed him enough aesthetic distance from his subject, and from himself, to transform the merely personal and whimsical into art of a kind enormously admired in its day though rather dated in our own.

By far the great majority of writers who use pseudonyms, of course, are genre writers; there are eleven hundred listings for writers of mystery-detective fiction alone. (The record would seem to belong to a contemporary British science fiction writer named Robert Lionel Fanthorpe, who publishes under twenty-eight pseudonyms, all male.) Multiple-name writers tend to publish their quality work under their own names but may have a descending order of quality among their pseudonyms: Erle Stanley Gardner, for instance, has written under seven pseudonyms in addition to his own name, with "A. A. Fair" at the top of his list: John Creasey has published under thirteen pseudonyms, in addition to his own name, with "J. J. Marric" at the top of his. Evan Hunter, whose baptismal name is Salvatore A. Lombino, also publishes under the names Hunt Collins, Richard Marsten, and, most prominently, Ed McBain. Isaac Asimov, a rival of Simenon's in terms of sheer writerly abundance, has also published under the name "Paul French." "Ellery Queen" and "Ellery Queen, Jr." (joint pseudonyms of Daniel Nathan and Manfred Lepofsky) have published dozens of books, and Stephen King, our most prodigiously successful writer of horror stories, has recently sired a sort of sorcerer's apprentice in "Richard Bachman"—a pseudonym so little a secret that King's name is listed with "Bachman" in advertisements. No less prolific are science fiction writers Robert Heinlein, who published under four pseudonyms in addition to his own, and Barry Malzberg, who has also published under the name "K. M. O'Donnell." Highly regarded as masters of their mystery-genre are "John Le Carré" (David Cornwall) and "P. D. James" (Phyllis James White). Perhaps because most genre fiction is gamesmanship of a writerly sort, the author's intention being to outmaneuver the reader—to plunge forward into "plot" while at the same time impeding "plot" at every plausible turn—such writers employ pseudonyms as a matter of course. However serious, if not frankly obsessive, the underlying motives for writing of death as a component in a puzzle, the act can be passed off casually: it is only "entertainment" after all.

There endures an old aristocratic tradition, in any case, of not taking authorship seriously; or not allowing oneself to be charged with thinking so: as if the natural impulse is to shrink from seeming to suggest we might have something to say of interest or value to others. For all its strategies, art is an offensive maneuver from this perspective; it moves into another's private space, demands his attention if not his respect and admiration. To bring it off is so daring, so arrogant, so fraught with peril, the most ingenious defenses are required. It is appropriate that Nabokov, our most knottily "defensive" writer, anxious to hide his sentimental nature behind a shell of glittering artifice and hauteur, wrote an early novel, as "V. Sirin," titled *The Defense*.

In the end, it is probable that the cultivation of a pseudonym is not so very different from the cultivation *in vivo* of the narrative voice that sustains any work of words, making it unique and inimitable. Choosing a pseudonym as the work's formal author simply takes the mysterious process a step or two further, erasing the author's social identity and supplanting it with the pseudonymous identity. For who among us, identified with such confidence by others, has not felt uneasy, if not an impostor, knowing that, whatever they know of us, *we* do not somehow share in that knowledge? Fame's carapace does not allow for easy breathing.

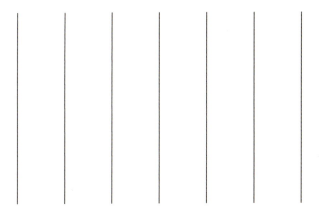

ACKNOWLEDGMENTS

The essays below originally appeared in much different forms as lectures, papers, formal essays, and feature articles. To the editors and conference organizers involved, all thanks and gratitude are due.

"Beginnings" appeared in an early version under the title "A Terrible Beauty Is Born: How?" in *The New York Times Book Review* (July 1985), given, in longer form, as the 1987 University of Michigan Hopwood Address, and published in *The Michigan Quarterly Review* (Winter 1987).

ACKNOWLEDGMENTS

"(Woman) Writer: Theory and Practice" was given as the keynote address at the Twentieth-Century Women Writers' Conference at Hofstra University, April 1982, and published, in longer form, in *Crosscurrents* (Spring 1987).

"The Art of Self-Criticism" was given as a paper at the Comparative Literature Conference at New York University, May 1986, and published in *The New York Times Book Review* (July 1986).

"The Dream of the 'Sacred Text'" was published, in an earlier version, in *The Generation of 2000: Contemporary American Poets* (Ontario Review Press, 1984), edited by William Heyen.

"Does the Writer Exist?" was published, in an earlier version, in *The New York Times Book Review* (1984).

"Literature as Pleasure, Pleasure as Literature" was published in *Antaeus* (Fall 1987).

"Against Nature" was published in *Antaeus* (Fall 1986) and reprinted in *The Pushcart Prize XII: The Best of the Small Presses* (New York, 1987).

"Wonderlands" was published in *The Georgia Review* (Spring 1985).

"Frankenstein's Fallen Angel" was published in a special illustrated edition of *Frankenstein* (Pennyroyal Press, 1984).

"Jane Eyre: An Introduction" was published as a preface to *Jane Eyre* (Bantam Classic, 1988); it appeared in an earlier version under the title "Romance and Anti-Romance: From Brontë's *Jane Eyre* to Rhys's *Wide Sargasso Sea"* in *Virginia Quarterly Review* (Winter 1985).

ACKNOWLEDGMENTS

"Looking for Thoreau" was given as a paper at the annual Thoreau Society conference, July 1985.

"Soul *at the White Heat:* The Romance of Emily Dickinson's Poetry" was given as a paper at the 1986 Emily Dickinson Conference, University of North Carolina at Chapel Hill, and published in *Critical Inquiry* (Summer 1987).

"Pleasure, Duty, Redemption Then and Now: Susan Warner's *Diana"* was given at the Modern Language Association Convention, December 1983, and reprinted in *American Literature* (Fall 1987).

"Jekyll/Hyde" was published in *The Hudson Review* (Winter 1987) and will be reprinted as the preface to a special limited edition of the novel in 1988 by Pennyroyal Press.

"Kafka as Storyteller" was published as a preface to *Franz Kafka: Collected Stories* (Quality Paperback Book Club, 1983).

"Mike Tyson" was published in *Life* (March 1987).

"Blood, Neon, and Failure in the Desert" was published in *The Village Voice,* 24 March 1987.

"Tyson/Biggs: Postscript" was published in *The New York Times* (as the "Views of Sport" essay), 25 October 1987.

"Annie Johnson: A 'Lost' New England Artist" was published in *Art & Antiques* (January 1986).

" 'Life, Vigor, Fire': The Watercolors of Winslow Homer" was published in *Art & Antiques* (February 1987).

"George Bellows: The Boxing Paintings" was published in *Art & Antiques* (Summer 1987).

ACKNOWLEDGMENTS

"The Hemingway Mystique" was published in *TV Guide*, 8 December 1984.

" 'Food' as Poetry" was published in *The New York Times*, 19 November 1986.

" 'Where Are You Going, Where Have You Been?' and *Smooth Talk:* Short Story Into Film" was published in *The New York Times*, 23 March 1986.

" 'State-of-the-Art Car': The Ferrari Testarossa" was published in *Quality* (November 1986).

"Visions of Detroit" was published in *Michigan Quarterly Review* (Spring 1986).

"Meeting the Gorbachevs" was published in *The New York Times Magazine*, 3 January 1988.

Preface to *them* was published in the Franklin Library edition of the book, 1979; *Mysteries of Winterthurn*, 1984; *Marya: A Life*, 1986; and *You Must Remember This*, 1987.

Preface to *Bellefleur* was published in the First Edition Society edition, 1980.

"Pseudonymous Selves" was published in *The New York Times Book Review* (December 1987).